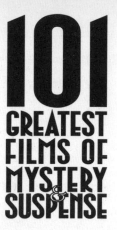

101 GREATEST FILMS OF MYSTERY & SUSPENSE

OTTO PENZLER is the founder and proprietor of The Mysterious Bookshop in Manhattan, New York, the founder of The Mysterious Press, as well as The Armchair Detective Library. Penzler received an Edgar Award for *The Encyclopedia of Mystery and Detection*, and was honored with the prestigious Ellery Queen Award by The Mystery Writers of America for his many contributions to the field. As an editor in the mystery field, Penzler's work includes *Murder and Obsession*, *The 50 Greatest Mysteries of All Time*, and *The Best American Mystery Stories of the Century* (edited with Tony Hillerman). Penzler lives in New York.

The films in this book are ranked in decli~~ng~~ ~~~~ lowest) to #1 (the best).

AVAILABLE NOW

COMING SOON

101
GREATEST FILMS OF MYSTERY & SUSPENSE

Otto Penzler

ibooks
new york
www.ibooksinc.com

DISTRIBUTED BY SIMON & SCHUSTER, INC.

To my friends Jane, John, and Pam Burgoyne
Who have made my life so much better in so many ways

An Original Publication of ibooks, inc.

Pocket Books, a division of Simon & Schuster, Inc.
1230 Avenue of the Americas, New York, NY 10020

Published by arrangement with Byron Preiss Visual Publications, Inc.

An ibooks, inc. Book

ibooks, inc.
24 West 25th Street
New York, NY 10010

The ibooks World Wide Web Site Address is:
http://www.ibooksinc.com

ISBN 0-7434-0717-2
First ibooks, inc. printing November 2000
10 9 8 7 6 5 4 3 2 1
POCKET and colophon are registered trademarks of Simon & Schuster, Inc.

Edited by Dinah Dunn

Cover design by Jay Vita
Cover photographs © 2000 Photofest
Interior design by Mike Rivilis

PRINTED IN THE U.S.A.

TABLE OF CONTENTS

INTRODUCTION

The truth of the matter is, although I've seen thousands of mystery movies over the years, I'm not a film expert.

What I do know about are stories, believable characters, and good dialogue. Get all three of those into a movie and you're going to have a pretty good one. Even if you know every single thing in the world about every camera and every lens ever created, if you don't pay attention to the story, character, or dialogue, you'll make a lousy movie.

Yes, yes, I know that reviewers and critics will write in glowing terms about some Polish film that must be played backward to fully appreciate the interplay of light and dark, and they may indeed be right. But that's not for me. I want to be entertained when I go to the movies, and I've never found a type of film that, when it is well done, is as compelling as a mystery.

My definition of a mystery, by the way, is any movie in which a crime, or the threat of a crime, is central to the plot or the theme. It's a broad definition, to be sure, but I think it's a fair one. A film doesn't have to be a detective story to be a mystery, and there are a lot of films discussed in these pages that aren't detective stories. Sometimes, even if a detective is present, the movie is not a mystery. Noir films tend to be about the criminals more often than they are about the people trying to catch them. Espionage counts, because a crime against the state is as much or more of a crime than a crime against an individual.

Some groups of movies were eliminated for various reasons. No foreign language films are included. It's personal. I don't like to read a movie, as subtitles require, and dubbing is a travesty. If foreign films were included, *Les Diaboliques* might have made the list, and possibly *High and Low* and *Purple Noon*, and probably *M.* But there aren't any, so don't look for them.

There are no silent films either. I just don't think it's possible to objectively compare films that are nearly different media. At the least, every aspect of a film made three-quarters of a century ago is so much clumsier, so much more primitive, that even a well-written story from the silent era pales when contrasted with the superior technical qualities of film from more modern times.

Finally, there are no made-for-television motion pictures. Mostly, of course, they aren't good enough to compete with theatrical releases because of the bigger film budgets with which the best actors, writers, directors, and others work. Also, as a practical matter, I simply haven't seen enough of them in recent times to be fair in judging. Certainly *Tinker, Tailor, Soldier, Spy* with Alec Guinness could have been considered, and so could *Prime Suspect* with Helen Mirren. There may be others. But don't look for them here; that is another book. A different book.

Is this a subjective listing? Well, of course it is. What else could it be? You may have a favorite that didn't make the cut. I'd be shocked if it were otherwise. You may disapprove of some selections. Ditto.

All I can say in that regard is, if a picture didn't make it into this book, it wasn't an oversight. After compiling an exhaustive list of every possible film, I screened nearly three hundred of them, making notes along the way. I was surprised how some favorites from another time did not hold up well on a later viewing, and I was equally amazed that some of the great ones seemed as fresh and intelligent after multiple viewings as they did when first released. That's what makes them great, I suppose.

I would like to acknowledge the help I received with this book from Harlan Ellison, Stuart Kaminsky, Natalie Kirpalani, Lorraine Lamm and Pamela Burgoyne-DeYoung, without whom this book would have been less than it is, and delivered even later than it was.

—Otto Penzler
New York

CHARLIE CHAN AT THE OPERA
1936

TYPE OF FILM: Detective

STUDIO: Twentieth Century-Fox

PRODUCER: Sol W. Wurtzel

DIRECTOR: H. Bruce Humberstone

SCREENWRITERS: Scott Darling and Charles S. Belden; story by Bess Meredyth

SOURCE: Characters created by Earl Derr Biggers

RUNNING TIME: 66 minutes

PRINCIPAL PLAYERS:

Warner Oland . . . . .Charlie Chan
Boris Karloff . . . . .Gravelle
Keye Luke . . . . .Number One Son, Lee Chan
Charlotte Henry . . . . .Mlle. Kitty
Thomas Beck . . . . .Phil Childers
Margaret Irving . . . . .Mme. Lilli Rochelle
Gregory Gaye . . . . .Enrico Barelli
Nedda Harrigan . . . . .Mme. Lucretia Barelli
Frank Convoy . . . . .Mr. Whitely
Guy Usher . . . . .Inspector Regan
William Demarest . . . . .Sergeant Kelly

DID YOU KNOW? Warner Oland, the first screen Charlie Chan, was born in Sweden. His vaguely Oriental appearance got him several roles as Asians, usually villains, before he was cast as the Honolulu detective in *Charlie Chan Carries On*, a film now lost. He played the much-loved character from 1931 to 1938 in sixteen movies, all of which were successful and earned Twentieth Century-Fox about a million dollars a year in profits, even during the height of the Depression.

Oland used virtually no makeup for his screen appearances, adding only the goatee to give him his identifying physical characteristic. He lived in Santa Barbara even during filming, driving sixty-five miles each way every day so that he could live at home.

He became more and more of an alcoholic in later life, and his wife divorced him in 1937. Later that year, in the midst of filming his seventeenth Chan movie, *Charlie Chan at the Ringside*, he walked off the set one day and never came back. He was not seen again until he turned up in his native Sweden, where he died in his mother's bed at the age of fifty-eight.

THE STORY: An amnesiac in an asylum plays piano and sings opera. After seven years of incarceration, an attendant brings him a newspaper, and the "maniac" recognizes the picture on the front page of an opera star, Mme. Lilli Rochelle, which seems to bring back his memory. He overpowers the guard and escapes, setting off a massive manhunt.

Charlie Chan, on his way home to Honolulu with his Number One Son, Lee, stops into the local police station just before Mme. Lilli bursts in and tells of a death threat for that night's performance. The police promise a major presence, and Chan joins them.

Shortly before the opera, *Carnival*, is to begin, the escaped lunatic, skulking around the opera house, is recognized by Mme. Barelli as Gravelle, the great baritone whom she believed had died in an opera house fire years ago when he had been locked in his dressing room. He threatens to kill her if she reveals his identity, and he replaces Enrico Barelli onstage in the role of Mephisto, where his appearance so terrifies Mme. Lilli that she faints.

Believing that Lilli had truly been stabbed when she passed out, the police chase Gravelle to Barelli's dressing room, kick in the locked door, and find Barelli stabbed to death. While searching for the culprit, Sergeant Kelly falls through a trap door into Mme. Lilli's room to find that she, too, has been stabbed.

Although the police are immediately convinced that the sinister Gravelle is the murderer, Chan doesn't believe it and convinces the deranged singer to restage the stabbing scene with Mme. Barelli, who is so terrified of Gravelle that she panics and the police shoot him. The bullet, however, is not fatal, and Chan is able to point the finger at the guilty party.

* * *

A convoluted and irrational plot does not prevent *Charlie Chan at the Opera* from being the best of the many Chan movies. In addition to the numerous familiar situations and fortune-cookie bits of wisdom, the over-the-top performance of Boris Karloff makes

4

this an irresistible film. Although he does little besides skulking menacingly around the opera house, frightening everybody who sees him, Karloff is nothing less than the most obvious red herring in cinema history. *Charlie Chan at the Race Track* is better plotted, and the background of *Charlie Chan at the Olympics* is fascinating, but the appeal of *Charlie Chan at the Opera* remains unmatched. It was the favorite of Keye Luke, the popular Number One Son.

The opera, *Carnival,* was especially commissioned for this film from Oscar Levant; William Kernell wrote the libretto.

Several sources report authoritatively that Boris Karloff did his own singing and that his voice was not dubbed, as is reported in numerous other sources. Keye Luke, who was on the set, wondered who had done the dubbing but allowed the possibility that it was Karloff's own voice. Watching the movie and hearing the voice, however, it does not seem likely that such a strong operatic voice could have been Karloff's—who gave no evidence of such a powerful baritone in any other film.

In the forty-six Charlie Chan motion pictures (as well as the thirty-nine-episode television series), Chan has never been played by an Asian actor.

BEST LINE: After a seamstress screams because she saw a strange man in Madame Lilli's dressing room, the stage manager, trying to bring order to the chaotic scene, tells Sergeant Kelly, "You cops would make anybody hysterical. . . . This opera is going on tonight even if Frankenstein walks in."

BULLITT
1968

TYPE OF FILM:	Police
STUDIO:	Warner Brothers—Seven Arts
EXECUTIVE PRODUCER:	Robert E. Relyes
PRODUCER:	Philip D. Antoni
DIRECTOR:	Peter Yates
SCREENWRITERS:	Alan R. Trustman and Harry Kleiner
SOURCE:	*Mute Witness*, novel by Robert Pike (pseudonym of Robert L. Fish)
RUNNING TIME:	113 minutes

PRINCIPAL PLAYERS:

Steve McQueen . . . . .Frank Bullitt
Robert Vaughn . . . . .Walter Chalmers
Jacqueline Bisset . . . . .Cathy
Don Gordon . . . . .Delgetti
Robert Duvall . . . . .Weissberg
Simon Oakland . . . . .Captain Bennett
Norman Fell . . . . .Captain Baker
Carl Reindel . . . . .Stanton
Felice Orlandi . . . . .Renick
Pat Renella . . . . .Johnny Ross

DID YOU KNOW? In the most famous chase scene in movie history, four cars were used: a pair of Dodge Chargers and a pair of Mustangs (which were owned by the Ford Motor Company and lent to Warner Brothers as part of a promotional agreement). The cars were modified for the high speed chase and driven by two stunt drivers. Both of the Chargers were junked after the filming, as was one of the Mustangs. The other Mustang, not quite as battered as the other cars, was purchased by a Warner Brothers employee after the film was completed. Several years later, the car was in New Jersey and Steve McQueen tried to buy it, but the owner did not want to sell it and he put it into storage in a barn: It has not been driven for many years.

6

THE STORY: The ambitious politician, Walter Chalmers, requests Detective Lieutenant Frank Bullitt to guard Chicago hoodlum Johnny Ross, who has agreed to testify before a Senate subcommittee on organized crime. Two hoodlums break into the hotel room where Ross is hiding and shoot him. Ross is rushed to the hospital but dies, and Bullitt convinces the doctor to keep the death secret while he sets out to investigate how the Mafia knew where Ross had been sequestered.

The gangsters chase Bullitt throughout San Francisco until their car crashes into a gasoline pump and explodes. He soon learns that the gunned-down Ross was really an impostor and that the real criminal is planning to leave the country. Bullitt finally catches up with him at the San Francisco airport, where Chalmers admits that he had sent the police to guard the decoy, but that he wants Ross taken alive now. Bullitt chases him from a plane just before it is about to take off and finally catches up with him, shooting him dead as he tries to escape.

* * *

Bullitt is remembered today mainly for two things: Steve McQueen's best-known role, the one with which he is most often associated, and the fabulous chase scene through the streets and over the hills of San Francisco. Only the chase scene in *The French Connection* bettered it, and neither required the crashes of dozens, or even scores, of cars that inevitably exploded in chase scenes in the less imaginative pictures that followed.

Director Peter Yates called for his stunt drivers to hit speeds of 70 to 80 miles per hour in the chase scene, but in the excitement of the moment, they often hit as high as 110 miles per hour (as did the cars containing the cameras, of course). While the scene took less than ten minutes in the film, it required three weeks of shooting.

Yates had wanted to set part of the chase on the Golden Gate Bridge but was denied permission.

BEST LINE: Chalmers to Bullitt: "We both know how careers are made. Integrity is something you sell the public."

ANATOMY OF A MURDER
1959

TYPE OF FILM:	Courtroom
STUDIO:	Columbia
PRODUCER:	Otto Preminger
DIRECTOR:	Otto Preminger
SCREENWRITER:	Wendell Mayes
SOURCE:	*Anatomy of a Murder* by Robert Traver, pseudonym of John D. Voelker, a judge
RUNNING TIME:	160 minutes

PRINCIPAL PLAYERS:

James Stewart . . . . .Paul Biegler
Lee Remick . . . . .Laura Manion
Ben Gazzara . . . . .Lieutenant Frederick Manion
George C. Scott . . . . .Claude Dancer
Arthur O'Connell . . . . .Parnell McCarthy
Eve Arden . . . . .Maida
Kathryn Grant . . . . .Mary Pilant
Orson Bean . . . . .Dr. Smith
Russ Brown . . . . .Mr. Lemon
Murray Hamilton . . . . .Alphonse Paquette
Joseph N. Welch . . . . .Judge Weaver
Brooks West . . . . .Mitch Lodwick

DID YOU KNOW? The judge in this compelling courtroom drama did a splendid job in his role, which actually came fairly easily to him. In real life, he was not an actor but a judge who played a key role in the famous hearings in which Senator Joseph McCarthy questioned members of the Hollywood movie-making community and others before the House Un-American Committee. The author, John D. Voelker (using the pseudonym Robert Traver), was in real life a judge as well, in the upper peninsula of Michigan.

THE STORY: Lieutenant Frederick Manion is arrested and brought to trial for killing the bartender he claims beat and raped his wife Laura. Former prosecutor Paul Biegler reluctantly agrees to defend the arrogant and insolent soldier. The prosecution, including Claude Dancer, charges that Laura was a woman of easy virtue who had been having an affair with the murdered man and that Manion found out about it, beat the truth out of his wife, and then killed her lover.

Biegler's researcher finds a comparable case from the nineteenth century in which a man killed his wife's attacker, citing "an irresistible impulse," and the man had been acquitted, so Biegler decides to use the same defense.

His prize witness is the murdered man's stepdaughter, who testifies that the dead man had been fond of the young woman and offers physical evidence: a pair of torn panties that belonged to Laura Manion, missing since the alleged attack but found among the bar's laundry, proving that her stepfather had tried to hide them.

Lieutenant Manion is acquitted but, when Biegler goes to collect his fee at the trailer where the Manions lived, he finds a note stating that they had "an irresistible impulse" to leave without paying him.

* * *

Lana Turner had been hired to play Laura Manion but walked off the set after a few days. Producer/director Otto Preminger claimed she didn't like the clothes she'd been given to wear. Turner responded by saying, "I would not walk out of a picture for something as trivial as a costume. It was simply impossible to deal with Mr. Preminger's unpredictable temper."

Preminger then vowed to take an unknown actress and make her a star, which he did with Lee Remick.

At the time the film was released, it was extremely shocking for its frequent use of language rarely spoken in polite company. Words like "panties," "climax," "intercourse," and "contraceptive" were too strong for Richard Daley, the mayor of Chicago, who banned its showing in his city until a court order forced him to allow it.

Anatomy of a Murder was nominated for six Academy Awards in the year in which *Ben-Hur* swept most of them. It lost to *Ben-Hur* for Best Picture, James Stewart lost to Charlton Heston for Best Actor (though Stewart was named Best Actor by the New York Film Critics), and both George C. Scott and Arthur O'Connell lost to Hugh Griffith for Best Supporting Actor.

9

BEST LINE: At the murder trial in which a charge of rape is a major element, the subject of the alleged victim's underwear is raised and Judge Weaver asks the lawyers if another word can be used instead of panties. Claude Dancer, a prosecuting attorney, volunteers that he'd been overseas during the war and learned a French word for them, but believed the word might be slightly suggestive. "Most French words are," says Weaver.

THE SPY WHO CAME IN FROM THE COLD

1965

TYPE OF FILM:	Espionage
STUDIO:	Paramount
PRODUCER:	Martin Ritt
DIRECTOR:	Martin Ritt
SCREENWRITERS:	Paul Dehn and Guy Trosper
SOURCE:	*The Spy Who Came In from the Cold*, novel by John le Carré
RUNNING TIME:	112 minutes

PRINCIPAL PLAYERS:

Richard Burton . . . . .Alec Leamas
Claire Bloom . . . . .Nan Perry
Oskar Werner . . . . .Fiedler
Peter Van Eyck . . . . .Hans-Dieter Mundt
George Voskovec . . . . East German defense attorney
Sam Wanamaker . . . . .Peters
Cyril Cusack . . . . .Control
Rupert Davies . . . . .John Smiley
Michael Hordern . . . . .Ashe
Robert Hardy . . . . .Carlton
Bernard Lee . . . . .Patmore

DID YOU KNOW? Although it is perhaps the most influential espionage movie ever made, *The Spy Who Came In from the Cold* was a failure at the box office. Cinematic spying traditionally used such standard features as beautiful women who turned out to be ruthless double agents, posh surroundings, and international locales. The lack of all those colorful elements in the film, plus the realistic depiction of the ordinariness of everyday life as a spy and its commensurate lack of action, made audiences less than enthusiastic about this cinematic experience. They made it clear that they preferred the unrealistic but exciting world of James Bond.

THE STORY: Alec Leamas, the head of British Intelligence in Germany, is near retirement when he is sent home to explain why so many of his agents have been killed. They appear to be the victims of ex-Nazi Hans-Dieter Mundt, now the head of the East German counterintelligence unit. The British Secret Service, led by Control, wants to eliminate him.

Leamas, burned out after so many years at the job, lacking family and close ties, has become a disillusioned drunk. Using that apparent weakness as a good cover, Leamas is given the assignment of making himself appear ready to defect so that he can infiltrate the East German organization.

He takes a job in a library to become involved with known Communist Nan Perry. When he is offered money to tell his secrets to Mundt's second in command, the brilliant but devious Fiedler, Leamas accepts. Fiedler, eager to replace his superior, plans to frame him as a double agent and uses Leamas in his plot.

When a secret tribunal is held and Nan is called as a surprise witness, Leamas suddenly realizes that the entire purpose of his mission to East Berlin was to set up Fiedler and strengthen the position of Mundt, who is actually a British double agent.

Mundt arranges for Leamas to escape over the Wall, but Nan, a security risk, must be shot. Knowing the life to which he will return, the embittered Leamas decides that escape is pointless and stays behind the Wall to be shot and killed.

* * *

The film version of *The Spy Who Came In from the Cold* was a faithful adaptation of John le Carré's 1963 novel, which, unlike the film, was an enormous success and catapulted the author onto best-seller lists from then on.

Much as *The Godfather* created a view of the Mafia that was so real that it seemed the only accurate definition of that world, so, too, did le Carré make his depiction of the espionage world appear to be the only true one. His inventive use of language sounded so authentic that it has seeped into common usage, and terms like *circus* and *control* are used knowingly as genuine "spy speak," but were created in that context by le Carré.

The success of the book and the fame of the film produced several takeoffs and spoofs, notably *The Spy Who Came* (1969), a black-and-white sex film, and *The Spy with a Cold Nose* (1966), in which a dog is used as a secret agent.

Paul Dehn and Guy Trosper received Edgar Allan Poe Awards from the Mystery Writers of America for their screenplay.

BEST LINE: Fiedler has offered Leamas a woman. Leamas tells him that he doesn't need one. Fiedler reminds him that he had one in England—the girl in the library. Leamas says, "Oh, yes, yes. She was a Communist too. She believed in free love. At the time it was all I could afford."

DEAD END
1937

TYPE OF FILM: Crime

STUDIO: United Artists

PRODUCER: Samuel Goldwyn

DIRECTOR: William Wyler

SCREENWRITER: Lillian Hellman

SOURCE: *Dead End*, play by Sidney Kingsley

RUNNING TIME: 93 minutes

PRINCIPAL PLAYERS:

Sylvia Sidney	Drina Gordon
Joel McCrae	Dave Connell
Humphrey Bogart	"Baby Face" Martin
Wendy Barrie	Kay
Claire Trevor	Francey
Marjorie Main	Mrs. Martin
Allen Jenkins	Hunk
Billy Halop	Tommy Gordon
Huntz Hall	Dippy
Bobby Jordan	Angel
Leo B. Gorcey	Spit
Gabriel Dell	T.B.
Bernard Punsley	Milty

DID YOU KNOW? Sidney Kingsley's play, *Dead End*, which opened on Broadway in October of 1936, was a launching pad for the successful Hollywood careers of more than a dozen stars. The Dead End Kids went on to screen stardom under that name, as well as the names The East Side Kids, The Little Tough Guys, and The Bowery Boys. The play also featured Humphrey Bogart and Marjorie Main, who reprised their roles in the film version, along with Sidney Lumet and Martin Gable, who went on to become famous directors, and Dan Duryea, a staple in many films noir and other Hollywood productions for decades. The screen rights to the play were sold for $165,000—more than the entire production budgets for many motion pictures of that time.

THE STORY: "Baby Face" Martin, a notorious gangster, returns to his boyhood neighborhood, New York's East Side, which is undergoing changes as some of the dilapidated old tenements are torn down to make way for luxurious apartment houses. He has come to see his mother and former girlfriend, Francey. Since his mother, ashamed and angry at his career, rejects him, and Francey has turned to prostitution, Martin realizes that he cannot escape his own crimes and settle down as he had hoped.

Dave, an unemployed architect who lives on the same street, dreams of a better life for himself and the girl he loves, Kay. Drina, Dave's friend who has been secretly in love with him for years, struggles to keep her kid brother, Tommy, from becoming a criminal like his friends. When the gang of street toughs steals a watch from Philip, one of the wealthier boys, Tommy returns it to the boy's father, who nonetheless wants to press charges. Tommy wants to run away and Drina wants to go with him.

Meanwhile, Martin plots to kidnap Philip for a ransom, but Dave kills Martin first, earning a large reward that he thinks will buy that better life for him and Kay, only to learn that she just wants to spend it all on a short binge of high living. Instead, Dave offers to use his money to pay for a good lawyer to keep Tommy (whom Drina has convinced to turn himself in) out of prison. As Tommy walks to the police station, he is accompanied by Drina and Dave.

* * *

Dead End was a seminal film in that it was the first to show that gangsters and hoodlums are not necessarily born that way, but that they may be the products of poverty, broken homes, parental neglect, government indifference, and lack of education. For the first time, the behavior of criminals was seen not as a genetic mutation, but as the direct result of external forces. This influential film inspired many others of its kind, notably Lewis Seiler's *Crime School* (1938) and Michael Curtiz's *Angels With Dirty Faces* (1938).

There were several differences between the stage and motion picture versions. Apparently a bit of toning down was necessary to make the film palatable to the censors. On stage, for example, Francey has syphilis, but in the movie she is merely "sick" with a hacking cough. Another difference is that in the stage version, the crippled artist becomes Dave's romantic interest.

Four Academy Award nominations went to *Dead End:* Best Picture, Best Supporting Actress (Claire Trevor), Best Cinematography, and Best Art Direction. It was named Best Picture of the Year by the *Film Daily Yearbook*.

BEST LINE: Not much credit to the screenwriter, but memorable nonetheless, is the closing moment as Tommy walks to the police station to face his fate, while the rest of the Dead End Kids, resigned to their lives in the slums, sing: "If I had the wings of an angel, over these prison walls I would fly."

THE HOUND OF THE BASKERVILLES

1939

TYPE OF FILM:	Detective
STUDIO:	Twentieth Century-Fox
PRODUCER:	Gene Markey
DIRECTOR:	Sidney Lanfield
SCREENWRITER:	Ernest Pascal
SOURCE:	*The Hound of the Baskervilles*, novel by Arthur Conan Doyle
RUNNING TIME:	80 minutes

PRINCIPAL PLAYERS:

Basil Rathbone . . . . .Sherlock Holmes
Nigel Bruce . . . . .Dr. Watson
Richard Greene .Sir Henry Baskerville
Wendy Barrie . . . . .Beryl Stapleton
Lionel Atwill . . . . .Dr. Mortimer
John Carradine . . . . .Barryman
Barlowe Borland . . . . .Frankland
Beryl Mercer . . . . .Mrs. Mortimer
Morton Lowry . . . . .John Stapleton

DID YOU KNOW? Basil Rathbone—an accomplished stage actor, especially in Shakespearean roles—played Holmes for the first time in this film, which was the first (after dozens of screen versions of Holmesian adventures) to be set in the Victorian Era. Rathbone, with Nigel Bruce as his Watson, went on to play Holmes in thirteen more full-length films, as well as 275 radio broadcasts and on the stage. Although he recognized that Holmes had made him famous, Rathbone also knew that he had, in fact, become typecast and that his career was ruined.

THE STORY: An ancient legend has it that a gigantic phantasmagoric hound prowls the Great Grimpen Mire, on which Baskerville Hall is located. Young Sir Henry has recently arrived from Canada to assume possession of the Baskerville estate after the mysterious death of his uncle. Dr. Mortimer, the physician of the Baskerville family, has come to Sherlock Holmes's rooms at Baker Street because he is afraid that Sir Henry will meet a similar end. When attempts on Henry's life are made in London, Holmes and Watson head to Dartmoor to prevent another death.

They arrive at Baskerville Hall and encounter the strange activities of Barryman, the butler, and his wife, who are caught signaling a strange man on the moor. When the man's torn and mutilated body is discovered soon after, it is learned that he was Mrs. Barryman's brother, an escaped convict, who had been wearing Sir Henry's old clothes. Holmes sets a trap for the killer, saying that he is returning to London, and that night Sir Henry is attacked by a monstrous dog on the moor, only to be saved when Holmes and Watson shoot it. Everyone returns to the manor house, where Holmes unmasks the killer—a distant relative of the Baskervilles intent on killing all who remain in the family, so that he can claim control of the Baskerville fortune.

* * *

Arguably the greatest mystery novel ever written, *The Hound of the Baskervilles* is also one of the most familiar, and it is a measure of its greatness that the film bears watching even if the viewer knows the murderer.

Extremely faithful to the book on which it is based and notable for introducing Rathbone and Bruce to the world as the definitive Holmes and Watson, the film has a superb cast, with such infamous screen villains as Lionel Atwill and John Carradine providing nice red herrings. Holmes aficionados have always resented the handsome new leading man, Richard Greene, being given top billing, and there is little chemistry between him and the pretty leading lady, Wendy Barrie. Barrie, incidentally, was a last-minute replacement for Anita Louise, because the head of foreign production at twentieth Century-Fox convinced the studio that British audiences would accept nothing less than an all-British cast.

Admittedly a trifle slow-moving at times, the film nonetheless abounds with atmosphere in spite of the lack of background music—virtually unknown for a suspense film because of the music's ability to heighten tension when properly used.

The magnificent, if creepy, Baskerville Hall was built entirely on Fox's lot. It had been used previously for a Charlie Chan movie and was later used in *The Man Who Wouldn't Die* (1942), a Mike Shayne film.

BEST LINE: Dr. Mortimer informs Holmes that Sir Charles Baskerville has been horribly murdered, and that all around the body were footprints. Holmes asks, "A man's or a woman's?" "Mr. Holmes," answers Mortimer, "they were the footprints of a gigantic hound!"

IN A LONELY PLACE
1950

TYPE OF FILM:	*Noir*
STUDIO:	Columbia
PRODUCER:	Robert Lord
DIRECTOR:	Nicholas Ray
SCREENWRITER:	Andrew Solt; adaptation by Edmund H. North
SOURCE:	*In a Lonely Place*, novel by Dorothy B. Hughes
RUNNING TIME:	91 minutes

PRINCIPAL PLAYERS:

Humphrey Bogart . . . . .Dix Steele
Gloria Grahame . . . . .Laurel Gray
Frank Lovejoy . . . . .Brub Nicolai
Robert Warwick . . . . .Charlie Waterman
Jeff Donnell . . . . .Sylvia Nicolai
Art Smith . . . . .Mel Lippman
Carl Benton Reid . . . . .Captain Lochner
Martha Stewart . . . . .Mildred Atkinson

DID YOU KNOW? Humphrey Bogart bought the rights to Dorothy B. Hughes' novel, *In a Lonely Place*, for his own production company, Santana Productions, because he loved the title and the premise. By the time the story made it to the screen, virtually nothing was left of the book he loved except the title. Still, his judgment proved excellent, as director Nicholas Ray helped shape Bogart's finest, most complex screen performance to date. Hughes was also the author of *Ride the Pink Horse*, which also became a noir classic, adhering more closely to the published version.

THE STORY: Dix Steele, a screenwriter having trouble getting work because he doesn't want to write screenplays that he doesn't like, and who has taken to drink and fits of violent behavior, decides to accept the job of adapting a popular potboiler. He knows he needs to do something, however distasteful, to salvage his dissolving career (and life). Rather than read the book, he has a hatcheck girl come to his apartment to tell him the story. The next day, she is discovered murdered and Steele is the prime suspect.

Dix's alibi is the young actress Laurel Gray, who has recently become his neighbor. They fall for each other and, inspired by her, he begins to write again. But his jealousy and the fits of anger that continually erupt frighten her, and she finally decides to leave him. Enraged, Dix chokes her, stopping just short of killing her when the telephone rings. It is the police, telling him that he is no longer a suspect as they have apprehended the real killer.

Laurel is nonetheless filled with terror, horrified at his behavior, and he realizes it's over. He simply turns and walks away.

When Dix, recognizing that he has just thrown away his life, walks from Laurel, the audience cannot know what he is walking toward. Is it suicide, another act of violence, the bottle, or a shrink? *In a Lonely Place* ends without the resolution so closely associated with noir films but only the most optimistic can believe, for even a moment, that Dix will move on to a happy and fulfilling life.

* * *

Nicholas Ray, the director, was married to Gloria Grahame while *In a Lonely Place* was being made. They had met in 1948 when they were making *A Woman's Secret,* and she apparently did for him in real life what she did for Bogart in the movie—inspired him to greater art in his work. They had an affair and she got pregnant, so Ray married her. The relationship soured, however, and Grahame reportedly spent her wedding night alone in a Las Vegas hotel room while Ray gambled the night away. Since they both were working in Hollywood, they attempted to maintain a polite, if superficial, professional relationship, but that became impossible when Grahame, well known for her promiscuity, had an affair with Ray's thirteen-year-old son from a previous marriage. (It all sounds like a B *noir* film, doesn't it?)

BEST LINE: Dix Steele, knowing it's over, to Laurel Gray: "I was born when you kissed me. I died when you left me. I lived a few weeks while you loved me."

TAXI DRIVER
1976

TYPE OF FILM:	Crime
STUDIO:	Columbia
PRODUCERS:	Michael and Julia Phillips
DIRECTOR:	Martin Scorsese
SCREENWRITER:	Paul Schrader
SOURCE:	Original
RUNNING TIME:	113 minutes

PRINCIPAL PLAYERS:

Robert De Niro . . . . .Travis Bickle
Cybill Shepherd . . . . .Betsy
Harvey Keitel . . . . .Sport
Peter Boyle . . . . .Wizard
Jodie Foster . . . . .Iris
Albert Brooks . . . . .Tom
Leonard Harris .Charles Palantine
Joe Spinell . . . . .personnel officer
Martin Scorsese . . . . .passenger

DID YOU KNOW? Talk about getting into a role! Robert De Niro, who plays the sociopath Travis Bickle, a New York City cab driver, drove a taxi for twelve-hour shifts for a month to prepare for the role. The film's most famous scene, and one which has lingered in the consciousness of filmgoers for nearly a quarter of a century, shows De Niro talking, or ranting, to himself in front of a mirror. "You talkin' to me? You're not talkin' to me! You're talkin' to me?" You remember it. Well, it was entirely ad libbed by De Niro.

Harvey Keitel, who plays the pimp, Sport, is from the same school of acting as De Niro. He rehearsed with real-life pimps to prepare for his role, and the scene in which he dances with Iris, the young prostitute, was improvised by Keitel and Jodie Foster.

THE STORY: Travis Bickle is a twenty-six-year-old Vietnam War vet on whom the service clearly had an impact. He is a loner, driving a New York City cab on the late night shift, where he is constantly confronted with the worst of society: hookers, pimps, druggies, and other low-life criminals. A self-styled moralist, he keeps a diary with his thoughts on this world, growing to hate it more with each passing night.

He meets a passenger in his cab, the pretty and decent Betsy, a campaign worker for a Senate nominee, and asks her for a date, which goes badly when he takes her to a pornographic movie. He later meets Iris, a fourteen year-old prostitute, and tries to convince her to go back home to her parents, without success. He even fails at getting her to leave her vile, brutal pimp, Sport, with whom she is in love.

In frustration, he buys guns and ammunition and practices with them as he sets out to rid the world of the scum that is epitomized by Sport, whom he shoots. He follows up that murder by going into a seedy hotel and shooting more pimps and sleazy criminals, making him a vigilante hero to the media and the public.

* * *

This is clearly not a motion picture for everyone. It is inexhaustibly ugly, vulgar, and violent, and it is impossible for just about any of the characters to speak a simple declarative sentence without peppering it with obscenities. The violence is omnipresent, whether simmering just below the surface or erupting in outrageous gore. In fact, *Taxi Driver* had been given a rating of "X", which is a box office death knell, until Scorsese agreed to reduce the level of violence. He accomplished this mainly by changing the color of the blood from a bright red to a more muted maroon color.

The famous Mohawk haircut that Bickle wore was not real. The make-up artist designed a bald skullcap for De Niro and made the hair out of coarse horsehair.

Brian De Palma, no stranger to violent films, was considered for the job of directing *Taxi Driver,* but when the producers saw *Mean Streets,* directed by Scorsese three years earlier and also starring De Niro, it was agreed that Scorsese could direct, but only if he was able to get De Niro to play the lead role.

Paul Schrader's screenplay was a hot property, and several other studios were interested in making the film. One of them had suggested (and I never joke!) Neil Diamond for the role of Travis Bickle.

Following in the footsteps of Alfred Hitchcock, Martin Scorsese has a small walk-on in each of his films, and so does his mother.

In *Taxi Driver*, Mrs. Scorsese can be seen in the photograph of Iris's parents that has been hung on Travis's wall. Scorsese is the irate husband in Bickle's taxi.

BEST LINE: Travis Bickle, writing in his diary: "I don't believe that one should devote one's life to morbid self-attention."

THE LAST SEDUCTION

1994

TYPE OF FILM:	Crime/*Noir*
STUDIO:	PolyGram
PRODUCER:	Jonathan Shestack
DIRECTOR:	John Dahl
SCREENWRITER:	Steve Barancik
SOURCE:	Original
RUNNING TIME:	110 minutes

PRINCIPAL PLAYERS:

Linda Fiorentino	Bridget Gregory/Wendy Kroy
Peter Berg	Mike Swale
J. T. Walsh	Frank Griffith
Bill Nunn	Harlan
Bill Pullman	Clay Gregory
Brian Varady	Chris
Dean Norris	Shep
Donna Wilson	Stacy
Mik Scriba	Ray
Serena	Trish Swale

DID YOU KNOW? In her personal life, Linda Fiorentino may be a lovely woman, but in movies she has quickly become type-cast as an evil monster of such relentlessly diabolical actions that it is difficult to imagine her as the sweet girl next door. In *The Last Seduction*, she calls her attorney and asks him if he's still a lawyer, and he responds by asking her if she is still "a self-serving bitch." Later, he asks her, "Anyone check you for a heartbeat lately?" And this is someone on *her* side! Over the course of her career, Fiorentino played similar roles in *Vision Quest*, a wrestling movie that was puerile and worth missing except for her icy performance, and the highly interesting Martin Scorsese film *After Hours*, in which she also plays a nearly nonhuman blackwidow spider, dooming every man who gets trapped (albeit willingly) in her web.

THE STORY: Bridget Gregory convinces her husband, Clay, a shady doctor, to make a drug deal, which is successful. He takes home $700,000, which she promptly steals, fleeing from New York City to a small town named Breston, near Buffalo. Stopping for gas, she hits the local bar and picks up Mike Swale, who is titillated by her beauty and sophistication, as well as her straightforward interest in him sexually—as evidenced when she opens his pants in the crowded bar and reaches in to see if his boasts about size are warranted.

Bridget decides to stay in Breston. Now using the name Wendy Kroy, she takes a job in an insurance company and maintains an affair with Mike. He has fallen for her, even though he is repelled by her cold-bloodedness and by her scheme for them to murder certain policyholders for large payoffs.

Clay is desperate to get the drug money back and hires Harlan, a private detective, to find Bridget, which he does. As they head back to New York, she presses her foot down hard on the gas pedal and aims the car at a pole, crashing into it head-on and sending Harlan through the windshield; she is saved by an air bag.

Bridget tricks Mike into going to New York with her and sets him up with an elaborate scheme to kill her husband. As Clay tells Mike more and more about Bridget, the naive upstater realizes he has been manipulated and refuses to go through with the murder, so Bridget kills her husband by spraying Mace down his throat. When Mike is outraged by her, she screams at him to rape her and, as he does, she surreptitiously dials 911 so that her rape is recorded, as well as her cries of "You killed my husband." With Clay dead and Mike arrested, Bridget heads off to an island paradise with the $700,000 and no hint of a conscience.

Although *noir* films are notorious for having bad women, never has any of them remained so one-dimensionally evil. Clearly influenced by James M. Cain and the other darkest of the dark writers, *The Last Seduction* provides a showcase for a diabolical character who never—not for an instant—displays any moral sense. As a tribute to Cain, Bridget Gregory identifies herself once as Mrs. Neff (Walter Neff is the man Phyllis Dietrichsonto lures into a plot to kill her husband in Cain's *Double Indemnity*).

The Last Seduction, now regarded as a noir masterpiece, had a tough time of it at first. Intended for theatrical release, initial response from the studio and theater owners was so lukewarm that it went directly to cable television, making it ineligible for an Academy Award. When it was released in England, the reaction to it from critics and viewers was so overwhelmingly positive that it crossed the Atlantic and was shown theatrically with reasonable success.

BEST LINE: Bridget Gregory stops at a bar and orders a Manhattan. When she is ignored, she yells in the general direction of the bartender, "Who does a girl have to suck around here to get a drink?"

HIGH SIERRA
1941

TYPE OF FILM: Crime

STUDIO: Warner Brothers

EXECUTIVE PRODUCER: Hal B. Wallis

DIRECTOR: Raoul Walsh

SCREENWRITERS: John Huston and W. R. Burnett

SOURCE: *High Sierra*, novel by W. R. Burnett

RUNNING TIME: 100 minutes

PRINCIPAL PLAYERS:

Ida Lupino . . . . .Marie Garson
Humphrey Bogart . . . . .Roy "Mad Dog" Earle
Alan Curtis . . . . .Babe Kozak
Arthur Kennedy . . . . .Red Hattery
Joan Leslie . . . . .Velma
Henry Hull . . . . .Doc Banton
Henry Travers . . . . .Pa Goodhue
Barton MacLane . . . . .Jack Kranmer
Jerome Cowan . . . . .Healy
Minna Gombell . . . . .Mrs. Baughman
Elisabeth Risdon . . . . .Ma Goodhue
Cornel Wilde . . . . .Louis Mendoza
Donald MacBride . . . . .Big Mac
Paul Harvey . . . . .Mr. Baughman
Willie Best . . . . .Algernon

DID YOU KNOW? George Raft is largely responsible for Humphrey Bogart's rise to stardom. Raft rejected the offer to play the lead in *Dead End* (1937) because he felt the gangster's portrayal was unsympathetic. Bogart took the role in the memorable film. When the role of Roy Earle was offered to Raft in *High Sierra*, he turned it down as well. He felt that his star status ought to give him the chance to be alive at the end of the film, instead of being gunned down, as had happened to him so many times before. Finally, Raft was offered the role of Sam Spade in

The Maltese Falcon (1941) and turned *it* down too, fearing that his modest acting skills would not be helped by a first-time director. The fact is, of course, that the director was John Huston, one of the greatest directors in the history of Hollywood, especially for crime movies. Raft was also considered for *Casablanca* (1943), and you know who got the part of Rick Blaine. Raft admitted that he didn't know much, so he listened to guys who were supposed to know something, like his agent. He was right about one thing: He didn't know much. Bogart's role in *High Sierra* propelled him to the top of Hollywood's list of stars, getting him top billing in *The Maltese Falcon* (after being billed behind Ida Lupino in *High Sierra*).

THE STORY: After serving eight years in prison, Roy Earle is given parole, bought for him by Big Mac, who wants Earle to help pull a big hotel robbery. As Roy drives to California, he encounters the Goodhue family on the road, befriends Pa Goodhue, and falls for his crippled granddaughter, Velma. When he gets to the mountain resort to hook up with Red and Babe, the other men who will pull off the robbery, Earle finds that they have brought along a girl named Marie from a dime-a-dance joint. Earle wants to get rid of her, knowing that the young crooks will fight over her, but he learns to accept and trust Marie far more than the small-time hoods.

Earle gives the Goodhues money for Velma's operation and goes to stick up the hotel. Earle gets away but the other getaway car crashes, killing Red and Babe and injuring Mendoza, the inside man who helped set up the job. Earle and Marie escape with the stolen jewelry. Traveling with them is Pard, the little dog with a reputation for bringing bad luck with him. A huge manhunt is begun, and Earle is identified by Mendoza, as his picture is now on every front page along with a $10,000 reward offered for his capture.

Earle stops to ask Velma, now healed, to marry him, and she turns him down, saying that she's in love with a man from back home. Believing he'll be safer on his own, Earle sends Marie and Pard to Las Vegas, promising to meet them as soon as he's received the money for the fenced jewels, but he is spotted. The police set up roadblocks, forcing him into the mountains, where he is surrounded. Marie returns in time to see him shot to death by a sniper. Knowing that Earle would rather have been killed than

29

return to prison, she is comforted by the notion that at last Earle is free.

* * *

High Sierra is notable as one of the rare noir films that is not set in the city and that sees much of its action occur during the day. Also unusual is that the femme fatale truly loves the main character and remains loyal to him.

Roy Earle was very loosely based on John Dillinger, who is given homage by being quoted in the film.

In spite of the nickname "Mad Dog," pinned on him by the newspapers, Earle was an extremely sympathetic character. While tough and violent with other crooks, he was extremely gentle and kind to Velma, the woman with whom he fell in love, and to Marie, the woman who loved him. His eventual undoing may have been his kindness to the bad-luck dog, Pard—he kept trying to leave him behind but relented every time, even taking him along on the big heist.

Raoul Walsh directed an excellent remake of the same story in 1949, this time as a western, with Joel McCrea as the outlaw on the run, and Virginia Mayo and Dorothy Malone as the two women in his life.

Less successful was the 1955 version, filmed again as a contemporary gangster melodrama, titled *I Died a Thousand Times*, starring Jack Palance as the vicious killer who falls for a crippled girl, played by Lori Nelson; Shelley Winters is the moll.

Other actors who were offered the role after Raft turned it down and before Bogart accepted it were: Paul Muni, James Cagney, and Edward G. Robinson.

BEST LINE: Doc Banton to Roy Earle: "Remember what Johnny Dillinger said about guys like you and him? He said you were just rushing toward death. Yeah, that's it. Just rushing toward death."

THE WOMAN IN THE WINDOW
1944

TYPE OF FILM: *Noir*
STUDIO: International Pictures
PRODUCER: Nunnally Johnson
DIRECTOR: Fritz Lang
SCREENWRITER: Nunnally Johnson
SOURCE: *Once Off Guard*, novel by J. H. Wallis
RUNNING TIME: 99 minutes

PRINCIPAL PLAYERS:
Edward G. Robinson . . . . .Professor Richard Wanley
Joan Bennett . . . . .Alice Reed
Dan Duryea . . . . .Heidt
Raymond Massey . . . . .District Attorney Frank Lalor
Edmond Breon . . . . .Dr. Barkstane
Thomas E. Jackson .Inspector Jackson
Dorothy Peterson . . . . .Mrs. Wanley
Arthur Loft . . . . .Claude Mazard/Frank Howard

DID YOU KNOW? Fritz Lang's noir masterpiece was one of a pair of bookends he made a year apart and with essentially the same cast. In *The Woman in the Window*, a mild-mannered professor who has unwittingly risked his future for an innocent evening with a femme fatale is saved in a comic ending when he wakes to find that the quicksand in which he had figuratively been trapped was all a dream. He never meant to do wrong, so Lang spared him. In *Scarlet Street*, released the following year, a mild-mannered businessman readily succumbs to the temptations of a cheap but beautiful girl and chases her, even sinking to stealing money from his job to keep her. When he finds that she loves another man, he kills her and allows her sleazy boyfriend to be executed for the murder. In this film, Lang lets the male protagonist suffer because he made the wrong decision. He did mean to do wrong and wanders the streets endlessly, mad with guilt. Edward G. Robinson played the milquetoast both times, Joan Bennett convincingly played the alluring sex object twice, and Dan Duryea excelled at his specialty—playing a cheap woman-beating hood—in both films.

THE STORY: A middle-aged psychology professor, Richard Wanley, sees his family off for the summer and returns to his club to meet friends, one of whom is District Attorney Frank Lalor. They discuss the loss of adventure as they've aged and the professor is warned against seeking it. Later, leaving the club, he stops to stare at the portrait of a beautiful woman in an art gallery window, only to be surprised when he finds Alice Reed, the model, standing next to him. She invites him to her apartment to see more sketches of her, and he accepts.

While Wanley and Alice are innocently chatting, her jealous boyfriend, Frank Howard, enters the apartment and attacks the professor, choking him. Unable to get Howard to stop, Alice hands the professor a pair of scissors, with which he stabs his attacker, killing him. Rather than call the police, they decide to dispose of the body. Wanley drives it into the country and throws it in the underbrush, scratching his hand on a barbed-wire fence in the process.

Put in charge of the case, the D. A. takes his friend Wanley to the scene of the crime, and they comment on his scratched hand and the poison ivy nearby, which also appears on the professor's hand.

The murdered man had a bodyguard, Heidt, who has figured out that the murder took place at Alice's apartment, and shows up, demanding $5,000. She and the professor raise the money, but when Heidt comes to collect, she tries to poison him, which infuriates him. He searches her apartment and finds incriminating evidence which he pockets, demanding another $5,000. Distraught, she calls to tell the professor of the new demand, and he takes an overdose of sleeping powder. While sitting on her bed, sobbing in despair, she hears gunshots in the street and runs out to find that Heidt has been shot to death by the police, who find the money and other evidence on him. She calls the professor, but he cannot be roused. Finally his eyes open, and he realizes that he has fallen asleep at the club and dreamed the entire adventure.

* * *

Parting from film *noir* tradition, Alice Reed, though a beautiful and provocative woman and clearly the mistress of the murdered man, does not lead the male hero into hopeless desire and ultimate doom. She is as much an innocent victim of circumstance as Professor Wanley.

The film also diverges from traditional *noir* sensibility by having a comic ending. Only the despised murder victim and the cheap blackmailer die, while the two stars are able to resume their normal lives.

Fritz Lang's original version of *The Woman in the Window* had a very different ending, much more in keeping with noir expectations. When Heidt tries blackmail in the earlier version, Professor Wanley kills him and later commits suicide. But Lang felt the price that Wanley had to pay for merely going home with a woman was too high and changed the ending to the more upbeat one that was in the final print. Lang thought it was a good cautionary tale, warning audiences that they must always be on guard.

The original working title of the motion picture was *Once Off Guard*. Merle Oberon had been the original choice to play Alice Reed but was replaced by Joan Bennett.

BEST LINE: District Attorney Frank Lalor about a female suspect: "She's got something on her conscience . . . but what woman hasn't?"

THE KILLING
1956

TYPE OF FILM: Crime/*Noir*

STUDIO: United Artists

PRODUCER: James B. Harris

DIRECTOR: Stanley Kubrick

SCREENWRITER: Stanley Kubrick

SOURCE: *Clean Break*, novel by Lionel White

RUNNING TIME: 83 minutes

PRINCIPAL PLAYERS:

Sterling Hayden . . . . Johnny Clay
Coleen Gray . . . . Fay
Vince Edwards . . . . Val Cannon
Jay C. Flippen . . . . Marvin Unger
Ted Corsia . . . . Randy Kennan
Marie Windsor . . . . Sherry Peatty
Elisha Cook, Jr. . . . . George Peatty
Timothy Carey . . . . Nikki Arane
Joe Sawyer . . . . Mike O'Reilly
Jay Adler . . . . Leo
Joseph Turkel . . . . Tiny

DID YOU KNOW? *The Killing* is the motion picture that made Stanley Kubrick famous, even though it had a minuscule budget. But this budget must have seemed positively gigantic to Kubrick after his first two films, *Fear and Desire* (1953) and *Killer's Kiss* (1955), which each had a budget of $40,000. Even in the 1950s, $40,000 was too tiny a sum to make a high quality picture.

When he made *The Killing*, Kubrick used the modest budget as a positive force. The sets, for example, had to be cheaply constructed, so as Kubrick moved his camera from one room to the next, he showed partitions as he went. Instead of building the fourth wall, the camera filled that function. The small spaces, crowded with gang members, reinforced the claustrophobic ambience, and scenes were shot from every imaginable angle, further illustrating the cramped space in which the actors (and, by extension, the robbers) had to work.

THE STORY: Ex-con Johnny Clay tells his girlfriend, Fay, that he will go straight after just one more job, a robbery at a racetrack that will net so much money that he'll never again have to be at risk. The other gang members are George Peatty, a cashier at the racetrack, who wants the money for his greedy and demanding wife, Sherry; Marvin Unger, who is retired and likes the idea of making a big score; Randy Kennan, a cop who owes money to the syndicate and figures the cash from the robbery will save his life; Mike O'Reilly, a bartender at the racetrack who needs money for his sick wife; and Nikki Arane, a brutal killer.

The heist is planned to take place during the seventh race. When Arane shoots one of the horses on the far turn to create a diversion, the rest of the gang loots the money room where the handle is kept, stuffing piles of bills into sacks and tossing them out a window to Kennan, who quickly throws them into his patrol car and drives away.

Kennan leaves the swag in a motel room for Clay to pick up and split with the rest of the gang. As they await Clay's arrival, Val Cannon, Sherry's secret lover, pulls out a gun and kills most of them but is himself shot to death in the gun battle.

George Peatty, badly wounded, manages to get home to Sherry and, realizing that she had set them all up in order to run away with Cannon, shoots the wife who betrayed him. Then he falls over dead.

Knowing of the shootout, Clay takes the suitcase full of money and heads for the airport with Fay. Just as their escape with the fortune seems assured, a clumsy porter drops the suitcase and it bursts open, scattering the cash along a windswept runway as the police close in to arrest him.

* * *

This cult classic features all the customary elements of noir films (bad girl who plays her guy for a sap, multiple murders, hopelessness for all, double-crosses), but it was also innovative. Audiences today are familiar with some of the technical feats achieved by Kubrick, but they were new at the time. His management of time, for example, is stunning, as he uses flashbacks and flashforwards with alacrity, managing never to confuse viewers. A voice-over helps keep all the action in context, and the suspense becomes nearly unbearable at times as quick cutting shows various characters in different locales acting simultaneously.

Given his tiny budget, Stanley Kubrick might have been expected to use unknown actors, but instead he hired familiar faces whose careers had either languished or had never taken off. Sterling Hayden, Elisha Cook, Jr., Marie Windsor, and Ted Corsia, among others, had had numerous roles but none ever attained the stardom that might have been expected.

One of the racehorses at the track is named "Stanley K" for director Stanley Kubrick.

BEST LINE: As Johnny Clay and his girl friend Fay watch a fortune in cash being blown away by the wind as the police close in, the gangster watches in despair and futility, saying, "What's the difference?"

RESERVOIR DOGS
1992

TYPE OF FILM:	Crime/*Noir*
STUDIO:	Miramax
EXECUTIVE PRODUCERS:	Richard N. Gladstein, Monte Hellman, Ronna B. Wallace
PRODUCER:	Lawrence Bender
CO-PRODUCER:	Harvey Keitel
DIRECTOR:	Quentin Tarantino
SCREENWRITER:	Quentin Tarantino
SOURCE:	Original
RUNNING TIME:	99 minutes

PRINCIPAL PLAYERS:

Harvey Keitel . . . . .Larry/"Mr. White"
Tim Roth . . . . .Freddy Newendyke/"Mr. Orange"
Michael Madsen .Vic Vega/"Mr. Blonde"
Chris Penn . . . ."Nice Guy" Eddie
Steve Buscemi . . . ."Mr. Pink"
Lawrence Tierney . . . . .Joe Cabot
Randy Brooks . . . . .Holdaway
Kirk Baltz . . . . .Marvin Nash
Eddie Bunker . . . ."Mr. Blue"
Quentin Tarantino . . . ."Mr. Brown"
Michael Sottile . . . . .Teddy

DID YOU KNOW? Director Quentin Tarantino had wanted James Woods, the quintessential modern hard-boiled actor, to appear in *Reservoir Dogs*. He wanted him so badly that he made five different offers to Woods, all of which were rejected by his agent, who never told Woods that they were made because the fees were all dramatically less than Woods was making. Some time after the film was completed, Tarantino and Woods met, and when the actor learned of the offers, he was so angry that he fired his agent. Naturally enough, Woods was a great fan of the film and wanted to know which role Tarantino had had in mind for him, but Tarantino refused to tell him, explaining only that "the actor who played the role was magnificent." It appears to be widely known inside Hollywood that the role Tarantino had in mind for Woods was "Mr. Orange," which was indeed played superbly by Tim Roth.

THE STORY: A jewelry robbery organized by Joe Cabot has gone terribly wrong. A gang of thugs, strangers to each other and using aliases assigned by Cabot, return to the abandoned warehouse that serves as their headquarters after the botched heist. "Mr. Orange" has been seriously wounded and driven back to the rendezvous by "Mr. White," where they meet up with "Mr. Pink," who had escaped with the loot. Pink is convinced that an informant has infiltrated the gang and suggests to White that they leave Orange to die and split the diamonds between them. As they debate the issue, "Mr. Blonde" returns with a cop he has taken hostage.

"Nice Guy" Eddie, Joe Cabot's son, arrives to try to clean up the mess that the gang of bunglers has created. He takes White and Pink with him to dispose of the car used in the robbery, while Blonde remains in the warehouse with the unconscious Orange and the cop, who Blonde tortures by slashing his face and cutting off his ear. As Blonde pours kerosene on the hostage, Orange wakes up and shoots Blonde, revealing to the cop that he is an undercover detective. Cabot shows up, certain that Orange is the traitor, but Orange convinces him that Blonde admitted that *he* was a cop, which is why Orange killed him. White returns and sizes up the situation. He trusts Orange, so he pulls a gun on Cabot as Eddie pulls a gun on *him*. They open fire on each other, Eddie and Cabot are killed.

Meanwhile, Pink decides to flee with the diamonds, not realizing that the warehouse is surrounded by police who have been waiting for Orange's signals, and is shot to death. When Orange reveals his true identity to White, White shoots him and is in turn shot by the police. The only survivor of the warehouse massacre is the young cop who, having also survived the torture, is concerned that his good looks have been destroyed.

* * *

This is not a film for everyone. In addition to flat moments, the amount and degree of violence may be off-putting to all but the most hardened. However, for all its *noir*-ish elements and the fact that just about everyone dies, *Reservoir Dogs* is filled with original and memorable characters and dialogue that, in its absurdity, is often hilarious.

The jewelry robbery at the core of the picture is never seen. Flashbacks are used to show what the plan had been and also to show snippets of isolated incidents to illustrate how badly the plan went awry.

The film, Quentin Tarantino's first, entirely his idea and his script, was shot on a very small budget. One money-saving opportunity presented itself when Robert Kurtzman offered to do the special effects makeup for no fee—on the condition that Tarantino write a script of Kurtzman's story. It was filmed in 1996 as *From Dusk Till Dawn,* and you may send up a prayer of thanks if you missed it.

If the title seems to make little sense, there's a good reason. It was inspired by *Au Revoir, Les Enfants*, a 1987 French film whose title Tarantino was unable to pronounce while he was working as a clerk in a video store.

The woman who was shot by Mr. Orange was Tim Roth's dialogue coach. He insisted that she play the role because she had been so tough on him that he wanted to see her killed.

A curiosity: there are no female speaking parts in *Reservoir Dogs*.

BEST LINE: When Mr. Pink comes into the warehouse, he sees that Mr. Orange has been shot. He asks him, "Is it bad?" Mr. White looks at Pink and asks, "As opposed to good?"

THE IPCRESS FILE
1965

TYPE OF FILM:	Espionage
STUDIO:	Universal
EXECUTIVE PRODUCER:	Charles Kasher
PRODUCER:	Harry Saltzman
DIRECTOR:	Sidney J. Furie
SCREENWRITERS:	Bill Canaway and James Doran
SOURCE:	*The Ipcress File,* novel by Len Deighton
RUNNING TIME:	108 minutes

PRINCIPAL PLAYERS:

Michael Caine . . . . .Harry Palmer
Nigel Green . . . . .Dalby
Guy Doleman . . . . .Major Ross
Sue Lloyd . . . . .Jean
Gordon Jackson . . . . .Carswell
Aubrey Richards . . . . .Radcliffe
Frank Gatliff . . . . .Bluejay
Thomas Baptiste . . . . .Barney
Oliver MacGreevy . . . . .Housemartin

DID YOU KNOW? The most unlikely producer of *The Ipcress File* and the subsequent espionage films made from Len Deighton's books is Harry Saltzman. He is also the co-producer of most of the James Bond movies, and is it possible for two heroes to be more unalike? Bond, handsome and suave, committed to defending freedom and democracy, especially for England, is well-trained and eager to take on the most dangerous assignments, no matter how much derring-do is required. Harry Palmer, on the other hand, is an overweight myopic who became a spy because he had been caught trafficking in the black market while he was a sergeant in the British armed forces and he was given the choice of jail or espionage. His allegiances are not exactly ideological; they are to girls, books, music, cooking, and Gauloise cigarettes, in roughly that order.

The executive producer, Charles Kasher, was a long-time friend of Saltzman's and earned his fortune in the 1950s with the Charles Antell line of hair products ("made with lanolin," as the commercials said, relentlessly).

THE STORY: When an important scientist is kidnapped and the British Central Intelligence operative who is guarding him is killed, the agent's replacement is the unlikely Harry Palmer, himself a borderline criminal who is transferred from a desk job to Major Ross' military division. The scientist is only one of several who have been kidnapped recently, but he is doubly important because of a valuable top secret file in his possession, which must not reach the wrong hands.

Palmer locates a deserted warehouse where he and his superior, Carswell, discover a tape marked *Ipcress*. Carswell is killed and Palmer is subjected to grueling and brutal brainwashing, though he manages to survive and escape. He then calls Dalby, the head of the civil intelligence division, and Ross, head of the military intelligence division, to the old factory building and confronts them, knowing one is a traitor. When Dalby is identified as the man who had tried to set up Palmer, he is shot.

* * *

The Ipcress File, like all of Len Deighton's stories about Harry Palmer, is complex and abstruse. Whereas in a James Bond movie the villain is so easily identified that he might as well be wearing a banner across his chest, Palmer's foes may be anyone on either side in what was then the Cold War. Subtlety and deception drive the stories, with Palmer's character dominating them.

In Len Deighton's novels, the protagonist (it would be overly stretching the concept to call him the hero) is never named. He is an Everyman, with neither special skills nor the desire to enter the largely boring but frequently dangerous world of espionage, but who is thrust into it anyway, much like so many of the characters in Alfred Hitchcock's films. Thus, the anonymity of a nameless man suited Deighton's desire to project that image of ordinariness, though ultimately he is anything but ordinary, of course.

When it came time to make the film, it was agreed that, while it may work in a novel, the notion of the central character being unnamed would be too awkward for a motion picture, so a name had to be created. Michael Caine suggested "Harry" as the perfect commonplace name, and the producers added "Palmer."

Christopher Plummer had initially been considered for the role of Harry Palmer but dropped out to star in *The Sound of Music* (1965).

Of the hundreds, even thousands, of action films made, the star of *The Ipcress File* was the first to wear glasses. In real life, Michael Caine is myopic and needs to wear them.

Two sequels to *The Ipcress File* were made, both starring Michael Caine. *Funeral in Berlin* (1966) was directed by Guy Hamilton, who did a far better job as the director of *Goldfinger* (1964). *The Billion Dollar Brain* (1967) was an incoherent mishmash directed by Ken Russell, bad enough to kill the series. Well, almost, but—alas—not quite. Two made-for-cable television films were made in 1997, *Bullet to Beijing* and *Midnight in St. Petersburg*. It is devoutly hoped that you missed them.

BEST LINE: Harry Palmer comes home unexpectedly early to find his apartment being searched by a fellow agent, who says, "You're supposed to be at work." Palmer responds, "And you are, of course."

THE KENNEL MURDER CASE
1933

TYPE OF FILM: Detective

STUDIO: Warner Brothers

DIRECTOR: Michael Curtiz

SCREENWRITERS: Robert N. Lee and Peter Milne

SOURCE: *The Kennel Murder Case*, novel by S. S. Van Dine

RUNNING TIME: 73 minutes

PRINCIPAL PLAYERS:

William Powell	Philo Vance
Mary Astor	Hilda Lake
Eugene Pallette	Sgt. Ernest Heath
Ralph Morgan	Raymond Wrede
Robert McWade	District Attorney Markham
Helen Vinson	Doris Delafield
Jack LaRue	Eduardo Grassi
Paul Cavanagh	Sir Thomas MacDonald
Robert Barrat	Archer Coe
Frank Conroy	Brisbane Coe
Etienne Girardot	Dr. Doremus
James Lee	Liang

DID YOU KNOW? One of the greatest of all film historians, William K. Everson, in his important book, *The Detective in Film* (1972), identified three films as the greatest detective movies ever made: *The Kennel Murder Case, The Maltese Falcon,* and *Green for Danger.* His criteria were that the films bring the same scrupulous attention as the book to planting fair clues and a cerebral resolution to the case, while remaining entertaining and fast-paced throughout, and keeping the ending a surprise until the very last.

THE STORY: When wealthy and heartless Archer Coe is found dead—an apparent suicide—Philo Vance and New York police sergeant Ernest Heath suspect murder. They join forces and attempt to sift through the myriad suspects, all of whom had ample reason to wish Coe dead. Hilda Lake, Coe's ward, hated his tight control over her money. Sir Thomas MacDonald wanted to marry Hilda and shared her anger at Coe; further, he blamed Coe for the death of his prize show dog and threatened vengeance. Raymond Wrede was Coe's secretary and believed Coe was all that stood between himself and Hilda, with whom he was in love. Doris Delafield was Coe's mistress but was preparing to run away with Eduardo Grassi, an art dealer; when Coe caught them together, he canceled a big deal with Grassi and dumped Doris. Liang, Coe's cook, had helped his employer illegally obtain ancient Chinese art; when Liang hid evidence, he, too, became a suspect. After an attempt is made on Sir Thomas's life, Vance arranges a scenario to prod the killer into another murder attempt. With the use of a fierce Doberman pinscher and a carefully constructed miniature house, Vance proves who the murderer was and how he or she accomplished the apparently impossible crime.

* * *

There were seventeen full-length feature films about Philo Vance, four of which—*The Canary Murder Case* (1929), *The Greene Murder Case* (1929), *The Benson Murder Case* (1930), and *The Kennel Murder Case*, starred William Powell. Powell was easily the best Vance, the detective role with which he was most associated until he began *The Thin Man* series in 1934. Other Vance portrayals were made by Basil Rathbone in *The Bishop Murder Case* (1930), Warren William, a bit more nondescript in *The Dragon Murder Case* (1934), Paul Lukas in *The Casino Murder Case* (1935), and Edmund Lowe in *The Garden Murder Case* (1936). *The Kennel Murder Case* was remade in 1940 as *Calling Philo Vance,* starring a lackluster James Stephenson as the detective updated to an American agent trying to solve the murder of the traitorous Coe.

Warner Brothers was paying Powell the star quality sum of $6,000 a week when the Depression hit and his pay was reduced to $4,000, making him unhappy enough to leave the studio. Although his departure was publicized as a desire on Powell's part to work as a freelance actor rather than a contract player, the fact is Warner was happy to see him go, because his box office take did not justify his large salary demands. Within a few years, the enormous success of *It Happened One Night* (1934) and *The Thin Man* (1934) catapulted him to the top of Hollywood's box-office attractions.

BEST LINE: The medical examiner, after closely inspecting the corpse, who had apparently shot himself to death in a locked room, states, "Gentlemen, when that bullet entered this man's head, he had been dead for hours."

THE GLASS KEY
1942

TYPE OF FILM: Detective

STUDIO: Paramount

PRODUCER: Fred Kohlmar

DIRECTOR: Stuart Heisler

SCREENWRITER: Jonathan Latimer

SOURCE: *The Glass Key*, novel by Dashiell Hammett

RUNNING TIME: 85 minutes

PRINCIPAL PLAYERS:

Brian Donlevy . . . . .Paul Madvig
Veronica Lake . . . . .Janet Henry
Alan Ladd . . . . .Ed Beaumont
Joseph Calleia . . . . .Nick Varna
William Bendix . . . . .Jeff
Bonita Granville . . . . .Opal Madvig
Richard Denning . . . . .Taylor Henry
Frances Gifford . . . . .Nurse
Donald MacBride . . . . .Farr
Margaret Hayes . . . . .Eloise Matthews
Moroni Olsen . . . . .Ralph Henry
Eddie Marr . . . . .Rusty

DID YOU KNOW? Alan Ladd, who played Ed Beaumont, and William Bendix, the actor who plays Jeff, the thug who beats him up, were best friends. They even lived in houses across the street from each other. The argument that broke up their friendship for good occurred when Ladd went into the Navy and served on a base in San Diego. When he complained to his friend Bendix about the difficulties of military life, Bendix joked that he had no right to complain and that he had it pretty soft. Ladd didn't respond, but his wife and agent, Sue Carol, retorted quickly that Bendix was in no position to talk, as he hadn't even joined any of the armed forces. Bendix, who was an asthmatic and ineligible for military duty, stormed off, and the two actors never spoke again.

THE STORY: Paul Madvig, a powerful politician, aids the corrupt Senator Henry in his bid for reelection, much against the wishes of Ed Beaumont, Madvig's loyal aide. When Madvig finally acts in a moral way and closes down the gambling joint run by a pal of Henry's, he is framed for the murder of the senator's son by the gangster. Although Madvig and Beaumont are competing for the same girl, the senator's daughter, Janet, when his boss is arrested for murder, Beaumont turns detective to find the real killer. After Beaumont is mercilessly beaten by Jeff, he manages to turn the thug against his boss and the gangster is killed. Beaumont manages to locate the real killer of Henry's son and get Madvig freed.

* * *

The Glass Key is a hybrid between the private eye novels that were popular in the 1930s and the noir films that had not yet clearly defined their genre. Although Beaumont works in the manner of the traditional detective, trying to solve the murder for which his boss has been framed, the normal structure of the detective story is lacking. In the classic private-eye tale, the detective is presented with a problem and he seeks the answer to that problem by asking questions and sifting the truth from the lies he inevitably will be told. When he learns the truth, the problem is solved and all is right with the world.

In *The Glass Key*, however, all the characters are morally ambivalent, and, when Beaumont reveals the identity of the perpetrator, the sense of satisfying closure that the traditional mystery offers is lacking: The greater criminal—in this case an intertwined society of crooked officials, gangsters, and all the people who connive to make the entire city corrupt—cannot be arrested and punished.

This is the second version of Dashiell Hammett's best novel. The first was produced in 1935, starring George Raft as Ed Beaumont (he was Ned in the novel), Edward Arnold as Madvig, Claire Dodd as Janet Henry, and Rosalind Keith as Opal Madvig. Although not as tough and violent as the 1942 version, it, too, is a first-rate film that can be viewed with pleasure today.

"The Glass Key" is underworld jargon for an invitation that is insincere.

When Hammett lived in San Francisco in 1925, he lived in an apartment on Eddy Street on which he based Beaumont's rooms.

Akira Kurosawa identified *The Glass Key* as the inspiration for his famous film *Yojimbo*.

BEST LINE: Jeff threatens Beaumont: "I've got a little room upstairs that's too small for you to fall down in. I can bounce you around off the walls; that way we won't be wasting a lot of time while you get up off the floor."

SLEUTH
1972

TYPE OF FILM: Crime

STUDIO: Twentieth Century-Fox

PRODUCER: Morton Gottlieb

DIRECTOR: Joseph L. Mankiewicz

SCREENWRITER: Anthony Shaffer

SOURCE: *Sleuth,* play by Anthony Shaffer

RUNNING TIME: 138 minutes

PRINCIPAL PLAYERS:

Laurence Olivier . . . . .Andrew Wyke

Michael Caine . . .Milo Tindle/ Inspector Doppler/ the voices of Detective Sergeant Tarrant and Police Constable Higgs

DID YOU KNOW? In an attempt to keep secret the fact that only two actors appear in the entire film, several names are listed in the opening credits, including Eve Channing, who is then listed as Margo Channing in the closing credits. Margo Channing, of course, is the name of the famous character played by Bette Davis in *All About Eve*, the classic film directed by Joseph L. Mankiewicz in 1950. She is supposed to have played Laurence Olivier's wife, Marguerite, but the character is never seen except in an idealized painting and a single photograph on the wall of the mansion. The person seen in that photo is actually Joanne Woodward.

THE STORY: Milo Tindle, owner of a couple of moderately successful hair salons in London, is invited to the country estate of Andrew Wyke, the fabulously successful writer of best-selling detective novels. Wyke makes it clear that he knows Tindle is having an affair with his wife but, instead of being angry or pained, is delighted to be rid of her and offers financial help to Tindle so that he'll be able to keep the spendthrift Marguerite in the style to which Wyke has allowed her to become accustomed.

Wyke, inordinately fond of games, the more complex the better, suggests that Tindle steal Marguerite's jewels, worth a quarter of a million pounds, and he'll help Tindle fence them while he, Wyke, collects the insurance money. To make the theft more interesting, he insists that Tindle wear a disguise, and they settle on an outrageous clown costume. Tindle follows all of Wyke's carefully worked out plans, including using a ladder to sneak through a window and blowing the safe open with dynamite. Suddenly, the novelist reveals that he has no plans to give up his wife and that he concocted the scheme so that he could shoot Tindle as an intruder. In spite of the younger man's pleas, Wyke holds a handgun to his head and pulls the trigger.

Soon after, a police inspector arrives to question the wealthy novelist about Tindle's disappearance and, searching the premises, finds evidence that the hairdresser had been there and met a bad end—Wyke's claims that he had shot his rival with a blank notwithstanding. Just as the case against Wyke seems certain, the policeman reveals himself to be Tindle in disguise.

Although the aging Wyke, close to a heart attack, is relieved to know that he was merely the victim of the younger man's trick and that he won't be arrested for murder, there is still a surprise in store for him. Tindle tells him that he has murdered Wyke's mistress, providing enough evidence to convince Wyke that he is telling the truth, and tells him that he has called for the police to arrive in fifteen minutes. Four clues have been planted in the house that will prove that Wyke committed the murder and he must find them, using Tindle's hints, in order to save himself.

Wyke's frantic search unearths the clues, and Tindle tells him it was all a hoax after all and that his mistress was an ally. The unrelieved pressure has been too much for the normally rational Wyke, and he grabs Tindle's gun and shoots him with it, just as the police sirens are heard and their lights come into view. Just before he dies, Tindle says, "Tell them it was only a game."

* * *

As perhaps the greatest mystery play ever written, *Sleuth's* cleverness was changed hardly at all for its motion picture version by Anthony Shaffer, who wrote both versions. The twists and turns of plot are rivaled only by *Witness For the Prosecution* for the honor of being the most distinguished stage presentation of a mystery.

At the time of the filming of *Sleuth,* Sir Laurence Olivier was the only actor ever named to be a lord, and Michael Caine was nervous about how to address his costar. Shortly before filming be-

50

gan, Caine unexpectedly received a letter from Olivier, announcing that "One minute after we meet, I shall call you Michael and you will call me Larry, and that's how it will remain forever." In fact, Sir Laurence Olivier insisted that everyone with whom he worked call him "Larry" throughout his extraordinary career.

Sleuth was the last film directed by Joseph L. Mankiewicz, whose many other successes included *Dragonwyck* (1946), *The Ghost and Mrs. Muir* (1947), *A Letter to Three Wives* (1949), *The Barefoot Contessa* (1954), *Guys and Dolls* (1955), *The Quiet American* (1958), *Suddenly, Last Summer* (1959), and the less successful *Cleopatra* (1963).

Director Mankiewicz asked Olivier during a rehearsal if he could think of a way to make the now-aging actor seem more attractive, and more "literary" while he was at it. The great actor suggested a simple thin mustache, and it gave him exactly the look Mankiewicz was seeking.

Sleuth was nominated for an Academy Award for Best Picture, and both its stars, Olivier and Caine, also received nominations for Best Actor, losing to Marlon Brando's portrayal of Don Vito Corleone in *The Godfather*, which also won as Best Picture. Anthony Shaffer won an Edgar Allan Poe Award from the Mystery Writers of America for his screenplay.

BEST LINE: Inspector Doppler to a smug Wyke: "Is there nothing you would not consider a game, sir? Duty, work, even marriage?" Wyke replies, "Oh, please, inspector, don't include marriage. Sex . . . sex is the game. Marriage is the penalty."

THE GRIFTERS
1990

TYPE OF FILM:	Crime/*noir*
STUDIO:	Miramax
EXECUTIVE PRODUCER:	Barbara De Fine
PRODUCERS:	Martin Scorsese, Robert A. Harris, Jim Painter
DIRECTOR:	Stephen Frears
SCREENWRITER:	Donald E. Westlake
SOURCE:	*The Grifters*, novel by Jim Thompson
RUNNING TIME:	119 minutes

PRINCIPAL PLAYERS:

John Cusack . . . . Roy Dillon
Anjelica Huston . . . . Lilly Dillon
Annette Bening . . . . Myra Langtry
Pat Hingle . . . . Bobo Justus
J. T. Walsh . . . . Cole
Henry Jones . . . . Sims, the desk clerk
Gailard Sartain . . . . Myra's landlady
Charles Napier . . . . Hebbing

DID YOU KNOW? Annette Bening, nominated for an Academy Award for her role as Myra Langtry, owes the jump-start to her career to Melanie Griffith. Anjelica Huston had been approached to star in *The Grifters* and, after thinking about it for a while, turned it down. Cher, approached next, also passed on the opportunity. Melanie Griffith took the role of Lilly Dillon but, after about three weeks of work, left the production. During that three week period, Annette Bening, who had little screen experience, having been trained as a stage actress, auditioned for the role of Myra, and it was given to her largely because she resembled Griffith. This was of great importance for the scene in which Lilly Dillon disguises herself as Myra. After Griffith quit, Huston was again offered the role and, for whatever reason, changed her mind and accepted. Although both actresses were superb in the roles, the disguise scene is ludicrous because, quite obviously, Huston and Bening do not resemble each other in the slightest.

THE STORY: The lives of three con artists—each the same in attitude but entirely different in style—are inextricably woven together. Lilly Dillon is a hardened professional whose entire career has been spent working for a bookmaking syndicate. Her son, Roy, learned the art of the grift from a small-timer who taught him two things: never take a partner, because then you have to share the take, and never get involved with the "long con,"—a swindle that is big and complex—because even if the take is big, so is the risk. Myra Langtry, the sexy girlfriend of Roy, has worked only the long con with another partner for a decade and raked in huge sums. She wants to get back into that game and has been searching for a new partner ever since her old one went insane; she thinks she's found him in Roy.

Lilly was very young when Roy was born and she wanted no part of him, so he left home at the age of seventeen. After eight years of separation, Lilly shows up unexpectedly and tries to get Roy out of the crooked life but is unable to do so. When she meets Roy's girlfriend, she instantly dislikes her for complicated reasons, not the least of which is the undercurrent of sublimated incestuous feelings on the part of both Lilly and Roy.

Roy is in the hospital because of a petty swindle that failed to work, getting him injured by a bartender who caught him. The young-looking Lilly is at his side when Myra shows up, and Roy introduces his mother. Myra exclaims, "That's impossible!" and Lilly responds, "Not quite." When Lilly insults her, Myra withdraws her friendly attitude. "Oh, oh, of course," she says. "Now that I see you in the light you're plenty old enough to be Roy's mother."

The mobster for whom Lilly works, Bobo Justus, becomes suspicious that Lilly may have tried to rip him off and brings her back to his hotel room. He threatens her with serious injury, but lets her off lightly with a nonetheless vicious warning, pressing his lighted cigar into her hand.

Myra, having been rebuffed by Roy, is convinced that Lilly is responsible and learns that, in fact, her "rival" *has* been stealing from Bobo and informs on her. Lilly flees with her stolen money. Myra follows her and attempts to strangle her in her sleep, but Lilly pulls a gun out from under her pillow and shoots her. Dressing in Myra's clothes, Lilly goes to her son's house and tries to steal his money, only to have him catch her and stop her. Desperate to get away from Bobo's henchmen with the money, she swings the suitcase full of cash at her son's head as he is drinking water and smashes the glass, which cuts an artery in his neck, killing him. Lilly scoops up the cash, shoves it into the suitcase, and drives away.

* * *

This *noir* masterpiece was a critical and commercial success—a surprise to more than a few people. Although wonderfully acted and with a brilliant screenplay, it resembled *Sea of Love* in style and texture. *Sea of Love* had been released just a year before *The Grifters,* and it, too, had a wonderful screenplay by Richard Price and was sensationally acted by Ellen Barkin and Al Pacino. It sank without a trace, ignored by audiences, critics, and award-givers, most notably the Academy of Motion Picture Arts and Sciences.

Anjelica Huston wasn't the only person to turn down the film. Donald E. Westlake had been offered the project and initially rejected it, saying the film was too gloomy. Director Stephen Frears met with Westlake and tried to convince him to write the screenplay, because Frears was a fan of Westlake's noir novels about the criminal Parker, written under the pseudonym Richard Stark. Westlake finally agreed to write the screenplay.

Frears, who is British, was making his first American film and loved that the *Boston Globe* had called Jim Thompson's novel "strong meat." He wanted to make a film that wallowed in American English and knew Westlake could give it to him. If the film is approached as the son's story, he admitted, it was all gloom and doom. However, if it is seen as the mother's story, it could easily be taken as an uplifting illustration of the price of survival. Both Huston and Westlake were nominated for Oscars.

The numerous scenes that make a motion picture are, of course, shot out of sequence, and director Stephen Frears has always maintained that an actor should never have to appear in a scene after he plays a scene in which he dies. It psychologically depresses them, sucking the energy out of their performance, he feels. Since there is a high body count among the leading characters in *The Grifters*, the last day of shooting saw virtually everybody of importance die.

In addition to the Academy Award nominations for Stephen

Frears (Best Director), Anjelica Huston (Best Actress), Annette Bening (Best Supporting Actress), and Donald E. Westlake (Best Adapted Screenplay), numerous other awards were showered on those connected to the film.

Donald E. Westlake won the Edgar Allan Poe Award from the Mystery Writers of America for his screenplay. Anjelica Huston was nominated for a Golden Globe Award as Best Actress and won the award in that category from the National Society of Film Critics and the *Los Angeles Times* Film Critics. Annette Bening was nominated for a British Academy Award as Best Supporting Actress and won the National Society of Film Critics Award.

BEST LINE: Myra, admiringly describing Cole, her former partner in the long con, to Roy Dillon: "He was so crooked he could eat soup with a corkscrew."

BULLDOG DRUMMOND
1929

TYPE OF FILM:	Espionage
STUDIO:	United Artists
PRODUCER:	Samuel Goldwyn
DIRECTOR:	F. Richard Jones
SCREENWRITERS:	Sidney Howard and Wallace Smith
SOURCE:	*Bulldog Drummond*, novel by H. C. McNeile, and *Bulldog Drummond,* play by H. C. McNeile and Gerald Du Maurier
RUNNING TIME:	89 minutes

PRINCIPAL PLAYERS:

Ronald Colman . . . . .Hugh "Bulldog" Drummond
Joan Bennett . . . . .Phyllis Benton
Lilyan Tashman . . . . .Irma
Montagu Love . . . . .Peterson
Lawrence Grant . . . . .Dr. Larkington
Wilson Benge . . . . .Danny
Claud Allister . . . . .Algy Longworth
Charles Sellon . . . . .John Travers
Adolph Milar . . . . .Marcovich

DID YOU KNOW? This was Ronald Colman's first talking picture. He had already become a screen idol in silents because of his good looks, but when audiences heard his unique voice with its perfect diction and unparalleled timing, they immediately made him one of the biggest stars in Hollywood.

THE STORY: Bored with life after World War I and seeking adventure, Captain Hugh "Bulldog" Drummond places an advertisement in the personals section of the newspaper. He is drawn to the response of Phyllis Benton, whose uncle, John Travers, has been taken prisoner and confined to an asylum by the villainous Dr. Larkington and his associates, a gang of international crooks who are trying to force the uncle to turn over his fortune to them.

Drummond and Phyllis head off to the countryside to rescue

the helpless Travers, only to have Phyllis captured as well. Drummond manages to rescue her briefly, but then he, too, is captured, though he finally manages to escape and kill the malevolent Dr. Larkington.

* * *

Bulldog Drummond was one of the most popular figures in British fiction during the 1920s and '30s. H. C. McNeile, using the pseudonym "Sapper" (British military argot meaning engineer), wrote *Bulldog Drummond*, a novel, in 1920. It had immediate success and was adapted for the stage the following year starring Sir Gerald Du Maurier in London. The play was then brought to Broadway for a grand opening, a long run, and a successful touring company. Eleven more Drummond novels were published during the next seventeen years by McNeile and, when he died, Gerard Fairlie continued to write about the adventurer until 1954.

The book character is tough and violent, allowing nothing—not the law, not scruples, not overwhelming odds—to stand in the way of the justice that lax laws and incompetent police officers are unable to provide. In the motion pictures, particularly with Colman but also when the role was played by Ralph Richardson, Ray Milland, John Lodge, and John Howard, he was more urbane and lighthearted—thoroughly enjoying the sport of it all.

While this was Colman's first talking film, so, too, was it the first talkie Samuel Goldwyn produced. He did not use McNeile's novel as the source for the film but instead used the stage play because, he reckoned, audiences for a talking picture would want lots of, well . . . talking.

The film was an immediate smash hit and earned Colman an Academy Award nomination for Best Actor, one of *two* nominations he received that year; however, he lost to George Arliss for his titular role in *Disraeli*.

There were several silent film versions before the classic 1929 film and eighteen additional talking pictures, the best by far being the only other one in which Colman starred, *Bulldog Drummond Strikes Back* (1934). Based on McNeile's novel *Knock-Out*, it costarred Loretta Young as Colman's love interest (although Myrna Loy had been sought for the role, which she spurned) and cost more than a half-million dollars to make—a staggering sum in 1934.

Ian Fleming once admitted that Bulldog Drummond was his inspiration for James Bond.

BEST LINE: Drummond has gone to an inn to meet Phyllis Benton, whose letter intrigued him because of the danger in which she believed her uncle to be. As Drummond awaits her arrival, his friend Algy shows up with the intention of protecting Drummond. "Algy," Drummond says, "If I'd wanted a bodyguard, I'd have sent for my maiden aunt." Algy objects, "Oh, I say. Why not?" Drummond replies. "She's more of a man than you are."

THIS GUN FOR HIRE
1942

TYPE OF FILM:	Crime/Espionage
STUDIO:	Paramount
PRODUCER:	Richard M. Blumenthal
DIRECTOR:	Frank Tuttle
SCREENWRITERS:	Albert Maltz and W. R. Burnett
SOURCE:	*This Gun for Hire*, novel by Graham Greene (U.K. title: *Gun for Sale*)
RUNNING TIME:	80 minutes

PRINCIPAL PLAYERS:

Veronica Lake . . . . .Ellen Graham
Robert Preston . . . . .Michael Crane
Alan Ladd . . . . .Philip Raven
Laird Cregar . . . . .Willard Gates
Tully Marshall . . . . .Alvin Brewster
Marc Lawrence . . . . .Tommy
Pamela Blake . . . . .Annie
Mikhail Rasumny . . . . .Slukey
Olin Howlin . . . . .Blair Fletcher
Roger Imhof . . . . .Senator Burnett
Frank Ferguson . . . . .Albert Baker

DID YOU KNOW? Sometimes coincidence, good luck, and fortuitous timing can have a greater impact on the making of a movie star than mere talent. In the film's opening credits, Alan Ladd is listed as being introduced to the screen in the role of Philip Raven, although he had in fact previously appeared in many small and unmemorable roles. His first bit of unpredictably superb timing was that the country was ready for noir films as war raged in Europe. Pictures with garrulous, cheerful leading men and snappy patter certainly continued to be popular, but there was now a place for silent, damaged, unemotional actors, of which Ladd, with his flat voice and immobile face, was the perfect archetype.

His second piece of good fortune was in being cast with Veronica Lake, who was as blond and as tiny as he was. When the couple stand next to the very large Laird Cregar, they look like small children, but when they are alone, they are perfectly matched. (Actually, when they are running, they seem to be the same size; when they are standing and talking to each other, Ladd towers over Lake, undoubtedly because he is standing on a box.)

And wouldn't his career have been different if the first actor to be considered for the role, Peter Lorre, had been cast?

Finally, Ladd's role became not only memorable but hugely influential and iconographic. As the film's tough guy, he wore a trench coat, which soon became standard dress for every hard-boiled movie hero.

THE STORY: Philip Raven, a cold-blooded contract killer, is hired to murder Albert Baker. Baker is blackmailing the Nitrochemical Corporation, which had sold a formula for poison gas to the Japanese, who had recently bombed Pearl Harbor. When Raven arrives to do the job, he finds Baker with his secretary and shoots them both. Paid with marked bills to do the killing, he realizes that he has been set up by Willard Gates, an executive with Nitrochemical, and sets out to kill him and the boss who gave the order.

On the train from San Francisco to Los Angeles, where the chemical company is headquartered, Raven meets Ellen Graham, the fiancée of Michael Crane, a police lieutenant. Ellen, coincidentally hired by Gates to appear in a nightclub he owns, is working as an undercover agent for Senator Burnett.

When Gates sees them together, he wires the police to meet the train but Raven escapes with Ellen, whom he has taken hostage. Raven plans to kill Ellen in an old warehouse because she knows he is a killer, but he is interrupted by workmen and she escapes. Assuming that Ellen is an accomplice of Raven, Gates abducts her and also plans to kill her. Raven rescues her and realizing that she is not working with Gates, he now trusts her. Wanting revenge, Raven plans to kill Gates and his boss, but Ellen convinces him that it is his patriotic duty to get signed confessions instead.

Raven manages to get into the Nitrochemical building and exacts the signed confessions before the police break in and shoot him. With his last breath he looks up at Ellen and asks, "Did I do all right by you?"

* * *

The plot bears small resemblance to Graham Greene's novel, which was published in 1936. In the novel—set in cold, dark, rainy England, rather than the sunny California of the film—the protagonist is a social outcast with a harelip, not the handsome, if tightlipped, killer portrayed by Alan Ladd. In Greene's book, the victim is a socialist minister, and the hit is paid for by a wealthy industrialist. In the film, the moneyman is again a businessman, but the reason for the hit is to avoid blackmail.

What George Orwell described as Greene's "usual left-wing scenery" is much in evidence in *This Gun for Hire*, not surprisingly. Greene, of course, was a Communist, whose social and political agenda infused all his fiction. The screenwriters, too, were overt left-wingers, especially Albert Maltz, who was later identified as one of the "Hollywood Ten." The evil head of the corporation, shown clumsily eating milksops, was even cast to physically resemble Henry Ford.

The great critical and commercial success of *This Gun for Hire* was largely credited to the pairing of Ladd and Lake, and they starred together again three more times, in *The Glass Key* (1942), *The Blue Dahlia* (1946), and *Saigon* (1948). They also made cameo appearances together in *Star Spangled Rhythm* (1943) and *Duffy's Tavern* (1945).

In 1957, Paramount remade *This Gun for Hire*, based on Burnett and Maltz's screenplay. The remake, titled *Short Cut to Hell*, starred Robert Ivers and Georgann Johnson, with James Cagney directing his first and only film. It was also absurdly remade in 1991 for cable television as a vehicle for Robert Wagner.

BEST LINE: When Willard Gates pays off Raven, the hitman wants assurance that the bills are all right. Gates is shocked at the notion that he could be distrusted, but then says he understands because, if there were any problem, Raven couldn't very well go to the police. Raven tells him, "I'm my own police."

STRANGERS ON A TRAIN
1951

TYPE OF FILM:	Suspense
STUDIO:	Warner Brothers—First National
PRODUCER:	Alfred Hitchcock
DIRECTOR:	Alfred Hitchcock
SCREENWRITERS:	Raymond Chandler and Czenzi Ormonde; adaptation by Whitfield Cook
SOURCE:	*Strangers On a Train*, novel by Patricia Highsmith
RUNNING TIME:	101 minutes

PRINCIPAL PLAYERS:

Farley Granger . . . . .Guy Haines
Ruth Roman . . . . .Ann Morton
Robert Walker . . . . .Bruno Anthony
Laura Elliott . . . . .Miriam Haines
Leo G. Carroll . . . . .Senator Morton
Patricia Hitchcock . . . . .Barbara Morton
Marion Lorne . . . . .Mrs. Anthony

DID YOU KNOW? Raymond Chandler, who had been nominated for two Academy Awards for his screenplays, had pretty much decided that Hollywood was not for him. He was frequently drunk, longing to get back to writing novels, nursing his dying wife, and contemptuous of the collaborative process. Nonetheless, he was lured back to screenwriting because he wanted to work for Hitchcock. He received $2,500 a week with a five-week guarantee to write the screenplay of *Strangers On a Train* and had the contractual right to work at home, forcing Hitchcock to fly from Los Angeles to San Diego and then take a limousine to La Jolla for meetings with him. In no time, Chandler regretted his decision, complaining loudly and often about Hitchcock's willingness to subjugate story and logic for a dramatic cinematic effect. As the relationship became more and more strained, Chandler openly defied Hitchcock, asking him, "If you know exactly what you want, why did you hire me?" It got worse. On one trip to La Jolla, Chandler watched Hitchcock pull up and said loudly, "Look at that fat bastard trying to get out of the limousine." When his secretary warned him that he might be heard (and apparently he was), he replied, "What do I care?" That was Hitchcock's last trip to La Jolla, and Chandler was replaced on the project by Czenzi Ormonde, an assistant to Ben Hecht (who also worked, uncredited, on the script). After working on only eight screenplays, this was Chandler's last involvement with Hollywood.

THE STORY: On a train trip, Guy Haines, a tennis player, meets Bruno Anthony, a ne'er-do-well who is a fan of his and seems to know a good deal about his life. As they chat, Guy reveals that he hates his wife, so Bruno amiably suggests that he will kill her, if Guy will reciprocate by killing his father. If both are strangers to the people they murder, he reasons, it will be impossible for anyone to suspect them. Guy rejects the idea, but when Bruno persists, he humors him, saying, "Sure, sure" just to get away from someone he perceives as an eccentric.

Guy goes to see his wife, bringing money for the divorce lawyer, but she takes the money and refuses to grant the divorce after all. Enraged Guy calls Ann Morton, the woman with whom he is in love, and tells her of Miriam's change of heart, saying he'd like to strangle her.

Bruno, in his madness, doesn't realize that Guy has no intention of living up to what Bruno perceives as an agreement, and he follows Miriam to an amusement park, where he strangles her. Guy, just returned to Washington, has an alibi, having met a man on the train who turns out to have been too drunk to remember meeting him. Since Guy is a prominent athlete and engaged to a senator's daughter, the police put an around-the-clock surveillance on him. His behavior becomes more and more suspicious to the police and to Ann, as he knows the identity of the murderer and is being harassed by him to live up to the bargain and kill his overbearing father.

To bring the situation to an end, Guy goes to Bruno's house with a gun, sneaks up to his father's bedroom, and begins to tell him of his son's sinister plot, when Bruno reveals himself to be in his father's bed. Now outraged, Bruno swears to implicate Guy by putting his cigarette lighter at the scene of the crime and informing the police.

Guy races through a tennis match to stop Bruno before he can plant the incriminating evidence, catching up to him at the amusement park. He chases him to a merry-go-round that careens out of control, going faster and faster as the two men fight. When it finally crashes, it crushes Bruno to death and the lighter is discovered clutched in his hand—proof that he was the killer.

* * *

After a string of failures, at least by Hitchcock's standards (*The Paradine Case*, 1947; *Rope*, 1948; *Under Capricorn*, 1949; and *Stage Fright*, 1950), *Strangers On a Train* was a terrific commercial and critical success that ushered in a dozen years of unabated triumphs. There are scenes of technical virtuosity, such as: watching Miriam be murdered through her fallen glasses; suspenseful crosscutting, as the tennis match is intercut with Bruno's attempt to retrieve the vital evidence, Guy's lighter, from a sewer; and a frantic finale as a huge merry-go-round spins wildly out of control in a complex scene that was also very dangerous to film.

Patricia Highsmith, a young American author, sold the rights to her first novel for only $7,500. She did not realize the purchaser was a front for Hitchcock, and resented him for ever after.

The motion picture was remade in 1969 as the incomprehensibly dreadful *Once You Kiss a Stranger* and served as the inspiration for *Throw Momma from the Train* (1987) with Danny DeVito and Billy Crystal, which isn't as funny as one might wish.

Hitchcock Alert: The director has his screen moment struggling with a large cello case as he boards the train.

BEST LINE: Guy is discussing the murder of his wife with Ann, her sister Barbara, and her father, Senator Morton. When the senator exclaims, "poor girl," young Barbara replies, "She was a tramp." The senator pompously lectures her, saying, "She was a human being. And let me remind you that even the most unworthy of us has a right to life and the pursuit of happiness." "From what I hear," retorts his daughter, "she pursued it in all directions."

A SHOT IN THE DARK

1964

TYPE OF FILM:	Detective/Comedy
STUDIO:	United Artists
PRODUCER:	Blake Edwards
DIRECTOR:	Blake Edwards
SCREENWRITERS:	Blake Edwards and William Peter Blatty
SOURCE:	*A Shot in the Dark*, play by Harry Kurnitz, and *L'idiote*, play by Marcel Achard
RUNNING TIME:	101 minutes

PRINCIPAL PLAYERS:

Peter Sellers . . . . .Inspector Jacques Clouseau
Elke Sommer . . . . .Maria Gambrelli
George Sanders . . . . .Benjamin Ballon
Herbert Lom . . . . .Chief Inspector Charles Dreyfus
Tracy Reed . . . . .Dominique Ballon
Burt Kwouk . . . . .Kato
Graham Stark . . . . .Hercule Lajoy

DID YOU KNOW? Although it is a hilarious film, *A Shot in the Dark* produced one less-than-hilarious result. As the pratfalling Inspector Jacques Clouseau, Peter Sellers insisted on performing most of his own stunts, falling repeatedly, banging into walls and doors, and fighting with his valet in extremely lively battles. The strain of this relentless activity was largely responsible for Sellers's serious heart attack, which stopped him from working for a long time. He did not take on the rigors of another Pink Panther movie for eleven years.

THE STORY: The famously inept Inspector Jacques Clouseau is accidentally assigned to a very important murder case—to the shock and dismay of his superior, Chief Inspector Charles Dreyfus. Maria Gambrelli,the parlor maid of the prominent Benjamin and Dominique Ballon, is the likely suspect in the murder of her lover, but Clouseau believes her innocent and refuses to arrest her. Dreyfus removes him from the case and jails Maria, but powerful influences force Clouseau back onto the case and he immediately has Maria released. She returns to her job and is immediately found, murder weapon in hand, with the dead gardener. Arrested for murder again, Maria is released by Clouseau, who still believes in her innocence. Maria next visits a nudist colony, followed by the uncomfortable Clouseau. Another corpse turns up, but Maria is not arrested. When Lafarge, the Ballons' butler, is murdered, Maria is again arrested; still undaunted by the evidence, Clouseau releases her.

Later, Clouseau takes Maria nightclubbing. Several attempts on his life are made while he is oblivious to the innocent bystanders who are accidently murdered in his stead. Clouseau becomes convinced that he knows who the real murderer is and gathers all the suspects in the Ballon house. They take turns blaming and accusing each other of the murders until the lights go out and all six make a run for it, piling into Clouseau's car. It explodes, as a bomb had been placed in it in yet another attempt to kill him. Only he and Maria survive.

Dreyfus, too, remains alive, but he has gone insane. Hoping to rid himself of Clouseau, he has repeatedly tried to kill him, causing a rash of deaths that succeeds only in Clouseau being perceived as a hero.

* * *

A Shot in the Dark is the sequel to The Pink Panther, made earlier in the same year and equally hilarious. The comic brilliance of Peter Sellers made the bungling Clouseau one of the most memorable screen detectives of all time, in spite of the fact that several of the later films were absolutely dreadful.

The third film in the series, Inspector Clouseau, did not come out until 1968, but it starred Alan Arkin as Clouseau and was a failure, as Sellers had already been so closely identified with the role.

The fourth film, The Return of the Pink Panther, starred Sellers after an eleven year hiatus, after which he quickly made the excellent The Pink Panther Strikes Again (1976), The Revenge of the Pink Panther (1978), and the weak The Trail of the Pink Panther (1982). The ill-conceived The Curse of the Pink Panther (1983) was Blake Edwards's attempt to keep the series alive in spite of the death of Sellers. Ted Wass played Clouseau, and David Niven

66

made his last screen appearance, his voice dubbed by impressionist Rich Little.

If you look closely at *A Shot in the Dark*, you will see a photograph on the wall of Clouseau shaking hands with General Charles De Gaulle.

In addition to Sellers's memorable portrayal, the series is remembered for the cartoon character who appears with the opening credits and went on to have a life of his own as a Saturday morning cartoon series, and for the very famous and perfectly appropriate score by Henry Mancini.

BEST LINE: Chief Inspector Charles Dreyfus, contemplating the havoc caused by the unimaginably stupid detective: "Give me ten men like Clouseau and I could destroy the world."

I WAKE UP SCREAMING
1941

TYPE OF FILM: *Noir*

STUDIO: Twentieth Century-Fox

PRODUCER: Milton Sperling

DIRECTOR: H. Bruce Humberstone

SCREENWRITER: Dwight Taylor

SOURCE: *I Wake Up Screaming,* novel by Steve Fisher

RUNNING TIME: 82 minutes

PRINCIPAL PLAYERS:

Betty Grable . . . . .Jill Lynn
Victor Mature . . . . .Frankie Christopher/Botticelli
Carole Landis . . . . .Vicky Lynn
Laird Cregar . . . . .Ed Cornell
William Gargan . . . . .Jerry McDonald
Alan Mowbray . . . . .Robin Ray
Allyn Joslyn . . . . .Larry Evans
Elisha Cook, Jr. . . . . .Harry Williams

DID YOU KNOW? Even though he was one of the most brilliant of the Hollywood producers, it seems likely that Darryl F. Zanuck never quite got it when it came to film *noir*. In keeping with the style, tone, characters, and plot of the entire narrative, *I Wake Up Screaming* had a downbeat ending—pretty much what one would expect from a dark tale of crime, murder, obsession, and misguided passion. However, Zanuck insisted that the picture end with a sprightly song-and-dance number by Hollywood's hottest star, Betty Grable. The ending was so ludicrously unsatisfactory that director H. Bruce Humberstone was permitted to make a change to the version that was released. After seeing what a lousy ending he had concocted, Zanuck told Humberstone to come up with a different one. The director pondered for hours and finally fell asleep without a satisfactory solution, but when he awoke, the entire last scene, in best Hollywood fashion, was completely laid out in his mind. Zanuck thought it was a brilliant solution but blasted Humberstone for wasting so much production time with that silly Grable songfest! Zanuck's hand, incidentally, was in another major change from the original plan. The film was originally a Hollywood story but Zanuck had forbidden any of his pictures to be set there, so it was moved to New York, indulging Zanuck's affection for the swanky nightclubs, theaters, and apartments of Gotham.

THE STORY: Frankie Christopher, a promoter, goes to a luncheonette with his friends Robin Ray, a washed-up actor, and Larry Evans, a newspaper columnist, where they meet Vicky Lynn, a beauty with ambitions to be a star. Impressed with her, they decide to try to make it happen. Frankie takes her out to a ritzy nightclub, introduces her around, and she gets two modeling offers that very night. This is just the beginning, as more offers and publicity come her way, but then she suddenly tells Frankie that she has accepted an offer to go to Hollywood—without him. Disappointed and angry, Frankie meets up with Ray and Evans, who share his feelings because they, too, have fallen for the lovely Vicky.

That night, Vicky is murdered and Frankie is questioned, as is her sister, Jill, who doesn't care for Frankie but believes him innocent. She is telling the police about a sinister man who seemed to be stalking her sister when she spots him; he turns out to be Ed Cornell, one of the best cops on the force.

The assistant district attorney releases all the suspects because he is convinced that Vicky was murdered by Harry Williams, the switchboard operator at the hotel where she lived, who disappeared the night she was killed.

Jill, eager to exonerate Frankie while learning who the real killer is, finds out that Williams was picked up for questioning but released because he said he'd gone to visit his parents. Cornell believes Jill is withholding evidence, and she is—an angry letter that Frankie wrote to Vicky when he learned that she was leaving for Hollywood. Jill goes out with Frankie to learn more and falls for him. Just as she is about to give him the incriminating letter, Cornell bursts in and arrests Frankie, but Jill helps him escape. She is arrested briefly, but when released, she and Frankie become convinced that Williams is the murderer and decide to trap him into confessing, which he does. Williams admits that he was madly in love with Vicky, but he tells them that Cornell knows he's guilty but let him off so that Frankie would be arrested for the crime. Frankie goes to Cornell's apartment and finds the walls covered with pictures of Vicky and a shrine on the mantel.

When Cornell returns, he denounces Frankie for changing Vicky, with whom he'd been in love and hoped to marry. His plan to frame Frankie gone awry, Cornell drinks poison and dies.

* * *

I Wake Up Screaming is one of the first noir films and one of several motion pictures in which Laird Cregar played a crazed killer, obsessive fetishist, or oily villain, as in such films as *This Gun for Hire, The Lodger,* and *Hangover Square*. In despair over his obesity and unattractiveness, he committed suicide. In 1948, the beautiful Carole Landis also committed suicide.

Steve Fisher wrote the story for *I Wake Up Screaming* as a film treatment and then wrote a novelization of it afterward, so the film is not based on the book, as is usually stated, but rather the book was planned to coincide with the release of the film.

The character of Ed Cornell received his last name as an homage to the greatest of all noir writers, Cornell Woolrich.

I Wake Up Screaming was originally titled *Hot Spot* and was first released that way, getting reviews under that title. As studio executives debated about which title they preferred, the editor of *Photoplay* magazine, Ernest Heyn, requested permission to serialize the story as *I Wake Up Screaming*, and the dilemma was resolved.

The story was loosely remade in 1953 as *Vicki*, with Jean Peters in the titular role, Jeanne Crain as her sister, and Richard Boone as the obsessive detective.

BEST LINE: Detective Ed Cornell is in Jill Lynn's apartment and sees a picture on the wall titled "The Garden of Hope". Jill wonders what would be the good of living without hope. In a dead voice, the lonely detective responds, "It can be done."

FARGO
1996

TYPE OF FILM: Crime
STUDIO: PolyGram
PRODUCER: Ethan Coen
DIRECTOR: Joel Coen
SCREENWRITERS: Joel and Ethan Coen
SOURCE: Original
RUNNING TIME: 97 minutes

PRINCIPAL PLAYERS:

Frances McDormand . . . . .Marge Gunderson
William H. Macy . . . . .Jerry Lundegaard
Steve Buscemi . . . . .Carl Showalter
Harve Presnell . . . . .Wade Gustafson
Peter Stormare . . . . .Oscar Grimsrud
John Carroll Lynch . . . . .Norm Gunderson
Kristen Rudrüd . . . . .Jean Lundegaard
Tony Denman . . . . .Scotty Lundegaard
James Gaulke . . . . .state trooper
Cliff Rakerd . . . . .Officer Olsen

DID YOU KNOW? The motion picture opens with the stark and unequivocal statement:

This is a true story.
The events depicted in this film took place in Minnesota in 1987.
At the request of the survivors, the names have been changed.
Out of respect for the dead, the rest has been told exactly as it occurred.

In fact, none of it is true and the Coen brothers made up the statement, just as they made up the rest of the film. (This is not unlike the preamble to *Return of the Living Dead*, which also claimed to be a true story, with not even the names being changed. The fact that the film was about zombies and the dead returning to life suggested to many filmgoers that they were witnessing a spoof.)

THE STORY: Badly in debt and desperate, car salesman Jerry Lundegaard hires two crooks, Carl Showalter and Oscar Grimsrud, to kidnap his own wife, counting on her wealthy father to come up with the ransom demand. He tells the hoods that he will seek a ransom of $80,000 and that he will pay them half of that, plus a new car. They agree and drive off. When they are stopped by a patrol car for not having proper license plates, Grimsrud shoots the trooper in the face, killing him. As Showalter drags the body off the road, a young couple in a car happens by and they flee but skid off the icy road. Grimsrud chases them, finds the overturned car, and shoots them both.

Chief of Police Marge Gunderson is called in the middle of the night and, when she arrives at the crime scenes, deduces exactly what happened, recognizing that two men were responsible. "I'll tell you what. From his footprint he looks like a big fella," she says of the shooter. She checks the slain policeman's log, and finds the car he stopped had dealer plates, and traces them to the Twin Cities.

Meanwhile, the kidnappers tell Lundegaard they want the whole $80,000 ransom because they had to kill people. Lundegaard protests, but not too much, as he has actually told his father-in-law the ransom demand is $1,000,000. It is his plan to take the million and deliver $80,000, keeping the rest. The plan goes awry when his father-in-law, recognizing what a bungler Lundegaard is, insists that he wants to deliver the money himself. Showalter shoots him dead but is also shot in the face. When he opens the suitcase, he sees a million dollars and decides to bury all but $80,000 of it, which he brings back to his partner, who insists they split the car, one buying out the other's half. Showalter refuses, saying he got shot so he'll take the car, and is shot by Grimsrud, who has killed the kidnapped woman. He is feeding his partner into a wood chipper when Officer Gunderson captures him, shooting him in the leg as he attempts to flee.

* * *

There are many similarities in structure between this relentlessly escalating botched crime and the first film made by Ethan and Joel Coen, *Blood Simple*, in which a bar owner hires a man to kill his wife and lover, only to be killed himself by the hired gunman. When the body is discovered by the wife's lover, he believes she committed the murder and tries to cover it up, with disastrous results.

Frances McDormand, who made her film debut in *Blood Simple*, won an Oscar for Best Actress in *Fargo*, and the Coen brothers won a statue for Best Original Screenplay. Nominations went to the film for Best Picture, to Joel Coen for Best Director, and to William H. Macy for Best Supporting Actor.

BEST LINE: Marge Gunderson has discovered that the two killers had been with a couple of young prostitutes and she asks them for a description. One describes the smaller one as "kinda funny lookin'." Marge asks, "In what way?" "I don't know," she says, "just funny lookin'." "Can you be any more specific?" Marge prods. "I can't really say," the girl answers. Wanting to be helpful, she offers, "He wasn't circumcised." Marge asks, "Was he funny lookin' apart from that?" Unable to further articulate a physical description, the prostitute concludes, "Like I say, he was funny lookin'. More than most people even," as her friend nods in agreement.

HARPER
1966

TYPE OF FILM: Detective

STUDIO: Warner Brothers

PRODUCERS: Jerry Gershwin and Elliott Kastner

DIRECTOR: Jack Smight

SCREENWRITER: William Goldman

SOURCE: *The Moving Target*, novel by Ross Macdonald

RUNNING TIME: 121 minutes

PRINCIPAL PLAYERS:

Paul Newman . . . . .Lew Harper
Lauren Bacall . . . . .Mrs. Elaine Sampson
Julie Harris . . . . .Betty Fraley
Shelley Winters . . . . .Fay Estabrook
Robert Wagner . . . . .Alan Taggert
Janet Leigh . . . . .Susan Harper
Arthur Hill . . . . .Albert Graves
Pamela Tiffin . . . . .Miranda Sampson
Strother Martin . . . . .Claude
Robert Webber . . . . .Dwight Troy
Harold Gould . . . . .Sheriff Spanner

DID YOU KNOW? As many mystery readers know, Paul Newman's titular character was based on Ross Macdonald's quintessential American private eye, Lew Archer. Why was his name changed from Archer to Harper? Newman appears to be superstitious. He had just had great success as the star of *Hud* and *The Hustler,* and wanted his character's name to begin with an H again. Because of those successes, he had enough box-office power to get the change that he wanted.

THE STORY: At the recommendation of his lawyer friend, Albert Graves, private investigator Lew Harper is hired by Elaine Sampson to find her husband, whom she believes is merely off on another fling with a woman. The bitter Elaine, crippled from a fall off a horse many years earlier, tells Harper that she doesn't want information so that she can divorce him, she just wants to outlive him. "I only want to see him in his grave," she says. "What a terrible thing to say." Harper replies, "People in love will say anything."

While at the estate, he meets Sampson's sexy young daughter, Miranda, and his private pilot, Alan Taggert, the handsome (Harper persists in calling him "Beauty") love interest of Miranda.

Harper searches the hotel suite that Sampson keeps for his private use and finds a photograph of a former movie star, Fay Estabrook, who is now an overweight drunk. He finds her at the bar where she spends too much time and takes her home. When she passes out, he searches her apartment, only to be interrupted by a phone call from the drug-using bar singer, Betty Fraley, and a visit from Dwight Troy, Estabrook's husband.

He interviews Fraley, and she leads him to a religious cult led by the charlatan Claude, whose mountain retreat had been a gift from Sampson.

Elaine receives a ransom note for Sampson, and the $500,000 is left at the designated place where Fraley picks it up. Harper goes to Fraley's place—where Troy is torturing her to learn the location of the money—breaks in, and shoots Troy, who had been operating a Mexican alien smuggling racket with Claude from the religious retreat. Harper forces Fraley to take him to the tanker where Sampson has been held captive, only to find the millionaire dead and his friend Graves at the location.

Fraley tries to escape in Harper's car but is killed when she loses control of the speeding car. As they drive back to Sampson's estate with the ransom money, Graves admits to being the killer. Harper says he has to turn him in. Graves says in that case he has to kill his best friend. He can't pull the trigger, and some doubt remains whether Harper will ultimately report Graves.

* * *

Harper is a classic, almost old-fashioned private-eye story, with Newman filling the role so memorably played by Humphrey Bogart in several films. Even Lauren Bacall, the widow of the legendary Bogart, was cast in the film, perhaps intending to help evoke the memory of Bogie as Sam Spade and Philip Marlowe.

The attractiveness of Lew Archer as *the* motion-picture detective of the then-modern era could not be denied. Although it had taken seventeen years to get *The Moving Target* filmed as *Harper*, it was a solid box-office success, and talk of sequels began almost instantly.

The Chill, perhaps Ross Macdonald's greatest book, was acquired and Newman was announced for the sequel, with Jack Smight again directing. No suitable script was forthcoming, however, so the project was dropped. A few years later, *The Drowning Pool*, Macdonald's second novel, was acquired, and a screenplay was turned in by Tracy Keenan Wynn, Lorenzo Semple, Jr., and Walter Hill—a lot of high-priced talent that produced a mediocre result. Newman again starred, this time with his wife, Joanne Woodward, who suggested that the locale be moved from Los Angeles to New Orleans. It was released in 1976 to lukewarm reviews and attendance in spite of the box office attraction of Newman.

In 1974, NBC telecast *The Underground Man*, a two-hour pilot starring Peter Graves as a stone-faced Archer. It was received well enough to warrant a series, but with Brian Keith replacing Graves. The 1975 series lasted only for seven one-hour episodes.

William Goldman won an Edgar Allan Poe Award from the Mystery Writers of America for his screenplay.

BEST LINE: Albert Graves, infatuated with the sexy young Miranda Sampson, asks Harper to put in a good word for him with her, saying that he's a nice guy. "The bottom is loaded with nice people, Albert." Harper tells him. "Only cream and bastards rise."

THE FALLEN IDOL
1948

TYPE OF FILM:	Suspense
STUDIO:	British Lion
PRODUCER:	David O. Selznick
DIRECTOR:	Carol Reed
SCREENWRITERS:	Graham Greene, Lesley Storm, and William Templeton
SOURCE:	"The Basement Room," short story by Graham Greene
RUNNING TIME:	94 minutes

PRINCIPAL PLAYERS:

Ralph Richardson . . . . .Baines
Michele Morgan . . . . .Julie
Bobby Henrey . . . . .Phillipe
Sonia Dresdel . . . . .Mrs. Baines
Jack Hawkins . . . . .Detective Lake
Bernard Lee . . . . .Detective Hart
Denis O'Dea . . . . .Inspector Crowe
Walter Fitzgerald . . . . .Dr. Fenton
Karel Stepanek . . . . .First Secretary
Joan Young . . . . .Mrs. Barrow
Dandy Nichols . . . . .Mrs. Patterson

DID YOU KNOW? When he got behind the camera for *The Fallen Idol*, Carol Reed was most famous for having directed *Night Train To Munich* (1940) and *Odd Man Out* (1947). He then had his greatest success with his next picture, *The Third Man* (1949). Indisputably a great director, he was additionally held in extremely high esteem for his ability to direct children, a tricky business for any director but a walk in the park for Reed, who had developed a special trick for this challenge. While child actors are generally able to remember and properly deliver their lines, they are notorious for missing their cues. Reed got around this by filming the adult actors doing the scene and then shooting a second take with the child actors as he delivered the cues to them. When the scene was complete, he simply intercut or dubbed the child's lines. Reed used this skill to great effect with Bobby Henrey as Phillipe in *The Fallen Idol* and again in *Oliver!* in 1968.

THE STORY: Young Phillipe is left by his father in the care of the family butler, Baines, whom the boy adores, and Baines's wife, the housekeeper, whom he does not. Baines has been having a clandestine affair with Julie, a typist at the embassy where they all live, but she has decided to end it. Phillipe overhears the conversation, not quite understanding it, and the information is pried out of him by the shrewish Mrs. Baines. After a violently jealous argument she subsequently has with her husband, she accidentally falls down a flight of stairs and dies.

When the police come to investigate, they question Phillipe but he is uncooperative, believing that Baines murdered his wife and wanting to protect him. Detective Lake persists, recognizing that the boy is withholding information that, ironically, if revealed would exonerate the butler, Phillipe's dearest friend.

Although the innocent Baines would prefer to accept blame for the crime and be sent to the gallows rather than implicate his lover, Julie, the lovely young woman finally admits she had been in the house that night with Baines and convinces the boy to stop trying to protect Baines by lying and to tell the truth.

As the police continue to investigate, they discover evidence that convinces them that Baines has been telling the truth all along and that his wife did indeed die from an accidental fall. Phillipe, in his enthusiasm for now telling a true story to the police, inadvertently tells them a story that would again throw suspicion on the innocent butler, but the police don't believe him, and Baines and Julie are free to be together.

* * *

The film is the polar opposite of the Graham Greene story on which it is based. In the fictional tale, the butler *is* guilty of murdering his wife, and the idolizing boy accidentally provides the police with the evidence they need to arrest him.

Carol Reed was nominated for an Academy Award for Best Director.

BEST LINE: Baines is returning to the embassy where he works after having had Julie, the woman he loves, tell him that their affair has to end. Young Phillipe, having intruded on their moment is told that Julie is Baines's niece. "Funny, isn't it," says Phillipe, "Julie working in the embassy, and all this time she's your niece." "Yes," Baines replies, "it's a scream."

IN THE LINE OF FIRE
1993

TYPE OF FILM: Suspense

STUDIO: Castle Rock/Columbia

EXECUTIVE PRODUCERS: Gail Katz, Wolfgang Petersen, David Valdes

PRODUCER: Jeff Apple

DIRECTOR: Wolfgang Petersen

SCREENWRITER: Jeff Maguire

SOURCE: Original

RUNNING TIME: 128 minutes

PRINCIPAL PLAYERS:

Clint Eastwood . . . . .Frank Horrigan
John Malkovich . . . ."Booth"/Mitch Leary
Rene Russo . . . . .Lilly Raines
Dylan McDermott . . . . .Al D'Andrea
Gary Cole . . . . .Bill Watts
Fred Dalton Thompson . . . . .Harry Sargent
John Mahoney . . . . .Sam Campagna
Gregory Alan Williams . . . . .Matt Wilder
Patrika Darbo . . . . .Pam Magnus
Steve Railsback . . . . .David Coppinger, uncredited

DID YOU KNOW? Decisions about the level of violence shown in the movie were not easy to make. In the United States, the scene in which Mitch Leary kills the bank clerk and her roommate by breaking their necks was shown. Although brief, it is quite explicit and very violent, with a single quick, hard twist clearly breaking each of the young women's necks. This was deleted from the film for its release in the United Kingdom. Actor John Malkovich wanted to go a step further and kill their dog too, but director Wolfgang Petersen decided that that was simply too much.

In another chilling moment, as Clint Eastwood is hanging from the top of a building and Malkovich comes to the edge and offers to save his life, Eastwood pulls out his gun and holds it up to

Malkovich's face. In an unscripted and unrehearsed bit of ad libbing, Malkovich takes the barrel of the gun into his mouth. The director liked this improvisation so much it stayed in the final cut.

THE STORY: Secret Service agent Frank Horrigan, on the scene in 1963 in Dallas, failed to protect President Kennedy from an assassin's bullet. He suddenly finds himself again in the position of protecting a President, even though he probably should have retired a long time ago. Still troubled by his perceived failure three decades earlier, Horrigan compensates by drinking excessively—and mostly alone, since his wife has left him.

Mitch Leary, a psychopathic former CIA operative, has decided to kill the President, not because of any philosophical or political position but mainly for the sport of it, "to punctuate the dreariness," as he puts it. When he learns that Horrigan is to be his chief adversary in the cat-and-mouse game, he becomes excited, calling the agent repeatedly to give him hints and clues and to gloat about his successes and Horrigan's failures. His taunts have an effect on Horrigan, who becomes more and more determined not to lose another President. The agent must also endure the arrogance of his much younger boss, who wants no part of Horrigan because he is not as by-the-book as he would prefer.

Also on assignment to protect the President is a young female agent, Lilly Raines, who has doubts about Horrigan, but soon learns to trust the politically incorrect dinosaur and falls in love with him. Horrigan's persistent sleuthing and reasoned deductions lead him to the killer, just in time to throw himself in front of the President as Leary fires his homemade handgun. He survives because of a bulletproof vest, which Leary later chides him for wearing. In their final confrontation in an elevator high above Los Angeles, Leary hangs from the edge and Horrigan offers to save his life, as Leary had saved his earlier, but the egomaniacal assassin lets go instead, plunging to his doom.

* * *

Although there is nothing original about a film in which there are two highly intelligent and well-motivated adversaries—one a vicious, amoral killer and the other an over-the-hill, drunken law enforcement maverick—it has rarely been done so well. The tension remains high, and the two primary protagonists, with wildly divergent styles (the frenzied pathology of John Malkovich and the laconic confidence of Clint Eastwood), mesh perfectly.

Verisimilitude for the filmed campaign shots was achieved by using actual scenes from the 1992 Presidential campaign of Bill Clinton.

In the scene where Horrigan's partner is killed, Clint Eastwood actually did hang from the edge of the building, six stories above the ground, at the age of sixty three, though he did wear a safety belt—just in case.

For such an expertly filmed and edited motion picture, there is one stunningly sloppy bit of filmmaking. When Horrigan breaks into Leary's house, he is seen smashing the top half of a large window. When he enters, however, he crawls through the bottom half.

Another slipup occurs when the Secret Service is able to trace a call from Leary to Horrigan. They discover that he is right across the street in Lafayette Park and race to catch him. There are, however, no pay telephones in Lafayette Park.

BEST LINE: When agent Lilly Raines asks Frank Horrigan if he has met the President and the First Lady yet, he replies, "I normally prefer not to get to know the people I'm protecting." "Oh yeah—why's that?" Lilly asks. "Well, you never know," Frank replies. "You might decide they're not worth taking a bullet for."

MURDER ON THE ORIENT EXPRESS
1974

TYPE OF FILM:	Detective
STUDIO:	Paramount
PRODUCERS:	John Brabourne and Richard Goodwin
DIRECTOR:	Sidney Lumet
SCREENWRITER:	Paul Dehn
SOURCE:	*Murder on the Orient Express* (U.S. title: *Murder on the Calais Coach*), novel by Agatha Christie
RUNNING TIME:	127 minutes

PRINCIPAL PLAYERS:

Albert Finney . . . . .Hercule Poirot
Lauren Bacall . . . . .Mrs. Hubbard
Martin Balsam . . . . .Bianchi
Ingrid Bergman . . . . .Greta Ohlsson
Jacqueline Bisset .Countess Andrenyi
Jean-Pierre Cassel .Pierre Paul Michel
Sean Connery . . . . .Colonel Arbuthnot
John Gielgud . . . . .Beddoes
Wendy Hiller .Princess Dragomiroff
Anthony Perkins .Hector McQueen
Vanessa Redgrave .Mary Debenham
Rachel Roberts .Hildegarde Schmidt
Richard Widmark . . . . .Ratchett
Michael York . . . . .Count Andrenyi
Colin Blakely . . . . .Hardman
George Coulouris .Dr. Constantine

DID YOU KNOW? After the Margaret Rutherford (playing Margaret Rutherford, not Miss Jane Marple) movies, the tepid 1966 remake of *And Then There Were None* titled *Ten Little Indians*, the incoherent *The Alphabet Murders* (1966), and the criminally terrible *Endless Night* (1972), Agatha Christie determined that there would be no more motion pictures made from her books. Only the intervention of Lord Louis Mountbatten, former Viceroy to India and the uncle of Prince Philip, Duke of Edinburgh, convinced Dame Agatha to allow one more try. Director Sidney Lumet spared no expense to make a good a film as he could, and the results paid off. Christie was delighted with it, and it took in $19,000,000 at the box office, becoming the most successful British picture ever made.

THE STORY: The famous Belgian detective Hercule Poirot boards the Orient Express on the Calais Coach. His fellow passengers are an interesting lot: Ratchett, an American businessman traveling with his secretary, Hector McQueen, his butler, Beddoes, and his bodyguard, Hardman; another obnoxious American, Mrs. Hubbard, who will not stop talking; a British Colonel, Arbuthnot; the Russian Princess Dragomiroff and her companion, Hildegarde Schmidt; a missionary from Sweden, Greta Ohlsson; and the Hungarian Count and Countess Andrenyi.

Ratchett is concerned that someone will try to kill him and offers Poirot $15,000 to protect him. Poirot refuses, and that night, Ratchett is murdered in his berth, stabbed repeatedly. In the morning, Poirot learns that an avalanche has caused a giant snowdrift on the tracks, stranding the passengers. With no footprints in the snow, Poirot recognizes that the murderer must be one of the people still in the Calais Coach.

One by one, and outside the earshot of the others, Poirot interrogates the passengers, learning from Ratchett's secretary that his employer had recently received threatening letters. When Dr. Constantine and the detective go to examine the body, the doctor tells Poirot that the stab wounds vary greatly, some deep, some shallow, some administered by the right hand, some by the left and, finally, that it is possible that Ratchett was already dead when he was stabbed. Various clues turn up in Ratchett's stateroom, including a piece of charred paper that Poirot is able to read by burning it again. It bears the words . . . *member Little Daisy Armstrong* and Poirot concludes that Ratchett was the kidnapper of the little American girl who had been held for $200,000 ransom but was then found dead, making headlines around the world.

As the questioning continues, Poirot learns that several of the passengers had known Ratchett and several others had had connections to the Armstrong family. Calling all the suspects together at last, Poirot informs them that no one person among them had killed Ratchett—they all had! Given ample reason, each passenger stabbed the callous killer in turn to avenge the murder of the baby.

* * *

Agatha Christie based her novel *Murder on the Orient Express* (in America titled *Murder on the Calais Coach*, 1934) on the Lindbergh kidnapping case, in which Anne and Charles Lindbergh paid a $50,000 ransom only to learn, some time later, that their baby had been murdered already.

Another plot element—the snowbound train unable to move forward or back—was also based on a real-life event. Five years before Christie wrote the book, the Orient Express had just crossed the Turkish border when an avalanche trapped it, keeping the train snowbound for six days.

Director Sidney Lumet might have been expected to have a difficult time with so many huge stars (and commensurate egos) on the same set, but that was not the case. Each of the principals behaved professionally and all were pleased to be there for their own reasons.

Richard Widmark made no attempt to hide the fact that he took the role because he was eager to meet the other stars. Sean Connery had been afraid of being typecast as James Bond, and Lumet had offered him very different roles in *The Hill* (1965) and *The Offence* (1973), so he was happy to pay him back by appearing in a minor role. The others, especially the more mature ones like Ingrid Bergman, Wendy Hiller, and John Gielgud, enjoyed playing interesting characters without committing to long shooting schedules or long-run plays.

The premier of the film was held in London and Queen Elizabeth attended. Indeed, members of the royal family had been regulars on the set, to the delight of everyone but Vanessa Redgrave, the political radical who disapproved of the special treatment given to them. She brought her own guest: Gary Healy of the Workers' Revolutionary Party.

Raymond Chandler, in his seminal essay "The Simple Art of Murder," wrote about *Murder on the Orient Express*: *M. Poirot decides that since nobody on a certain through sleeper could have done the murder alone, everybody did it together, breaking the process down into a series of simple operations like assembling an egg beater. This is the type (of book) that is guaranteed to knock the keenest mind for a loop. Only a halfwit could guess it.*

Numerous Academy Award nominations went to the film, including to Ingrid Bergman, who won for Best Supporting Actress, Albert Finney for Best Actor, and Paul Dehn for Best Adapted Screenplay.

BEST LINE: Ratchett offers Poirot "big money" to take on the job of protecting him. Poirot turns down $5,000, then $10,000, and finally $15,000. "I have made enough money to satisfy both my needs and my caprices," he tells Ratchett. "I take only such cases now as interest me and, to be frank, my interest in your case is . . . dwindling."

CHARADE
1963

TYPE OF FILM: Suspense/Comedy
STUDIO: Universal-International
PRODUCER: Stanley Donen
DIRECTOR: Stanley Donen
SCREENWRITER: Peter Stone
SOURCE: *The Unsuspecting Wife*, story by Peter Stone and Marc Behm
RUNNING TIME: 114 minutes

PRINCIPAL PLAYERS:

Cary Grant . . . . .Peter Joshua/Alexander Dyle/Adam Canfield/ Brian Cruikshank
Audrey Hepburn . . . . .Regina "Reggie" Lambert
Walter Matthau . . . . .Hamilton Bartholomew/ Carson Dyle
James Coburn . . . . .Tex Panthollow
George Kennedy . . . . .Herman Scobie
Ned Glass . . . . .Leopold Gideon
Jacques Marin . . . . .Inspector Grandpierre
Paul Bonifas . . . . .Felix

DID YOU KNOW? In addition to being one of the most clever and sophisticated comic thrillers outside the oeuvre of Alfred Hitchcock, *Charade* was a career-saver for several of the principals and a struggle for everyone else.

Cary Grant's career had been stalled in the early 1940s when he was still in his thirties, only to be rescued by Hitchcock with such superb suspense films as *Notorious* (1946), *To Catch a Thief* (1955), and *North by Northwest* (1959). But now it was the 1960s and Grant needed another lifeline, and *Charade* was it.

Meanwhile, director Stanley Donen, best known for such musicals as *Singin' in the Rain* (1952), hadn't had a big hit since that classic and hadn't worked at all in three years. He recognized the excellence of Peter Stone's script and saw it as his potential, badly needed smash when it was offered to him by Universal.

Meanwhile, Universal was looking for a director who could make successful Hitchcock-like motion pictures when the master was otherwise engaged. Sophisticated comic suspense films were surefire box-office hits, and having all the eggs in the Hitchcock basket was too risky. Donen, they hoped, might be their man.

Problem number one: Hitchcock was not at all pleased to think that someone else would move into his own highly personal sandbox to play and did everything he could think of to undermine Donen.

Problem number two: Grant was starting to look his age and needed lots of makeup to convince audiences that he would make a good husband—rather than a father substitute—for Audrey Hepburn.

Problem number three: Stone was rewriting daily as he battled with Donen, a good director whose background was in musicals and light comedies and who had no idea how to properly set up the elements in a traditional whodunit and, moreover, was no fan of the form in the first place.

Problem number four: Hepburn was getting a bit temperamental, demanding more and more expensive outfits designed for her by Givenchy.

Miraculously, everything came together to make this bright and intelligent film.

THE STORY: Fresh from a skiing trip in the Alps, Reggie Lambert returns to Paris to find her apartment empty, stripped of every piece of furniture and clothing, and her husband, Charles, dead. At the funeral, three Americans stop at the casket and make sure the corpse is really dead by stabbing it with a pin and holding a mirror to its mouth. The handsome Peter Joshua, whom she met on her holiday, helps Reggie find a hotel room.

Reggie is called to the U.S. Embassy, where Hamilton Bartholomew informs her that her husband and four accomplices stole a quarter of a million dollars in gold during World War II. He asks her help in retrieving the loot and warns her that her life might be in danger, as another of the crooks, Carson Dyle, had been killed but the other three were the sinister men who had attended the funeral.

She assures him that she has no idea where the money is and says the same to the three crooks, who threaten her. She seeks protection with Joshua, who now tells her that he is Carson Dyle's brother, Alexander, but when Bartholomew tells her Dyle

88

had no brother, she confronts him and he admits that he is a thief named Adam Canfield.

All three of the American crooks are killed and Reggie now believes Joshua, or Dyle, or Canfield, is actually the killer. But he isn't. He is really a U.S. Treasury agent named Brian Cruikshank. She then learns that the man passing himself off as Bartholomew is actually Carson Dyle, who, while in pursuit of Reggie to get the money, falls through a trap door at the Comedie Francais and plunges to his death.

After they figure out that the money has been converted into three fabulously valuable stamps, Reggie says to Cruikshank: "Oh, I love you, Adam . . . Alex . . . Peter . . . Brian . . . Whatever your name is. Oh, I love you. I hope we have a lot of boys and can name them all after you."

* * *

The plot, with its many twists and turns; the very high class stars, Audrey Hepburn and Cary Grant; the low-life villains; the wonderful chase scenes and suspenseful rooftop battle between Brian Cruikshank and Herman Scobie, the frequent use of comedy to leaven the suspense—all are so reminiscent of an Alfred Hitchcock motion picture that it is difficult to imagine that anyone else could have directed it, but clearly Stanley Donen was, this once, the equal to the master.

Peter Stone won an Edgar Allan Poe Award from the Mystery Writers of America for his screenplay.

The theme song by Henry Mancini and Johnny Mercer became a huge hit and was nominated for an Academy Award.

BEST LINE: A friend suggests to Reggie Lambert that she have affairs rather than get a divorce: "With a rich husband and this year's clothes, you won't find it difficult to make some new friends." "Look," Reggie replies, "I admit I came to Paris to escape American provincial, but that doesn't mean I'm ready for French traditional."

THE BLUE DAHLIA

1946

TYPE OF FILM:	*Noir*
STUDIO:	Paramount
PRODUCER:	John Houseman
DIRECTOR:	George Marshall
SCREENWRITER:	Raymond Chandler
SOURCE:	Original story by Raymond Chandler
RUNNING TIME:	99 minutes

PRINCIPAL PLAYERS:

Alan Ladd . . . . .Johnny Morrison
Veronica Lake . . . . .Joyce Harwood
William Bendix . . . . .Buzz Wanchek
Howard da Silva . . . . .Eddie Harwood
Doris Dowling . . . . .Helen Morrison
Tom Powers . . . . .Captain Hendrickson
Hugh Beaumont . . . . .George Copeland
Howard Freeman . . . . .Corelli
Will Wright . . . . .Dad Navell
Don Costello . . . . .Leo

DID YOU KNOW? Alan Ladd, a huge star for Paramount, was scheduled to serve a second hitch in the Navy in three months, and the studio desperately wanted to make another film with him before his departure. Raymond Chandler, fresh from his great success as the cowriter of *Double Indemnity* (for which he received an Academy Award nomination), had a partially completed novel. John Houseman read the pages and had the studio buy it and get a contract for Chandler to write the screenplay. The first half of the script was delivered quickly, and the studio liked it so much they began filming. New pages began to come very slowly, and with time running out on Ladd, Chandler appeared to have writer's block. He told Houseman that he could continue, but that he needed to write at home, not in his office, and that he had to be drunk to do it. Houseman hired nurses and limousines around the clock to be there if Chandler needed help, but he delivered the remainder of the script on time and received his second Oscar nomination, as well as the Edgar Allan Poe Award from the Mystery Writers of America.

THE STORY: Johnny Morrison comes home after military service in World War II to find his drunken wife in the arms of another man at a wild party in his home in the middle of the afternoon. He breaks up the party, and when she confesses that their son died because of her drunken driving, he leaves her. The war hero turns to the two buddies who returned from the war with him, Buzz Wanchek and George Copeland, and they decide to try to forget the past and start over. When Johnny's wife, Helen, is murdered, he becomes the prime suspect, so he realizes that he must find the killer or else he'll be arrested and the real killer will go free. He meets up with the beautiful Joyce Harwood, the wife of the man with whom his wife was having an affair, and they fall in love. With the help of Joyce and his two friends, Morrison finds the murderer and forces a confession out of him.

* * *

Chandler had conceived an unusual and philosophically perplexing ending. Johnny's pal Buzz had a war injury that required a steel plate to be imbedded in his skull, causing him intermittent memory loss, pain, and blackouts. In Chandler's story, Buzz actually killed his friend's wife but didn't remember doing it. The Department of the Navy wouldn't allow Paramount to release the film with that ending because it feared that it would reflect badly on the Navy. This decision forced Chandler to produce just the sort of humdrum ending that Chandler hated in other people's detective stories.

The Blue Dahlia is better than the several other *noir* films that use the similar motif of returning veterans being punished for their time in the service (Morrison loses his child, his wife, his home), much as returning convicts are seen as outsiders. Ironically, when Morrison is perceived to be a murderer, he must flee and hide from the very people he had fought to protect.

Alan Ladd and Veronica Lake were the perfect noir screen couple—both blond and beautiful, icy, nearly expressionless. No matter how beautiful she is, and no matter how tough he is, they both carry a sense of doom with them. The antithesis of William Powell and Myrna Loy, it would be difficult to have predicted happy endings for their film roles—which are unhappily reflected in their personal lives. Lake's career ended after only a decade or so, and Ladd's did not flourish after the 1950s. Both died young.

BEST LINE: Johnny Morrison, checking into a hotel room, to the desk clerk. "You call this dump a hotel?" To which the clerk replies: "That's what the sign says. Fresh sheets every day, they tell me." Morrison counters with, "How often do they change the fleas?"

TO KILL A MOCKINGBIRD
1962

TYPE OF FILM: Courtroom

STUDIO: Universal

PRODUCER: Alan Pakula

DIRECTOR: Robert Mulligan

SCREENWRITER: Horton Foote

SOURCE: *To Kill A Mockingbird,* novel by Harper Lee

RUNNING TIME: 129 minutes

PRINCIPAL PLAYERS:

Gregory Peck . . . . .Atticus Finch
Mary Badham . . . . .Scout Finch
Philip Alford . . . . .Jem Finch
John Megna . . . . .Dill Harris
Brock Peters . . . . .Tom Robinson
Robert Duvall . . . . .Arthur "Boo" Radley
Estelle Evans . . . . .Calpurnia
Frank Overton . . . . .Sheriff Heck Tate
Rosemary Murphy . . . . .Maudie Atkinson
Ruth White . . . . .Mrs. Duboses
Paul Fix . . . . .Judge Taylor
Collin Wilcox . . . . .Mayella Ewell
James Anderson . . . . .Bob Ewell

DID YOU KNOW? Of the many motion pictures made by Gregory Peck, he always maintained that *To Kill a Mockingbird* was his favorite. He liked the Pulitzer Prize-winning novel so much that he tried to buy the dramatic rights and quickly agreed when producer Alan Pakula offered him the role of Finch. "I can honestly say that in twenty years of making movies," Peck stated, "I never had a part that came close to being the real me until Atticus Finch." His own childhood was very much like those of the children in the film, through whose eyes the story unfolds. Though his childhood was in Southern California, rather than in the true South, Peck said that he nonetheless lived "in a small town where we ran around barefooted in the summertime and lived in trees and rolled down the street curled up in an old rubber tire." Peck was so deeply taken by the role of Finch that he once made a full nine-minute speech in a single take; the actors who were playing jurors broke into applause when he concluded.

THE STORY: In a small, racially divided Alabama town in the summer of 1932, an incorruptible lawyer, Atticus Finch, raises his two children—Scout, a six-year-old girl, and Jem, her ten-year-old brother—alone after the death of his wife. A primary endeavor in their carefree lives and that of their playmates is to get a look at Boo Radley, the retarded neighbor they have never seen and who, in local legend, is chained to his bed by his mean father.

Atticus agrees to defend Tom Robinson, a young black man accused of raping and beating a white girl, Mayella Ewell, creating a hostile environment for his children by the bigoted youngsters in town. Atticus proves that Tom is innocent and that the beating occurred at the hands of Mayella's father when he caught her making advances to the Negro, but the all-white jury still finds Tom guilty. Atticus plans to appeal, but before he is able to do so, Tom is killed when he allegedly tries to escape.

Mayella's father, seeking revenge against Atticus, attacks Scout and Jem, but they are saved when a strange man lurking in the woods attacks Ewell and stabs him to death. Scout is surprised to find Boo Radley standing quietly behind the door of her bedroom as her injured brother is attended by a doctor, and she identifies Radley as her protector. The sheriff, understanding the situation and sensitive to Boo's fragile mental state, decides to announce that Ewell fell on his own knife, so no trial will be necessary.

* * *

Harper Lee's only novel, *To Kill a Mockingbird,* was semiautobiographical. She grew up in a small southern town that had its racial problems, wrote sensitively about them, and saw them converted to the screen by Horton Foote, also a southern writer. Lee was that rare author whose novel had been made into a film who was able to say, "I am a happy author. They have made my story into a beautiful and moving motion picture. I am very proud and grateful." Foote won an Academy Award for his excellent screenplay.

The character of Dill, a schoolmate of Jem Finch, was based on the young Truman Capote, who had been a friend of Harper Lee while they were growing up. It is known, too, that Capote made major contributions to the writing of the book.

The narration is made by an adult Scout Finch, whose voice belongs to Kim Stanley.

Boo Radley is played by Robert Duvall in his screen debut.

Although *Lawrence of Arabia* swept most of the 1962 Academy Awards, Gregory Peck won an Oscar for Best Actor. *To Kill a Mockingbird* was nominated for Best Picture, Robert Mulligan was nominated for Best Director, and Mary Badham, who had never acted before, was nominated for Best Supporting Actress at the age of nine.

BEST LINE: Sheriff Heck Tate explaining to Atticus Finch how he is going to handle the death of the man who tried to harm his children, Scout and Jem: "Bob Ewell fell on his knife. He killed himself. There's a black man dead for no reason. Now the man responsible for it is dead. Let the dead bury the dead this time, Mr. Finch."

KISS ME DEADLY
1955

TYPE OF FILM:	*Noir*
STUDIO:	United Artists
EXECUTIVE PRODUCER:	Victor Savile
PRODUCER:	Robert Aldrich
DIRECTOR:	Robert Aldrich
SCREENWRITER:	A. E. Bezzerides
SOURCE:	*Kiss Me, Deadly,* novel by Mickey Spillane
RUNNING TIME:	105 minutes

PRINCIPAL PLAYERS:

Ralph Meeker . . . . .Mike Hammer
Albert Dekker . . . . .Dr. Soberin
Paul Stewart . . . . .Carl Evello
Cloris Leachman . . . . .Christina Bailey
Wesley Addy . . . . .Pat Chambers
Marian Carr . . . . .Friday
Maxine Cooper . . . . .Velda
Gaby Rodgers . . . . .Gabrielle/Lily Carver
Nick Dennis . . . . .Nick
Juano Hernandez . . . . .Eddie Yeager

DID YOU KNOW? When *Kiss Me Deadly* was filmed, Mickey Spillane, the author of the book on which it was based, was the most successful writer in the world. By the 1960s, his books had sold more than 100,000 copies worldwide, and by the 1970s, a survey of the best-selling fiction of the twentieth century showed seven of the ten top sellers of all time were written by Spillane (*The Godfather* topped the list).

The liberal media loathed Spillane and his work, and one critic asked him his opinion of a readership that would put him in such a rarefied position. Spillane warned him that, if the critic didn't watch out, he'd write three more books.

The motion pictures made from those books were another matter. United Artists, seeing the record-breaking sales of Spillane's novels, decided to capitalize on this extraordinary popularity and made a four-film contract. *I, the Jury* (1953), the first book, was also the first film, starring Biff Elliot as Spillane's hero, Mike Hammer. It was made in 3-D but, instead of being a box office smash as anticipated, grossed a respectable but unexciting $1,299,000.

The second and easily the best of the Mike Hammer films was *Kiss Me Deadly*, which grossed only $726,000—a failure.

The third, *My Gun Is Quick* (1957), starred Robert Bray as Hammer and had a U.S. gross of only $308,000—a disaster.

Finally, in 1963, Spillane himself played the tough Hammer in *The Girl Hunters,* doing a better job of it than most would have expected. There was a lot of publicity, but not much box office. The gross of *My Gun Is Quick* was not regarded warmly by United Artists, and they did not sign up any more Spillane films.

THE STORY: Driving along a dark, deserted road, Mike Hammer nearly hits Christina, a terrified blonde who is running barefoot down the middle of it. He picks her up, and soon his car is forced off the road and some hoods knock him out and torture the girl with pliers, eventually killing her. Her body and Hammer are put back in his car and pushed off a cliff. He survives and vows to find out who she was and why she was murdered.

His curiosity becomes inflamed when the FBI warns him to drop his investigations, and Hammer finds a gangster, Carl Evello, who is ostensibly in charge of the operation but who clearly has a powerful boss. In an attempt to get Hammer to lay off, the gangsters kill his mechanic and friend by dropping a car on him, crushing him, and kidnapping his secretary, Velda.

Hammer deduces that the murdered blonde had swallowed a key that may be at the center of the case and convinces a morgue attendant to get it for him. Hammer uses the key to open a locker with a box inside, and when he opens the box, a strong, eerie light emanates from it, burning his hand.

Christina's roommate, Lily Carver, manages to get the box and takes it to Dr. Soberin, the brains behind the operation. Hammer traces them to a beach house where Velda has been held hostage and where Lily insists that they open the box. Soberin explains that the nuclear material, recently stolen from Los Alamos to be sold to a foreign power, is too dangerous, so she shoots him dead and wounds Hammer. Just as Mike and Velda flee the little cot-

97

tage, Lily opens the box, the intense heat causing her to burst into flame and the house to explode.

* * *

A violent and exciting film, among the last of the films noir, *Kiss Me Deadly* became a major influence on French New Wave directors, fond as they are of the darkest side of mankind and relentlessly attracted to nihilism. Although it was not a box office success and was largely unloved by movie reviewers of the day, it has grown in stature over the years and is today a very large cult favorite.

Cloris Leachman made her film debut in *Kiss Me Deadly* as Christina Bailey, the escapeé from an insane asylum.

Much like *D.O.A.*, *Kiss Me Deadly* plays to the audience's fear of atomic power. No layperson knew how it worked (and certainly neither film provided any factual insight), but they knew they were afraid of it, which added an extra dose of terror to both noir classics.

The high level of violence, which pushed noir film elements to extremes never seen before, assured negative reviews in the view of the film's producer, Robert Aldrich. In an attempt to counteract those impending slams, he defended the film in a long article written for *The New York Herald-Tribune.* Ironically, while it was regarded as just another B picture when it opened in the United States, it was so enthusiastically received in France that it made Aldrich's reputation in Europe. Francois Truffaut, among others, thought it one of the greatest American films of all time.

BEST LINE: Mike Hammer picks up Christina Bailey, who was running terrified down the road, and asks her, "What's the matter? Were you out with a guy who thought no was a three-letter word?"

THE PETRIFIED FOREST
1936

TYPE OF FILM:	Crime
STUDIO:	Warner Brothers
EXECUTIVE PRODUCER:	Hal B. Wallis
DIRECTOR:	Archie Mayo
SCREENWRITERS:	Charles Kenyon and Delmer Daves
SOURCE:	*The Petrified Forest*, play by Robert E. Sherwood
RUNNING TIME:	83 minutes

PRINCIPAL PLAYERS:

Leslie Howard . . . . .Alan Squire
Humphrey Bogart . . . . .Duke Mantee
Bette Davis . . . . .Gabrielle Maple
Dick Foran . . . . .Boze Hertzlinger
Genevieve Tobin . . . . .Edith Chisolm
Charley Grapewin . . . . .Gramp Maple
Porter Hall . . . . .Jason Maple
Joseph Sawyer . . . . .Jackie
Paul Harvey . . . . .Mr. Chisolm

DID YOU KNOW? Robert E. Sherwood, the Pulitzer Prize-winning playwright, wrote *The Petrified Forest* as a play, which became a hit on Broadway starring Leslie Howard and Humphrey Bogart. When Howard was asked to star in the screen version, he accepted the role only on condition that Bogart, then a stage actor and a player mainly in B movies, be hired to again play Duke Mantee.

THE STORY: Alan Squire, a suicidal intellectual, is hitchhiking across the Arizona desert when he happens on the run-down Black Mesa Bar-B-Q. Were he to ask where he is, someone could reasonably tell him that he is in the heart of nowhere. Here he meets a pretty young idealist, Gaby Maple, who dreams of escaping the desolate gas station to go to France, where her mother still lives. They fall in love immediately, but the idyll is ended when a brutal killer, Duke Mantee, and his gang, running for the Mexican border, use the restaurant as their hideout. Mantee holds a small group of travelers and residents captive while waiting for the rest of his gang, especially Daisy, his girlfriend. The philosophic Squire spurs the "autobiographical impulse," and the people reveal their true feelings and hidden truths. Squire makes a deal with Mantee: Squire will sign over his life-insurance policy to Gaby if the gangster will kill him before he leaves, so that the girl will be able to escape her squalid life and find herself in France.

* * *

There is no doubting that the original form of *The Petrified Forest* was as a stage play, since the film is essentially confined to one set and has far more talk than action. Indeed, until the final shootout, there is *no* action. But it's a beautifully written play that eloquently makes a case for individualism.

Squire, for all his wordiness, never appears pedantic. Mantee, on the other hand, a man of action rather than thought, looks menacing but does not behave at all like the brutal killer he is reputed to be. When a rather thick young football player who is enamored of Gaby grabs a rifle, Mantee shoots him in the hand rather than killing him on the spot. When the restaurant is surrounded, he yells at his captives to get on the floor for their safety. He even has trouble living up to his bargain with Squire, finally shooting him only when the suicidal young man bars the door to Mantee's escape.

Two endings were shot, but the studio decided to remain true to the play and allow the hero to die.

A weak remake titled *Escape in the Desert* was made in 1945, without the superb writing and acting of the original. It starred Philip Dorn, Helmut Dantine, Jean Sullivan, and Alan Hale. In 1955, a television version starred Humphrey Bogart and Lauren Bacall.

The essential plot structure of a group of hostages held by gangsters is used equally effectively in *Key Largo* (1948) and *The Desperate Hours* (1955), both of which also starred Bogart.

BEST LINE: When Alan Squire asks Duke Mantee to talk about his life, Mantee tells him that most of it has been in prison, and "it looks like I'll spend the rest of my life dead."

THE ASPHALT JUNGLE
1950

TYPE OF FILM: Crime

STUDIO: Metro-Goldwyn-Mayer

PRODUCER: Arthur Hornblow, Jr.

DIRECTOR: John Huston

SCREENWRITERS: Ben Maddow and John Huston

SOURCE: *The Asphalt Jungle*, novel by W. R. Burnett

RUNNING TIME: 112 minutes

PRINCIPAL PLAYERS:

Sterling Hayden . . . . .Dix Handley
Louis Calhern . . . . .Alonzo D. Emmerich
Jean Hagen . . . . .Doll Conovan
James Whitmore . . . . .Gus Ninissi
Sam Jaffe .Doc Erwin Riedenschneider
Marilyn Monroe . . . . .Angela Phinlay
Marc Lawrence . . . . .Cobby
John McIntire . . . . .Police Commissioner Hardy
Barry Kelley . . . . .Lieutenant Ditrich
Anthony Caruso . . . . .Louis Ciavelli

DID YOU KNOW? Louis B. Mayer, then the head of Metro-Goldwyn-Mayer, hated *The Asphalt Jungle*. Director John Huston, collaborating on the screenplay with Ben Maddow, had contrived to make his gangsters sympathetic. Unlike earlier gangster films, in which the hoodlums were played broadly and one-dimensionally as ruthless or psychopathic thugs, the gang involved in the big heist in this influential film was composed of fairly commonplace men with fears and dreams and families, much like ordinary people. Mayer despised the liberal portrayal of the bad guys, saying that it was "full of nasty, ugly people doing nasty, ugly things. I wouldn't walk across the room to see something like that." The film was extremely successful, however, and Mayer's days as head of the giant studio were numbered.

THE STORY: Master criminal Doc Riedenschneider is released from prison and immediately heads to Alonzo Emmerich, a corrupt lawyer, to seek financing for a jewel robbery he meticulously planned while behind bars. Emmerich agrees to come up with the necessary $50,000 and will also fence the jewelry after the robbery. Doc then puts together a team to pull off the caper, bringing in Cobby, a bookie who actually puts up the cash promised by Emmerich; Dix Handley, the tough guy who just wants to go back home to Kentucky and live on a horse farm; Louis Ciavelli, the professional safecracker; and Gus Ninissi, the cat-loving hunchback who will serve as the driver.

In a wonderfully timed and executed heist, the gang succeeds, only to have the night watchman come across them and shoot Ciavelli, whom Ninissi drives home to die.

When a corrupt cop, Lieutenant Ditrich, suspects Cobby has been involved, he beats the truth out of him, and the bookie names his accomplices. Handley and Riedenschneider go to Emmerich with the purloined jewels to get their money, but the lawyer tries to double-cross them with the aid of his armed thug, who shoots Handley as he is himself shot dead.

Handley flees with some cash and tells Riedenschneider to escape quickly. The police show up at the apartment of Emmerich, who kills himself, and then Ninissi is arrested. Doc Riedenschneider hires a taxi to take him to Cleveland, stopping at a roadside café where he becomes entranced with watching a sexy young girl dance. He feeds nickels to the jukebox, and when he finally pulls himself away, the police have caught up with him. A couple of minutes—as long as it takes to play a phonograph record—he notes sadly have cost him his freedom. The wounded Handley drives furiously to reach Kentucky and arrives just in time to die, lying in the field of his dreams.

* * *

This enormously influential film, the first to break with the traditional gangster film in which the characters were largely stereotypes, was also the first to show a caper being planned and, in a long eleven-minute sequence, carried out. It served as the model for scores of caper films that followed it during the next half century.

In the W. R. Burnett novel on which the film was based, the story is told from the point of view of the police. For the film, director John Huston had his screenwriter, Ben Maddow, innovatively retell the tale from the novel perspective of the robbers. It has been reported that Huston hired real-life safecrackers as consultants to be certain the heist scene was accurate.

Lola Albright had been John Huston's first choice to play the small but important role of Angela Phinlay, Emmerich's "niece," but she was unavailable and the largely unknown Marilyn Monroe was cast instead.

There have been three remakes of *The Asphalt Jungle*. In 1958, it was set in the American West and titled *The Badlanders,* starring Alan Ladd and Ernest Borgnine. In 1963, it became a British production as *Cairo*, starring George Sanders and Richard Johnson. Finally, in 1972 it was made with an all-black cast as *Cool Breeze*, starring Thalmus Rasulala and Judy Pace.

Academy Award nominations went to John Huston for Best Director, Sam Jaffe for Best Supporting Actor, and Huston and Ben Maddow for Best Screenplay.

BEST LINE: "Experience has taught me never to trust a policeman," says the cynical mastermind behind the big robbery, Doc Riedenschneider. "Just when you think he's all right, he turns legit."

IN COLD BLOOD
1967

TYPE OF FILM:	Crime
STUDIO:	Columbia
PRODUCER:	Richard Brooks
DIRECTOR:	Richard Brooks
SCREENWRITER:	Richard Brooks
SOURCE:	*In Cold Blood,* a true but fictionalized book by Truman Capote
RUNNING TIME:	134 minutes

PRINCIPAL PLAYERS:

Robert Blake . . . . .Perry Smith
Scott Wilson . . . . .Dick Hickock
John Forsythe . . . . .Alvin Dewey
Paul Stewart . . . . .Reporter
Gerald S. O'Loughlin . . . . .Harold Nye
Jeff Corey . . . . .Mr. Hitchcock
John Gallanbet . . . . .Roy Church
James Flavin . . . . .Clarence Duntz
Charles McGraw . . . . .Tex Smith
James Lantz . . . . .Officer Rohleder
Will Geer . . . . .Prosecutor

DID YOU KNOW? Director Richard Brooks made every effort for the authenticity that a docudrama such as *In Cold Blood* requires. He took the crew to all the actual locations in Missouri, Colorado, Texas, Nevada, Mexico, and Holcomb, Kansas, including the Clutter house, where the four murders were committed. Nancy Clutter's horse Babe was used in several scenes. Brooks also filmed in the real-life courtroom in which the two murderers were tried, using six of the actual jurors who sat on the jury of their trial. Even the hangman who executed Perry Smith and Dick Hickock performed that role in the film.

THE STORY: On November 15, 1959, Perry Smith and Dick Hickock break into the remote farmhouse of the Clutter family in search of a safe and the $10,000 it is reputed to contain, and murder the entire family of four.

Smith and Hickock had met in jail and went to Holcomb, Kansas, with the intention of finding the money that a former cellmate had told Hickock was hidden in the house. After killing the Clutters and escaping with forty-three dollars, Smith and Hickock cash a series of bad checks on their way to Mexico, where Smith dreams about being a gold prospector. Hickock insists that they return to the United States, where they cash more worthless checks, not realizing that Hickock's former cellmate, aware of a reward, has informed on him.

The killers are caught in Las Vegas, and the alibi that they confidently regard as airtight unravels when the police question them separately and find that their stories don't quite mesh. When their footprints exactly match those that had stepped in Mr. Clutter's blood, there is sufficient evidence to convict them, and they are sentenced to die. After two stays of execution, they are hanged at the Kansas State Penitentiary in Lansing on April 14, 1965.

* * *

The cold-blooded murder of the very decent Clutter family sparked a national outrage and inspired Truman Capote to write *In Cold Blood* (1966). With that book, he created a new type of literary work, one that blended fact and fiction, telling a true story but inventing dialogue and making up or combining characters to enhance the narrative.

BEST LINE: A reporter (not local) asks Alvin Dewey, the detective on the case, how the killers got into the house. "Probably just walked in," he says. "Don't people around here lock doors?" the reporter persists. "They will tonight," Dewey replies.

THE 39 STEPS
1935

TYPE OF FILM:	Espionage
STUDIO:	Gaumont-British
PRODUCER:	Michael Balcon
DIRECTOR:	Alfred Hitchcock
SCREENWRITERS:	Charles Bennett and Alma Reville; additional dialogue, Ian Hay
SOURCE:	*The 39 Steps*, novel by John Buchan
RUNNING TIME:	86 minutes

PRINCIPAL PLAYERS:
Robert Donat . . . . .Richard Hannay
Madeleine Carroll . . . . .Pamela
Lucie Mannheim . . . . .Miss Smith, also Annabella
Godfrey Tearle . . . . .Professor Jordan
Peggy Ashcroft . . . . .Mrs. Crofter
John Laurie . . . . .Crofter, the farmer
Frank Cellier . . . . .sheriff
Wylie Watson . . . . .Mr. Memory
Helen Haye . . . . .Mrs. Jordan

DID YOU KNOW? The writer of the screenplay, Charles Bennett, worked for both the Federal Bureau of Investigation and U.S. Naval Intelligence during World War II. He was a tremendously gifted screenwriter who worked with Alfred Hitchcock on some of the master's most successful films (*The Man Who Knew Too Much*, 1934, *Sabotage*, 1936; *The Secret Agent*, 1936; and *Foreign Correspondent*, 1940).

THE STORY: When a shot is fired in a crowded British music hall, causing a panic, a young woman who calls herself Miss Smith pleads with Richard Hannay to take her back to his apartment. When they get there, she reveals to him that she is in fact a secret agent on the trail of spies who intend to smuggle government secrets out of the country. Soon after, she is murdered and Hannay is suspected of the crime. He is convinced that the only way he can clear himself is to find the real killers—the espionage agents. Based on the information given to him by Miss Smith, he heads for Scotland by train, on which he meets the lovely Pamela. Although attracted to her, he becomes increasingly irritated when she refuses to believe his story. When the spies catch him, they believe Pamela to be involved, so they handcuff the two together. Hannay and Pamela escape, still handcuffed, and are chased both by the police and the espionage agents. Finally realizing that Hannay's outré story is true, Pamela agrees to help him, and they return to London and the music hall where Mr. Memory is performing. Hannay asks him the right question and the performer unwittingly provides the solution to the crimes.

* * *

The 39 Steps is the film that made Alfred Hitchcock famous in America. He'd had a string of successes in England, but it took this highly suspenseful and accessible thriller to bring him the mass appeal that the film world requires.

As the most successful director of suspense films of all time, Hitchcock had several tricks that he used on numerous occasions. Notable in *The 39 Steps* is his familiar device of having the hero (and in this case the heroine) chased both by the police and the criminals. The reason for this double-barreled threat is entirely pragmatic. If the hero is chased by only the bad guys, he could simply go to the police. But if the police want him as well, he can't very well go to them for help, casting him as a far more vulnerable and sympathetic character. This classic chase film, in many ways reminiscent of Hitchcock's later *North by Northwest*, is a nonstop series of incidents that leave the heroes, as well as the audience, breathless.

The term "MacGuffin," so much associated with Hitchcock throughout his career, first came to be used in connection with this picture. The "MacGuffin" is the item (stolen jewels, government secrets—whatever) that causes all the activity to occur. As Hitchcock pointed out, it doesn't really matter what it is, so long as it's there.

When Robert Donat appeared in *The 39 Steps*, he was at the peak of his immense popularity, having just made *The Private Life of Henry VIII* (1933) and *The Count of Monte Cristo* (1934); he was about to make *Goodbye, Mr. Chips* (1939). Madeleine Carroll, too, was at the apex of her successful career, starring in such

107

films as *The Case Against Mrs. Ames* (1936), *The General Died at Dawn* (1936), and *The Prisoner of Zenda* (1937).

The 39 Steps has been remade twice, once in 1959 with Kenneth More, and again in 1978 with Robert Powell. Neither is memorable.

BEST LINE: "Mr. Memory" is a music-hall performer whose act is displaying his remarkable memory. In a ridiculous non sequitur, a patron repeatedly asks him, "How old is Mae West?" (Remember, this was in 1935!)

FREAKS
1932

TYPE OF FILM:	*Noir*
STUDIO:	Metro-Goldwyn-Mayer
PRODUCERS (UNCREDITED):	Irving Thalberg and Harry Sharrock
DIRECTOR:	Tod Browning
SCREENWRITERS:	Willis Goldbeck and Leon Gordon; additional dialogue by Edgar Allan Woolf and Al Boasberg
SOURCE:	"Spurs," short story by Tod Robbins
RUNNING TIME:	64 minutes

PRINCIPAL PLAYERS:

Wallace Ford . . . . .Phroso
Leila Hyams . . . . .Venus
Olga Baclanova . . . . .Cleopatra
Roscoe Ates . . . . .Roscoe
Henry Victor . . . . .Hercules
Harry Earles . . . . .Hans
Daisy Earles . . . . .Frieda
Rose Dione . . . . .Madame Tetrallini

DID YOU KNOW? M-G-M challenged Tod Browning, the director of the highly successful *Dracula* with Bela Lugosi, to come up with a film that would be even more terrifying—that would be the greatest horror movie of all time. Drawing on his own experiences as a runaway to a circus when he was eighteen years old, Browning produced *Freaks*, which was a box office flop in the United States and wasn't even released in the United Kingdom for thirty years.

A written prologue (attributed variously to Irving Thalberg and Dwain Esper, who acquired distribution rights) was reportedly added when the title was changed to *Nature's Mistakes*, but the early print screened from M-G-M's library has the prologue and was titled *Freaks*.

THE STORY: The happy engagement of Hans and Frieda, two of the carnival's dwarfs, is broken up when Cleopatra, the beautiful but wicked aerialist, flirts successfully with the wealthy Hans. Laughing at Hans behind his back, Cleopatra is having an affair with the equally hard-hearted strongman, Hercules, who has thrown over the sweet Venus. Knowing that Hans has a fortune, Cleopatra weds him, then cruelly tells him that their marriage is nothing more than a joke. Later, one of the other dwarfs overhears Cleopatra and Hercules plotting to kill Hans by poisoning him. Hans recovers from the poisoning, but the trapeze star plans to do it again—until the freaks plot their own revenge on her and Hercules. They attack Hercules with knives and kill him, and put the curse of the freaks on Cleopatra, who is mysteriously transformed into a "duck woman" and is now the most horrific of all the freaks in the carnival.

* * *

Generally grouped with horror films, *Freaks* in fact has only one brief event that is beyond the rational: the transmogrification of the aerialist beauty into a half duck–half woman. The rest of the horror has to do with the appearance of people born with defects, such as Siamese twins, the living torso (who has no lower half of his body), the half man–half woman, a bearded lady, pinheads, the bird girl, the armless girl, the human skeleton, and others—and the behavior of some of the "normal" people, which is far more "freakish" than that of those with greater reason, perhaps, to behave poorly.

The film was admired by some reviewers on release but was found overly disagreeable to others. Audiences, too, had mixed reactions, and it was reported that it was not uncommon for women to run screaming out of the theater. Today, of course, it is regarded as one of the great cult films.

There are reports of a different ending, in which Hercules is seen performing in a music hall in a falsetto voice, suggesting that the freaks emasculated him rather than killed him, but it does not appear to have been released.

Jean Harlow, then Myrna Loy, was considered for the part of Cleopatra before it was given to Olga Baclanova.

In the prologue, the statement is made that "Never again will such a story be filmed, as modern science and teratology is rapidly eliminating such blunders of nature from the world."

Some years after its initial release, it was distributed under the various titles *Nature's Mistakes, The Monster Show,* and *Forbidden Love.*

BEST LINE: Barker at a sideshow: "But for the accident of birth, you might be even as they are."

NOTORIOUS
1946

TYPE OF FILM:	Espionage/Suspense
STUDIO:	RKO
PRODUCER:	Alfred Hitchcock
DIRECTOR:	Alfred Hitchcock
SCREENWRITER:	Ben Hecht
SOURCE:	Original screenplay
RUNNING TIME:	103 minutes

PRINCIPAL PLAYERS:

Cary Grant . . . . .Devlin
Ingrid Bergman . . . . .Alicia Huberman
Claude Rains . . . . .Alexander Sebastian
Louis Calhern . . . . .Paul Prescott
Madame Leopoldine Konstantin. . . . . .Mme. Sebastian
Reinhold Schunzel . . . ."Dr. Anderson"
Moroni Olsen . . . . .Walter Beardsley
Ivan Triesault . . . . .Eric Mathis
Alex Minotis . . . . .Joseph
Wally Brown . . . . .Mr. Hopkins

DID YOU KNOW? Hollywood censors were still diligent about sex scenes, which included kissing. A stopwatch was put on the length of the kiss between John Garfield and Lana Turner in *The Postman Always Rings Twice* (1946) to insure that it wouldn't go beyond the perceived limit of propriety. In *Notorious,* made in the same year, the passionate kiss between Ingrid Bergman and Cary Grant, accompanied by lots of soft murmurs and an intimate embrace, was publicized by the Selznick studio as the longest kiss in the history of Hollywood movies.

THE STORY: Alicia Huberman, a fun-loving playgirl in Miami, finds her reputation questioned because her father had been convicted of being a German spy. She meets Devlin, a U.S. agent, who convinces her to go to South America with him to help his investigations into the highly dangerous activities in Rio de Janeiro. There a plot by a group of "former" Nazis to corner the world market in enriched uranium that is headed by Alexander Sebastian, who is a friend of Alicia's jailed father.

Devlin and Alicia have fallen in love, but soon a plan is devised that will enable the Americans to spy on Sebastian: Alicia is to marry him. Fearing that Devlin no longer loves her, and wanting to prove that she is a patriotic American and remove the taint of suspicion that clings to her because of her father's activities, she agrees.

At the party celebrating the marriage, Alicia slips Devlin a key to the wine cellar, where he discovers uranium ore samples hidden in old wine bottles. Sebastian, already suspicious of Alicia, discovers the truth and knows he must dispose of his wife to protect himself. Knowing that a sudden murder would alert the other members of the uranium cartel to his carelessness, he plots with his Nazi-sympathizing mother to slowly poison Alicia with arsenic. Too weak to alert Devlin, she lies helpless in bed until he finally realizes the truth and leads her away to safety.

* * *

In addition to being one of Alfred Hitchcock's greatest films, with moments of suspense so intense as to be nearly unbearable, *Notorious* is also one of his most morally ambiguous. The heroine, seen early to be a flirty good-time girl, is willing to marry and bed an enemy of her country. The hero, claiming to be in love with her, is perfectly willing to send her off to sleep with another man.

The characters are as aware of this dilemma as the viewer. Devlin recognizes that it is his duty to send her into the arms of his enemy. That same sense of patriotic duty forces her to agree. Doubt rears its ugly head when Devlin wonders how, if she truly loves him, she could sleep with another man. And she wonders, if Devlin truly loves her, how he could ask her to do such a thing. We wonder too.

To complete the picture of moral ambivalence, Sebastian is portrayed as a gentleman who finds himself in a position not entirely of his own making and who would, apparently, be far happier if he were able to extricate himself from it. Circumstances force him along, one step to the next, until he is cornered and, undoubtedly, doomed.

Inexplicably, someone thought it was a good idea to remake *Notorious* as a movie for cable television in 1992.

BEST LINE: Bergman (drunk) to Grant, suggesting a late-night drive: "My car is outside." Grant replies, "Naturally."

FATAL ATTRACTION
1987

TYPE OF FILM: Suspense

STUDIO: Paramount

PRODUCERS: Stanley R. Jaffe and Sherry Lansing

DIRECTOR: Adrian Lyne

SCREENWRITER: James Dearden

SOURCE: *Diversion*, a short subject by James Dearden

RUNNING TIME: 119 minutes

PRINCIPAL PLAYERS:

Michael Douglas . . . . .Dan Gallagher
Glenn Close . . . . .Alex Forrest
Anne Archer . . . . .Beth Gallagher
Ellen Hamilton Latzen . . . . .Ellen Gallagher
Fred Gwynne . . . . .Arthur
Mike Nussbaum . . . . .Bob Drimmer
Stuart Pankin . . . . .Jimmy
Ellen Foley . . . . .Hildy
Meg Mundy . . . . .Joan Rogerson
Tom Brennan . . . . .Howard Rogerson

DID YOU KNOW? As the second-most commercially successful film noir ever made (only *Basic Instinct* did greater box office, having the unfair advantage of an exquisitely—and frequently—naked Sharon Stone to lure audiences, especially men, into theater seats), *Fatal Attraction* nonetheless took severe critical flak for its ending. In customary Hollywood style, the philandering male receives only mild punishment for his sexual activity, while the sexually adventurous female pays with her life.

However, in the original version, director Adrian Lyne presented a far more complex portrait of Alex Forrest as the one night stand who is overly possessive, becoming a sympathetic woman rather than an obsessive monster. In frustration and despair, she kills herself. However, preview audiences so hated the ending and, by extension, the film, that a new ending was substituted, and the more traditional ending helped make it a box office smash.

THE STORY: A successful and happily married lawyer, Dan Gallagher, is required to attend a Saturday meeting at the publishing house for which he works, so his wife and young daughter leave him in New York while they visit her parents in the suburbs. After the meeting, he goes out to dinner with Alex Forrest, an editor, and they return to his apartment to have sex, which continues throughout the weekend. Alex immediately becomes overly attached to him, and when he tries to leave for his home, she cuts her wrists. He comforts her and they separate.

Although Gallagher has made it clear that there are to be no further involvements, Alex begins to show up unexpectedly, and calls him at the office and in the middle of the night at home. Finally, she informs him that she is pregnant as a result of their brief liaison. When he continues to want nothing further to do with her, she escalates her actions, ruining his car, invading his home, killing his daughter's pet rabbit, briefly kidnapping her, and ultimately attempting to stab his wife to death.

In a violent conclusion, he subdues her, holding her under the water of a bathtub until he believes her to be dead. With a last burst from the tub, large kitchen knife still in hand, she slashes at him, only finally to be shot dead by his wife.

* * *

Fatal Attraction was a huge success with audiences, but was attacked by various groups and critics. Feminist groups had a negative response to the film because they resented the portrayal of a sexually active woman as a violent schizophrenic. Others charged that the entire story line was manipulative, while conceding that it was suspenseful.

While certainly a film for its time, it would be impossible to argue that it's not old-fashioned in its values. A sexually loose woman is made to pay for her transgression with her life, while the man (far more guilty, as she is single and he's an adulterer) is free to return to his wife after a few tense days and resume his happy life.

Fatal Attraction has been accused (perhaps accurately) of inhibiting sexual activity in the 1990s because of the price the male protagonist paid for his little fling, not to mention the ultimate price paid by his sexual partner. It has further been described as a subliminal warning about the dangers of sexual activity in the era of AIDS.

Academy Award nominations went to the film for Best Picture, to Adrian Lyne for Best Director, to Glenn Close for Best Actress, and Anne Archer for Best Supporting Actress.

BEST LINE: Alex tells Gallagher that she's pregnant as a result of their weekend together. He asks her how she knows it's his. She responds (with a cold glare): "Because I don't sleep around."

D.O.A.
1950

TYPE OF FILM:	*Noir*
STUDIO:	United Artists
EXECUTIVE PRODUCER:	Harry M. Popkin
PRODUCER:	Leo C. Popkin
DIRECTOR:	Rudolph Maté
SCREENWRITERS:	Russell Rouse and Clarence Greene
SOURCE:	Original story by Russell Rouse and Clarence Greene
RUNNING TIME:	83 minutes

PRINCIPAL PLAYERS:

Edmond O'Brien . . . . Frank Bigelow
Pamela Britton . . . . Paula Gibson
Luther Adler . . . . Majak
Beverly Campbell (later Garland) . . . . Miss Foster
Lynn Baggett . . . . Mrs. Philips
Neville Brand . . . . Chester
William Ching . . . . Halliday
Henry Hart . . . . Stanley Philips
Laurette Luez . . . . Marla Rakubian

DID YOU KNOW? There have been four filmed versions of this unusual story. The noted 1950 motion picture was a remake of a 1931 German movie made by two of the greatest directors in cinema history, Billy Wilder and Robert Siodmak. In 1969, a modest remake was made by Australian director Eddie Davis under the title *Color Me Dead*. This uninspired little film starred Tom Tryon, Carolyn Jones, Patricia Connolly, and Rick Jason. Finally, there was the big-budget travesty of 1988, again titled *D.O.A.* — lots of money, lots of bright colors, lots of fast cutting, and lots of look-at-all-the-camera-tricks-I-learned-in-film-school directing by Rocky Morton and Annabel Jankel, who gave the world *Max Headroom*. It starred Dennis Quaid, Meg Ryan, Daniel Stern, and Charlotte Rampling, who should be ashamed of themselves.

THE STORY: Frank Bigelow, an accountant in the little desert town of Modesto, decides he needs a few days off in San Francisco, much to the dismay of his fiancée who thinks he might get into trouble, which is exactly what he has in mind. He immediately heads for a gin mill and spots a likely blonde. While distracted, a stranger drops poison in his drink. Frank heads home, not feeling well, and the next morning goes to a doctor, who tells him he's been poisoned and that he has a day or two, maybe a week, to live.

Bigelow, dying to know who poisoned him, finds that the basis of his murder occurred in his hometown. He innocently had notarized a bill of sale that, if it surfaced, could convict a woman and her lover of having killed her husband. The husband's death had been rigged to look like a suicide over a business failure, but the bill of sale would have discredited that scenario.

Reunited with his fiancée, whom he now realizes he truly loves, the doomed innocent bystander says, "All I did was notarize one little paper." He finally finds the man who fatally poisoned him and shoots him—more than once.

* * *

In this striking variation on the classic detective story, the victim and the detective are the same person. Talk about *noir*! The hero, the man the audience is rooting for, is already dead! A standard element of *noir* films is the sense of foreboding, the belief that there cannot be a happy ending for any of the principal players. In *D.O.A.*, the guesswork is gone. The hero is speaking from the grave.

Several minor roles were played by interesting choices. Two of the doctors were played by Larry Dobkin and Jerry Paris, both of whom went on to have very successful careers as directors. In an uncredited cameo, Hugh O'Brien appeared briefly; he went on the great fame as Wyatt Earp in the wildly popular television series.

The poison used to kill Bigelow, called luminous toxin, actually exists. It seemed a good choice of murder weapon, as audiences in America were slightly paranoid about the ramifications of atomic energy, radioactivity, and the substances involved, all of which had only recently come into public consciousness.

BEST LINE: At the beginning of the film, under the credits, Frank Bigelow walks into a police station. He tells the captain in charge, "I want to report a murder." "Sit down," the captain says. "Where was the murder committed?" "San Francisco. Last night." "Who was murdered?" Long pause. "I was."

FOREIGN CORRESPONDENT
1940

TYPE OF FILM:	Espionage
STUDIO:	United Artists
PRODUCER:	Walter Wanger
DIRECTOR:	Alfred Hitchcock
SCREENWRITERS:	Charles Bennett, Joan Harrison; dialogue by James Hilton and Robert Benchley
SOURCE:	Original screenplay
RUNNING TIME:	119 minutes

PRINCIPAL PLAYERS:

Joel McCrea . . . . .Johnny Jones/Huntley Haverstock
Laraine Day . . . . .Carol Fisher
Herbert Marshall . . . . .Stephen Fisher
George Sanders . . . . .Scott ffolliott
Albert Basserman . . . . .Van Meer
Robert Benchley . . . . .Stebbins
Edmund Gwenn . . . . .Rowley
Eduardo Ciannelli . . . . .Krug
Harry Davenport . . . . .Mr. Powers

DID YOU KNOW? The love scene aboard the ship during the violent North Sea storm was taken from Hitchcock's own life. Although the script was completed, Hitchcock added the scene in which the Joel McCrea character asks the Laraine Day character to marry him. There is nothing fancy about the scene, no sappy clinches and such, just the same straightforward proposal that Hitchcock made to Alma fifteen years earlier. McCrea: "I'm in love with you and I want to marry you." Day: "I'm in love with *you*, and I want to marry *you*." McCrae: "That cuts down our love scene quite a bit, doesn't it?"

THE STORY: At the beginning of 1939, John Jones, an American newspaper reporter, is sent to Europe under the name Huntley Haverstock. His mission is to learn more about the possibility of war, mainly by interviewing Van Meer, a Dutch diplomat who has committed to memory a key secret element in the Allied Peace Treaty. Jones meets Stephen Fisher, a member of the British upper class who is the head of a pacifist organization, and his daughter Carol, with whom Jones quietly falls in love. When Van Meer is kidnapped by foreign agents, Jones goes to Holland to find him. At a meeting in Amsterdam Square, Van Meer doesn't seem to recognize Jones and is shot and killed, while the assassin disappears in a sea of black umbrellas. With Carol and ffolliott, a British correspondent, Jones pursues the killer to a windmill in the Dutch countryside, which is the headquarters of a foreign spy ring.

Jones sends ffolliott for help, and finds a drugged Van Meer, proving that the murdered man was a lookalike impostor. The spies flee before the authorities return, so Jones goes back to London, where he goes to see Fisher. During the visit, Jones recognizes one of the men from the windmill. He realizes that Fisher is a traitor, and with ffolliott's help, he rescues Van Meer.

When war is declared between England and Germany, Carol and her father get on a plane for America and are surprised to meet Jones and ffolliott. The plane is shot down over the Atlantic, and Fisher, knowing he has been found out and facing arrest in America, sacrifices his life to save his daughter. An American ship rescues them, and Jones is able to report the story to his newspaper.

* * *

Producer Walter Wanger had purchased the rights to *Personal History*, the memoirs of foreign correspondent Vincent Sheean, and planned to make an important and timely film about the crisis in Europe, but he ran into endless problems—frequently of his own making—along the way. Numerous screenplays were rejected because they lacked plot and drama, and he couldn't get financing because of fears that the film might compromise America's position of neutrality.

He was eventually able to make a deal with David O. Selznick to borrow Alfred Hitchcock to direct. Hitchcock, his wife, Alma, Charles Bennett, and longtime collaborator Joan Harrison put together a script that was workable but had no similarity to the book, nor was it the anti-Nazi film Wanger had envisioned. Wanger wanted to see each development in the European crisis in the script. Hitchcock assured him this would be so, showing him the daily rushes, which pleased Wanger, and the show went on. In fact, Hitchcock added nothing to the script, and the film remains only mildly political, being transformed into a romantic adventure film with many comic moments. Only its ending, written by Ben Hecht and out of step with the rest of the film, urges America to be prepared. Five days after the last scene was shot, Germany dropped bombs on London. Ironically, the film was reported to be a personal favorite of Hermann Goering.

Foreign Correspondent was nominated for an Oscar for Best Picture, losing to another Hitchcock film, *Rebecca*. It also received other nominations, including several for technical categories, as well as one for Albert Basserman as Best Supporting Actor.

Hitchcock had wanted Gary Cooper to play Johnny Jones but was turned down because Cooper claimed thrillers were held in low regard. Years later, he told Hitchcock that he had made a mistake and should have taken the role.

BEST LINE: Mr. Powers, the editor of the *New York Morning Globe*, is disgusted with his foreign correspondents for failing to send any hard news to the paper and decides that he wants a real reporter to go to Europe, selecting the charming if slightly dim Johnny Jones, who admits that he knows nothing about Europe or any crisis. "What Europe needs," Powers exclaims, "is a fresh, unused mind."

SUSPICION
1941

TYPE OF FILM: Suspense
STUDIO: RKO
PRODUCER: Harry E. Edington
DIRECTOR: Alfred Hitchcock
SCREENWRITERS: Samson Raphaelson, Joan Harrison, and Alma Reville

SOURCE: *Before the Fact*, novel by Francis Iles (pseudonym of Anthony Berkeley Cox)

RUNNING TIME: 99 minutes

PRINCIPAL PLAYERS:

Cary Grant . . . . .Johnny Aysgarth
Joan Fontaine . . . . .Lina McLaidlaw
Cedric Hardwicke .General McLaidlaw
Nigel Bruce . . . . .Beaky Thwaite
Dame May Whitty . . . . .Mrs. McLaidlaw
Isabel Jeans . . . . .Mrs. Newsham

DID YOU KNOW? Alfred Hitchcock hated the title, writing in a memo that "*Suspicion* is such a cheap and dull title and makes it sounds like a B picture." He preferred the title of the book on which the film is based, *Before the Fact*, but polls showed a lukewarm response from audiences. At this time, George Gallup often polled moviegoers about potential titles for works in progress, and *Before the Fact* did poorly. Hitchcock suggested *Fright*. The studio suggested *Suspicious Lady*, and soon as many as fifty titles were being considered and polled, including *Search for Tomorrow*, *Girl in the Vise*, *Love in Irons*, *Men Make Poor Husbands*, and *Last Lover*. Finally, Hitchcock pushed hard for *Johnny*, but polls showed that *Suspicion* was a three-to-one choice over its nearest competitor and opened to great box-office success.

THE STORY: The charming and handsome Johnny Aysgarth meets the prim wallflower Lina McLaidlaw and they quickly fall in love and elope. After a long honeymoon, they return to a lavish house and furnishings ordered by Johnny, who turns out to be penniless, counting on his wife's income to support them. Lina insists that he take a job and, to placate her, he does, only to be fired for embezzling two thousand pounds. When she learns of his thievery and the frequent lies he has told her, Lina packs her bags to leave him, but then realizes she loves him too much to go away. Just as she tears up her farewell note, Johnny hands her a telegram informing her of her father's sudden death. At the reading of the will, Lina and her husband learn that he has left her nothing, clearly because he had always distrusted Johnny.

Soon after, Johnny's bumbling friend Beaky Thwaite comes for a weekend visit and Johnny draws Beaky into a real-estate deal that will require a large investment. Lina has visions of Johnny killing his friend for the money but is relieved to learn that, in fact, Johnny saved his life. A few days later, however, her fears resurface when Beaky and Johnny are in London together and Beaky dies. The cause of death is a glass of brandy, and Lina's neighbor, a writer of mystery novels, tells her that Johnny recently borrowed a book in which brandy is the murder weapon.

New fears arise when Lina discovers a letter in which Johnny has inquired about borrowing against her life insurance policy. Since he can collect only in the event of her death, she begins to fear for her life. At dinner, Johnny asks the mystery writer and her coroner husband about undetectable poisons, convincing Lina that that is how she will meet her end. Lina is unable to sleep that night and Johnny brings her a glass of milk, which she won't touch, convinced that it is lethal. She decides to stay with her mother for a few days and Johnny insists on driving her, speeding wildly along the coast. When the passenger side door swings open, Johnny reaches across the seat to grab her and she pulls away from him. She believes he was trying to push her out, while he furiously explains that he was trying to save her. Now she knows that Johnny wanted the poison to commit suicide because of his inability to pay his debts, and he admits he had considered it but decided that jail was a better choice. She begs his forgiveness for doubting him, and he turns the car around to return home.

* * *

From the beginning, the conclusion of the film was a problem, with the conflicting desires of the studio, Cary Grant, Hitchcock, the Production Code, and audiences.

In the book, Aysgarth poisons his wife with a glass of milk. The Production Code, however, prohibited a murderer from surviving and profiting from his crime. Furthermore, RKO was convinced such a downbeat ending would prove unsatisfactory to audiences. And, finally, Grant was not very pleased about being cast as a wife-killer.

A different ending was proposed in which Lina, pregnant, knows she is going to be poisoned but allows her husband to kill her and their unborn baby, because she doesn't want the blood of a murderer to flow into the next generation.

Yet another ending had Johnny confessing to his sins as a liar and a gambler who failed to pay his debts, then joining the RAF to try to atone.

Another proposal was that Lina meet another man, have an affair, and then allow herself to be poisoned, partly in contrition. Preview audiences openly laughed at this one.

Finally, the present ending, in which all thoughts of murder emanate from the imagination of Lina, was found to be the least objectionable. Audiences liked it, therefore RKO liked it, Grant liked it, the Production Code had no problem with it, and Hitchcock accepted it, though he always maintained that the ending he really wanted was to have Johnny poison Lina, who, knowing she was going to be murdered, had written a letter to her mother reaffirming her love for him but exposing him as the murderer: Just as she drinks the poisoned milk, Johnny drops the letter into a mailbox.

In the famous scene in which Johnny carries the glass of milk up the stairs and into his wife's bedroom, the camera focuses on it, just as Lina's eyes do. Hitchcock had placed a lighted bulb inside the glass to make it glow slightly but compellingly; it is impossible to take one's eyes from the menacing glass.

Suspicion was nominated for an Academy Award for Best Picture, and Joan Fontaine won for Best Actress, defeating her sister, Olivia de Havilland, who had been nominated for her role in *Hold Back the Dawn*. Forty years later, Fontaine assured the world that the famous feud between the two had never really existed and, besides, it was de Havilland's fault.

BEST LINE: Lina McLaidlaw has been afraid that her husband Johnny planned to murder his old friend Beaky in order to make a small fortune in a real estate deal. When Beaky tells her how Johnny saved his life, she is relieved and says, "Johnny, I can never tell you how much this means to me." Beaky responds, "It means a good bit to me too!"

CROSSFIRE
1947

TYPE OF FILM: *Noir*

STUDIO: RKO

PRODUCER: Adrian Scott

DIRECTOR: Edward Dmytryk

SCREENWRITER: John Paxton

SOURCE: *The Brick Foxhole*, novel by Richard Brooks

RUNNING TIME: 86 minutes

PRINCIPAL PLAYERS:

Robert Young . . . . .Finlay
Robert Mitchum . . . . .Sergeant Keeley
Robert Ryan . . . . .Monty Montgomery
Gloria Grahame . . . . .Ginny
Paul Kelly . . . . .The Man
Sam Levene . . . . .Joseph Samuels
Jacqueline White . . . . .Mary Mitchell
Steve Brodie . . . . .Floyd Bowers
George Cooper . . . . .Arthur Mitchell
Richard Benedict . . . . .Bill

DID YOU KNOW? Two of the principal players, both noted for distinguished roles in so many other *noir* films that they became typecast, worked totally against type in this film. Gloria Grahame, the ultimate victim in film after film—usually playing a sleazy prostitute or party girl—was actually a classically trained stage actress who longed to play Lady Macbeth. She was well known in Hollywood for having a lightning-fast wit and longed to get away from the roles for which she is now remembered. Her one chance came when she got the role of Billie Dawn in *Born Yesterday*, but RKO refused to loan her out to Columbia and the part went to Judy Holliday, who won an Oscar.

Similarly, Robert Ryan was nothing like the Neanderthals he so frequently played. An intellectual who loved Shakespeare, he attended Dartmouth and sought a career as a writer before attending acting school and signing with Paramount to act in B war movies.

THE STORY: The war has ended and four army buddies—Monty Montgomery, Floyd Bowers, Arthur Mitchell, and Leroy—go out to celebrate their imminent return to civilian life. They impose on Joe Samuels and go to his apartment to continue the party. As he gets drunker and more belligerent, Monty's anti-Semitism heats up and he beats the Jewish Samuels to death. Police Captain Finlay at first believes the killer is Mitchell, but Army Sergeant Peter Keeley, who knows all the men involved, enters the case and assures him that Mitchell isn't capable of such a crime. Monty, afraid that Bowers won't be able to stand up to the penetrating questioning and that he'll reveal the true killer, murders Bowers. Leroy and Mitchell go into hiding, but Keeley, aided by Ginny Tremaine, a prostitute, finds them and they set a trap for Monty, convincing him that Bowers is still alive. When Monty shows up to finish the job, he is arrested. As he breaks free and runs to escape, he is shot.

* * *

Crossfire is the first of the pure *noir* films to raise a serious social issue and as a result achieved the kind of critical acclaim that was never accorded equally good films that lacked a similar message. Producer Adrian Scott was committed to making socially conscious films and found this the perfect way to make a popular movie that would still deliver a strong anti-Fascist statement.

At a rival studio, Darryl F. Zanuck had acquired the rights to *Gentleman's Agreement*, a novel by Laura Hobson about anti-Semitism. The new head of RKO, Dore Schary, urged Scott to rush the film so that it could be released before Zanuck's project in order to get first crack at the liberal audience. It worked. The film was a smash at the box office, got rave reviews, and received tons of awards, many from humanitarian groups.

Both the producer, Adrian Scott, and the director, Edward Dmytryk, soon were hauled in front of the House Un-American Activities Committee, where they took Fifth Amendment pleas and were sent to jail. Both were fired by the studio and blacklisted in Hollywood for several years. Dmytryk reestablished himself by pointing a finger at other members of the Hollywood community. Ironically, the furthest left of all the players was Robert Ryan, who spent decades as an activist for left-wing causes but was never brought before HUAC.

Academy Award nominations went to *Crossfire* as Best Picture,

Dmytryk for Best Director, Gloria Grahame for Best Supporting Actress, and Robert Ryan for Best Supporting Actor.

BEST LINE: Capt. Finlay has just shot the fleeing Montgomery when Leroy asks, "Captain, is he dead?" Finlay answers, "He was dead for a long time. He just didn't know it."

KISS OF DEATH
1947

TYPE OF FILM: *Noir*

STUDIO: Twentieth Century-Fox

PRODUCER: Fred Kohlmar

DIRECTOR: Henry Hathaway

SCREENWRITERS: Ben Hecht and Charles Lederer

SOURCE: "Stoolpigeon," story by Eleazar Lipsky

RUNNING TIME: 98 minutes

PRINCIPAL PLAYERS:

Victor Mature . . . . .Nick Bianco/Nick Cavallo
Brian Donlevy . . . . .Louis D'Angelo
Coleen Gray . . . . .Nettie Cavallo
Richard Widmark . . . . .Tommy Udo
Taylor Holmes . . . . .Earl Howser
Howard Smith . . . . .Warden
Karl Malden .Sergeant William Cullen
Mildred Dunnock . . . . .Ma Rizzo

DID YOU KNOW? Perhaps the greatest performance as a psychopathic killer this side of James Cagney was given by Richard Widmark in his screen debut. He memorably played Tommy Udo, in a performance that made him an overnight star. Audiences were struck by Widmark's strange manner of speaking, his piercing eyes, his almost skeletal face, his overly energetic method of movement, but mostly by his laugh, a humorous giggle that was terrifying. In what may be the single most memorable scene in the history of film noir, Udo goes to the home of a stool pigeon that he has been sent to kill. When he realizes that the squealer has fled and that his wheelchair-bound mother has lied to protect him, he ties her to the chair with an electrical cord, wheels her to the top of a flight of stairs, and pushes her down, giggling maniacally the whole time.

It was a strange path to stardom for Widmark, who had been an all-American boy in his hometown of Sioux Falls, South Dakota. He was an honor student in high school, president of his senior class at Lake Forest College in Illinois, played on the football team, was captain of the debating team, and was a member of the drama department. When he came to New York in 1942, he got leading man roles on Broadway in *Kiss and Tell* and *Kiss Them for Me*. Nothing he did prepared the world for Tommy Udo.

THE STORY: On Christmas Eve, Nick Bianco and two other crooks hold up a jewelry store at the top of the Chrysler building and are caught. Although the Assistant District Attorney, Louis D'Angelo, repeatedly asks Bianco to cooperate in exchange for D'Angelo's help in getting to see his wife and two daughters, Bianco refuses, putting his faith in his lawyer, Earl Howser. When Bianco learns that his partners and his lawyer did not provide financial help as promised for his wife, causing her to commit suicide, he agrees to snitch on his jailmate, the psychopathic Tommy Udo, and his former cohorts, especially Pete Rizzo.

Bianco tells his crooked lawyer that Rizzo has squealed, and Howser sends Udo to kill Rizzo. When Udo finds him already gone, he kills Rizzo's mother instead by pushing the wheelchair-bound woman down a flight of stairs.

Given parole in exchange for information about the dangerous Udo, Bianco marries Nettie Cavallo, who used to baby-sit his daughters, and moves to a house in the suburbs. When Udo is unexpectedly acquitted in spite of Bianco's testimony, Bianco decides to protect his wife and children by sending them away and forcing a confrontation with the maniacal killer.

Bianco arranges with D'Angelo to have police nearby when he finds Udo in his favorite restaurant, taunting him until Udo pulls a gun and shoots him. Badly wounded but alive, Bianco goes back to his family and Udo is hauled away to prison.

* * *

The scene in which Udo pushes the old lady in a wheelchair down a flight of stairs was so shocking and repellent that many theaters edited it out. Even today, more than a half century later, it remains horrifying.

The original title of the picture was *Stoolpigeon*, the name of the story submitted by Eleazar Lipsky. It was changed to *Blind Date,* but when the head of production at Twentieth Century-Fox, Darryl F. Zanuck, spotted a reference in a Hedda Hopper column to an event in a politician's life as "the kiss of death," he liked the sound of it so much that he changed the film title again. Lipsky, an assistant district attorney in New York, submitted the story under a pseudonym, Lawrence L. Blaine.

The year after the film's release, novelist Lawrence B. Bachman sued Twentieth Century-Fox, Zanuck, producer Fred Kohlmar, Lipsky, and Penguin Books (which had published a novelization of the screenplay) for $125,000. He claimed that he had been damaged because he had published a book in 1946 called *The Kiss of Death* and that the public had been misled into thinking that the novelization, titled *Kiss of Death*, was his book. Three years later, Bachman dropped the suit.

Although Nick Bianco's wife, Maria, and his cohort Pete Rizzo are mentioned prominently in the movie, she is never seen and Rizzo appears only in the opening scene. All the other scenes in which they were featured ended up on the cutting room floor.

Richard Widmark received an Academy Award nomination for Best Supporting Actor for his compelling role as Tommy Udo. Eleazar Lipsky was also nominated for Best Original Story.

A western version of *Kiss of Death* was released in 1958, titled *The Fiend Who Walked the West*, starring Hugh O'Brian and Robert Evans. In 1995, *Kiss of Death* was remade starring David Caruso as Nick Bianco, Nicolas Cage as Tommy Udo, and Helen Hunt as Nick's wife. The film failed, but not as miserably as the usually first-rate Cage, who tried to out menace Widmark with such extremity that he became a bad cartoon.

BEST LINE: Tommy Udo, telling a crook's mother that he'll find her son, who he believes to be a stool pigeon: "You know what I do to squealers?" he asks her. "I let 'em have it in the belly, so they can roll around for a long time, thinking it over."

SPELLBOUND
1945

TYPE OF FILM: Suspense

STUDIO: Selznick International

PRODUCER: David O. Selznick

DIRECTOR: Alfred Hitchcock

SCREENWRITER: Ben Hecht

SOURCE: *The House of Dr. Edwardes*, novel by Francis Beeding

RUNNING TIME: 110/116 minutes

PRINCIPAL PLAYERS:

Ingrid Bergman . . . . .Dr. Constance Peterson
Gregory Peck . . . .John Ballantine/Dr. Anthony Edwardes/J.B./ John Brown
Michael Chekhov . . . . .Dr. Alex Brulov
Leo G. Carroll . . . . .Dr. Murchison
Rhonda Fleming . . . . .Mary Carmichael
John Emery . . . . .Dr. Fleurot
Norman Lloyd . . . . .Garmes
Bill Goodwin . . . . .house detective
Steven Geray . . . . .Dr. Graff
Donald Curtis . . . . .Harry
Wallace Ford . . . . .stranger in hotel lobby
Art Baker . . . . .Lieutenant Cooley
Regis Toomey . . . . .Sergeant Gillespie
Paul Harvey . . . . .Dr. Hanish

DID YOU KNOW? Alfred Hitchcock hired Salvador Dali, the famous Spanish surrealist painter, to design a dream sequence. Hitchcock wanted to do something different from the typical Hollywood dream sequence, which generally was little more than a hazy, blurry image created by rubbing Vaseline on the lens. The producer, David O. Selznick, thought Hitchcock had hired the artist as a publicity gimmick, but the director genuinely had done it for creative reasons. He wanted vividness and greater sharpness than in the main body of the film itself. Dali worked closely and directly with Hitchcock, who wrote a long and complicated sequence that lasted twenty minutes, but Selznick found it far too long and incomprehensibly complex, so it was edited down to about two minutes. Dali had created about a hundred sketches and five oil paintings—all at Hitchcock's instruction and constructed entirely from the director's imagination. Hitchcock left the set before the dream sequences had been entirely edited, so Selznick had to replace him with William Cameron Menzies after Josef von Sternberg turned him down. Menzies found the dream sequence so unappealing that he refused credit for the film. When the dream sequence got rave reviews and contributed to the overall success of the film, Hitchcock took credit himself. Dali received $4,000 for his two months of work.

THE STORY: The young and handsome psychologist Dr. Edwardes, who is replacing Dr. Murchison, the outgoing head of Green Manors mental hospital, finds a mutual attraction with Dr. Constance Peterson. She reads a signed book by him from the hospital library, goes to talk to him, and they become more romantically involved. All is not well, however, as the sight of parallel lines makes him dizzy and confused. Later, she compares the signature in the book with a note he'd written to her, and she realizes that he is an impostor, which he readily admits. He is an amnesiac who can't remember his own identity but is convinced that he killed the real Dr. Edwardes. Constance refuses to believe him, confident that he is delusional. He tells her that he found a cigarette case with the initials J.B. in a pocket, and she tells him that with her therapy they will be able to recover his memory.

He leaves for New York and she follows, taking him to Rochester to meet her much loved old mentor, Dr. Alex Brulov, whom she tells that she and J.B. are on their honeymoon. J.B. stares dazedly at his shaving cream when he prepares to shave and has an even more profound reaction to the sight of snow outside Brulov's house. Constance guesses that J.B. and Dr. Edwardes had been skiing together and helps him recall where, and they set off to Gabriel Valley.

While they are skiing together, he recalls a terrible incident from his childhood when he accidentally pushed his brother off a roof, causing him to be impaled on the spikes of a fence below. He then saves Constance from going over the edge of a precipice—the same one from which Dr. Edwardes fell to his death. The recalled memory of his childhood tragedy brings back his name; John Ballantine. He is arrested when the police find Edwardes's body exactly where J.B. told them it would be, but they discover that it has a bullet in it. He is convicted of murder, but Constance, still believing in his innocence, returns to Green Manors where she has a conversation with Dr. Murchison. Murchison inadvertently mentions that he knew the real Dr. Edwardes, thereby revealing that he must have known J.B. was an impostor though he acted as if he did not. She further realizes that Murchison must have shot Edwardes in view of J.B., who sublimated the action because of repressed guilt about his brother's death. She confronts Murchison and he pulls a gun on her, but she talks him out of killing her. As she leaves his office and closes the door, he turns the gun on himself.

* * *

A movie based on psychological themes was a pet project of producer David O. Selznick, and he wanted Hitchcock to direct it. Hitchcock went to London and bought all theatrical rights to *The House of Dr. Edwardes*, a novel by Francis Beeding, convinced Selznick this was the perfect vehicle, and sold the rights to him for a whopping profit.

Numerous psychiatric and psychological experts were consulted, and several were hired to help assure that the film would be scientifically accurate. As soon as Hitchcock hired Ben Hecht to write the screenplay, they toured mental institutions in Connecticut and New York, ending with the psychiatric wards at Bellevue Hospital. Additionally, Selznick hired his own analyst, Dr. May E. Romm, a distinguished psychiatrist in Beverly Hills, to serve as consultant on the film, and later added Dr. Karl Menninger, another noted psychiatrist.

Joseph Cotten had been planned to star as J.B., but Selznick cast him in another movie, *I'll Be Seeing You*, and he decided instead on the rising young star Gregory Peck for *Spellbound*. Dorothy McGuire was to have been Dr. Constance Peterson, but Ingrid Bergman became available and replaced her.

Academy Award nominations went to *Spellbound* for Best Picture, Alfred Hitchcock for Best Director, and Michael Chekhov for Best Supporting Actor.

Hitchcock Alert: When people emerge from a crowded elevator, Hitchcock is among them.

BEST LINE: Peck (suffering from amnesia) to Bergman: "Will you love me just as much when I'm normal?" Bergman: "I'll be insane about you."

TOPKAPI
1964

TYPE OF FILM: Crime/Comedy
STUDIO: United Artists
PRODUCER: Jules Dassin
DIRECTOR: Jules Dassin
SCREENWRITER: Monja Danischewsky
SOURCE: *The Light of Day,* novel by Eric
Ambler
RUNNING TIME: 120 minutes

PRINCIPAL PLAYERS:

Melina Mercouri . . . . .Elizabeth Lipp
Peter Ustinov . . . . .Arthur Simpson
Maximilian Schell . . . . .Walter
Robert Morley . . . . .Cedric Page
Akim Tamiroff . . . . .Geven
Despo Diamantidou . . . . .Voula
Gilles Segal . . . . .Giulio
Jess Hahn . . . . .Fischer
Titos Wandis . . . . .Harback
Ege Ernart . . . . .Major Tufan

DID YOU KNOW? Peter Ustinov won an Academy Award for
Best Supporting Actor for his role as the sleazy Englishman
Arthur Simpson. Along with his many other awards, he keeps the
famous gold statue, perhaps the most important award any actor
can win, in a glass case in his bathroom. Someone suggested to
the much-loved actor that this room seemed to be lacking in dig-
nity for something so important, but Ustinov maintained that it
was the only room in his house where he could comfortably ad-
mire the monuments to his achievements without appearing ego-
tistical.

THE STORY: Elizabeth Lipp (not her real name, she quickly
confides) has a passion to steal a fabulous jeweled dagger from Is-
tanbul's Topkapi museum and has her lover (though she hasn't
seem him for three years), William Walter, design the plan. He

decides that the other necessary members of the gang that will pull off the caper must be amateurs, and he recruits a strange coterie. Cedric Page is an inventor and electronic genius; Giulio is a mute acrobat; and Fischer is the muscle.

While still in Greece, where the plans have been laid, Elizabeth and William Walter hire Arthur Simpson, an unsuccessful con man, to drive their car across the border into Turkey. They fail to tell Simpson that a rifle and grenades are hidden in the car. When Simpson is caught at the Turkish border, he is forced to work undercover for the Turkish police—who believe they have uncovered a terrorist plot—or he will be sent to jail. Simpson infiltrates Elizabeth's gang of thieves. Their drunken cook misunderstands some overheard conversation, believes the crooks are a gang of Soviet spies, and imparts this information to Simpson, who passes it on to the Turks.

Meanwhile, Page has figured out that the floor of the museum is weight-sensitive once the alarms are turned on, so even the slightest pressure will set off the alarms. The plan is to enter from the roof, with Fischer holding a rope while Giulio is lowered and removes the dagger from its case without touching the floor. When Fischer's hands are injured, the gang decides to recruit Simpson, offering him $10,000 to lower Giulio instead. He writes a note to himself, resigning from the Turkish Secret Service, and flushes it away.

The meticulously planned robbery goes exactly as planned except that a small bird has flown in through the same window used by Giulio. When it lands on the floor, alarms go off and the theft is discovered, sending the entire gang good-naturedly into prison, where Elizabeth hatches a new scheme to steal the Russian crown jewels.

* * *

Although it is one of the handful of best comic caper films ever made, *Topkapi* was not a huge box office success. Clearly, the ending suggested that a sequel was planned, but it never happened, in spite of a decade of rumors.

Jules Dassin, the producer and director, was married to Melina Mercouri, the star. He had previously made a first-rate caper film in France, *Rififi*, which lacked the many comic elements of *Topkapi*.

The source novel for the screenplay, *The Light of Day*, is the only novel by Eric Ambler, one of the great espionage novelists of all time, that did not involve spies and international intrigue of a serious nature.

Bruce Geller, the creator of the immensely popular television show, *Mission: Impossible*, claimed that *Topkapi* was the inspiration for his series.

BEST LINE: The gang, secure in the knowledge that the caper has gone off as planned, go to the police station to tell them of their astounding discovery: weapons in their car. The alarm goes off during their visit and the police officer learns what has happened, and tells them, "I know now why you are here." The surprised Simpson says, "You do? Do you really, sir?" And the policeman replies, "Yes, Mr. Simpson. A little bird told me."

KEY LARGO
1948

TYPE OF FILM: Crime

STUDIO: Warner Brothers—First National

PRODUCER: Jerry Wald

DIRECTOR: John Huston

SCREENWRITER: John Huston and Richard Brooks

SOURCE: *Key Largo*, play by Maxwell Anderson

RUNNING TIME: 101 minutes

PRINCIPAL PLAYERS:

Humphrey Bogart . . . . .Frank McCloud
Edward G. Robinson . . . . .Johnny Rocco
Lauren Bacall . . . . .Nora Temple
Lionel Barrymore . . . . .James Temple
Claire Trevor . . . . .Gaye Dawn
Thomas Gomez . . . . .Curley Hoff
Jay Silverheels . . . . .Tom Osceola
Harry Lewis . . . . .Toots Bass
John Rodney . . . . .Deputy Clyde Sawyer
Marc Lawrence . . . . .Ziggy

DID YOU KNOW? In an early scene, Bogart (as Major Frank McCloud) visits the widow and father of a war buddy who was killed in action. Lionel Barrymore, as James Temple, is eager to hear of his son's exploits, so as his former commanding officer, McCloud tells him of his son's heroic actions. This speech, by writer/director John Huston, was largely drawn from *San Pietro*, a 1944 war documentary that he had also made.

THE STORY: Major Frank McCloud, recently returned from the war, goes to a hotel on Key Largo to visit the family of a soldier killed under his command and finds that it has been taken over by a gang of criminals. A hurricane hits, scaring the leader of the gang, the notorious Johnny Rocco. When the storm lets up, Sheriff Ben Wade comes looking for his deputy, whom Rocco has killed, intimating that two Indians had killed him. Wade finds the Indians, who are wanted for escaping from jail after a drunken spree, and kills them both.

Rocco plans to return to Cuba with his gang, and McCloud agrees to pilot the boat. Three of the gangsters go below and Mc-Cloud abruptly speeds up, throwing one of those on deck overboard and shooting the other. One of the thugs comes running up the stairs, and McCloud shoots him too. Rocco orders the remaining henchman up the stairs to deal with McCloud and, when he refuses, Rocco kills him. The frightened thug then tries to make a deal with McCloud, offering him all the money from his recently concluded deal, but McCloud simply waits for him to come up on deck and shoots him when he does. He turns the boat around and heads back to Key Largo and Nora, the widow of his slain army comrade.

* * *

If the plot of *Key Largo* sounds familiar, you are right. In *The Desperate Hours*, Bogart plays Glenn Griffin, an escaped gangster who, with his gang, holds a family hostage. In *The Petrified Forest*, Bogart plays an escaped gangster who, with his gang, holds a group of people hostage. Here, in *Key Largo*, Bogart plays one of the people held hostage by a gang of criminals.

Claire Trevor, as Gaye Dawn, the drunken girlfriend of Johnny Rocco, won an Academy Award for Best Supporting Actress.

For those unfamiliar with American geography, the film opens with a foreword explaining that: At the southernmost point of the United States are the Florida Keys, a string of small islands held together by a concrete causeway. Largest of these remote coral islands is Key Largo.

Key Largo has been portrayed as a political statement, a position enhanced by director/screenwriter John Huston's frequent contemporary and retrospective statements. The character of Johnny Rocco represented fascism, with a desire to return to the "good old days" when democracy and freedom were not allowed in his world. Bogart, a war hero, complains about America's postwar aimlessness and political corruption. Finally, of course, he realizes that he cannot allow the thugs to win and he takes up arms (in this case, a handgun slipped to him by Rocco's boozy mistress) to "cleanse the world of ancient evils," as the script portentiously puts it.

BEST LINE: The gangsters have just taken over the hotel owned by James Temple, a tough old bird confined to a wheelchair. As the hoods bully the hostages, Temple will have none of it, baiting one of the thugs. "That big gun in your hand," he says, "makes you look grown up—you think. I'll bet you spend hours posing in front of a mirror holding it, trying to look tough."

THE FUGITIVE
1993

TYPE OF FILM: Suspense

STUDIO: Warner Brothers

PRODUCER: Arnold Kopelson

DIRECTOR: Andrew Davis

SCREENWRITERS: Jeb Stuart and David Twohy; story by David Twohy

SOURCE: *The Fugitive*, TV series, created by Roy Huggins

RUNNING TIME: 127 minutes

PRINCIPAL PLAYERS:

Harrison Ford . . . . .Dr. Richard Kimble
Tommy Lee Jones . . . . . . .Deputy U.S. Marshal Samuel Gerard
Sela Ward . . . . .Helen Kimble
Julianne Moore . . . . .Dr. Ann Eastman
Joe Pantoliano . . . . .Cosmo Renfro
Andreas Katsulas . . . . .Sykes—The One-Armed Man
Jeroen Krabbé . . . . .Dr. Charles Nichols
Daniel Roebuck . . . . .Biggs
L. Scott Caldwell . . . . .Poole

DID YOU KNOW? The film version of *The Fugitive* was, of course, based on the hugely popular television series of the 1960s, the last episode of which was, at the time, the highest rated program in the history of television. Harrison Ford, who plays Dr. Richard Kimble, the role played by David Jansen in the TV series, never saw a single episode before starring in the motion picture.

While it has been popular in recent years to make big budget movies based on successful television series, the vast majority have been both critical and financial failures (think of *Leave It to Beaver, The Mod Squad, Twilight Zone—The Movie,* and *The Beverly Hillbillies*). *The Fugitive* was both commercially successful and critically acclaimed, perhaps because it changed so dramatically from one medium to the other. Whereas the TV program was a character-driven, modestly budgeted series of dramas about a thoughtful and sensitive man about whom audiences cared, the motion picture version was a big, fast-paced action thriller that kept audiences on the edge of their seats. Both good—but 180-degree opposites from each other.

THE STORY: Dr. Richard Kimble, an eminent surgeon, returns home from an emergency operation to find his wife murdered. He struggles with the intruder, a one-armed man, who escapes. Kimble is arrested, tried and convicted of the murder.

As a bus transports him to prison, an escape plan hatched by other convicts goes awry and the bus careens onto a train track. Just before the train smashes into the bus, Kimble rescues one of the guards, then escapes.

When Deputy U.S. Marshal Sam Gerard arrives, he questions the guards and learns that Kimble and another convict have escaped. Kimble, meanwhile, has made it to a hospital where he cleans up, shaves his beard, puts on doctor's clothing and steals an ambulance, with Gerard pursuing him in a helicopter. Trapped in a roadblocked tunnel, Kimble manages to escape through a drainage system, again with Gerard in pursuit. He gets Gerard's gun and yells to him, "I didn't kill my wife!" Gerard yells back, "I don't care!"

Kimble takes off with Gerard, who has pulled out a backup weapon, again in pursuit. When Kimble comes to a precipice above a dam, the marshal tells him to drop his gun, which he does, then leaps over the edge.

Kimble survives the death-defying leap and works his way back to Chicago, where he makes contact with his lawyer and a trusted colleague, Dr. Charles Nichols. After several other narrow escapes, Kimble learns that Nichols knew the one-armed man and had framed his friend in order to prevent him from discovering a scheme by which Nichols would have made a fortune by selling a highly dubious drug. Kimble soon catches up with the one-armed man and struggles with him on an elevated train, killing him, and later also confronts Nichols in a roof-top battle. Gerard finally acknowledges Kimble's innocence and removes the handcuffs from the exhausted doctor.

* * *

This is a chase movie, pure and simple, with little detection and not much in the way of clues, observation or deduction. Much like a James Bond film, the overall story serves mainly as a framework for a series of smaller vignettes and set-pieces. On those terms, it is one of the most exciting movies of the past several decades.

Harrison Ford actually hurt his leg during the filming of the sequence in the woods and decided to delay surgery until filming was completed so that his character would retain the limp. From that scene on, Dr. Kimble has a limp, barely noticeable when he walks but quite obvious when he runs.

In the scene in which the train crashes, director Andrew Davis used a real train (not a miniature, as is so often done) and crashed it. The engine was not destroyed and survives, now pulling a dinner train on which can be seen props from the film, including the prison bus.

Tommy Lee Jones won an Academy Award for Best Supporting Actor for his portrayal of Marshal Gerard. *The Fugitive* was nominated for Best Picture, losing to *Schindler's List*.

There was a sequel to *The Fugitive*. In 1998, Tommy Lee Jones again played Sam Gerard in *U.S. Marshals*, a decent thriller that makes up in breathless action what it lacks in originality.

BEST LINE: After the bus has been destroyed by the train and the U.S. Marshals are questioning a guard, Marshal Poole listens to the odd concoction and asks, "Care to revise your statement, sir?" The guard cleverly says, "What?" Poole, now slightly less friendly, replies, "Do you want to change your bullshit story, sir?"

THE MAN WHO KNEW TOO MUCH

1956

TYPE OF FILM:	Suspense/Espionage
STUDIO:	Paramount
PRODUCER:	Alfred Hitchcock
DIRECTOR:	Alfred Hitchcock
SCREENWRITERS:	John Michael Hayes and Angus McPhail
SOURCE:	Story by Charles Bennett and D. B. Wyndham-Lewis
RUNNING TIME:	120 minutes

PRINCIPAL PLAYERS:

James Stewart . . . . .Dr. Ben McKenna
Doris Day . . . . .Jo McKenna
Brenda De Banzie . . . . .Mrs. Drayton
Bernard Miles . . . . .Mr. Drayton
Ralph Truman . . . . .Buchanan
Daniel Gelin . . . . .Louis Bernard
Alan Mowbray . . . . .Val Parnell
Hillary Brooke . . . . .Jan Peterson

DID YOU KNOW? There were two versions of *The Man Who Knew Too Much*, both directed by Alfred Hitchcock. The first was made in England in 1934 and had a more action-packed ending than the later film, in which the kidnaped boy is rescued from a foreign consulate by his father, acting virtually alone. In the British version, the police attack the spy ring in a house, in a scene that recreates an actual historical event, the Sidney Street siege.

A few years before the first World War, some Russian anarchists had barricaded themselves in a house and were shooting at the police, who were trying to get them out. The police were making little progress so soldiers were called in, and Winston Churchill, then the head of the London police, was called in to take charge of the operation. The police had had little success because British policemen do not carry firearms, requiring the military presence. As the anarchists continued to hold out, Churchill was about to call in the artillery, when the house caught fire and the anarchists came running out.

When *The Man Who Knew Too Much* was made, Hitchcock ran into difficulty because British authorities did not want to see policemen carrying or using firearms. When Hitchcock asked how he was going to get the spy ring out of the house, it was suggested that water hoses be used—the same idea that Churchill had advanced many years before. Finally, it was agreed that the police could use firearms if the screen showed them going to the local gunsmith to pick out antique weapons, demonstrating that they were unfamiliar with modern weaponry. Hitchcock ignored the silly directive and had a truck loaded with rifles pull up to supply the policemen.

THE STORY: American tourists Dr. Ben McKenna, his wife Jo and their young son, Hank, are in Marrakesh on the bus from the airport where they meet a Frenchman and later befriend an English couple. Bernard, the Frenchman, is stabbed in a crowded marketplace and whispers dying words into Ben's ear, telling him that he is a French agent and giving him information about a planned assassination attempt of an important politician in London.

The McKenna's son is kidnapped soon after by the British couple, who are in fact foreign agents. Warned that their son will be harmed if they reveal a single word of the Frenchman's message, Ben and Jo head to London to try to recover their son and, if possible, prevent the assassination.

They learn that the attempt will be made at Albert Hall during a concert, at the precise moment that cymbals crash. Just before that musical moment, Jo screams, causing the assassin to miss his mark. A grateful prime minister invites the Americans to his embassy that evening. Knowing now that their son is captive there, they go. As Jo, a famous singer before her marriage, provides a concert, which includes "Que Sera, Sera," her signature song, her son hears it and whistles the same tune, leading Ben to the room in which he is being held. As the agent tries to sneak out of the embassy with Ben and Hank as hostages, he tumbles down the staircase and the family is happily reunited.

Film critics often state their preference for the earlier version, which is also excellent. It was made in 1934 and starred Leslie Banks, Edna Best, and Peter Lorre. A major reason given for finding the second version inferior is that it is longer, has more elaborate sets, and is dramatically bigger. Hitchcock himself, however, much preferred the second film. He told Francois Truffaut that "the first version is the work of a talented amateur, and the second was made by a professional."

"Que Sera, Sera," the song sung by Doris Day several times during the film, was a number one hit single in America and became her signature song. It won an Academy Award for Best Original Song.

The idea of the shot being fired just as the cymbals clash was inspired by a cartoon strip showing a man waking up in the morning and going through all the rituals of the day, getting on a bus to Albert Hall, carrying his instrument case (a flute, in this instance) into the hall, opening it, taking his seat, taking out the score, and dutifully turning pages until the conductor finally points to him and he blows out his single note, then packs up, puts on his hat and coat, and gets on the bus to go home, filling his entire day. Hitchcock thought it would be amusing to get a suspense effect from one clash of cymbals.

The Man Who Knew Too Much was a stunning financial success. After being released for only one week, it was already the most commercially successful film of the year. In his first year as an American citizen, Hitchcock earned $4,000,000, and his financial advisers arranged enough tax shelters so that he paid not a cent in income tax.

BEST LINE: Meeting the McKennas on a bus in Marrakesh, Louis Bernard tells them he is French. Hank asks if he eats snails, and Bernard says he does, when he is lucky enough. The young boy then tells him if he is ever hungry, their garden back home has a lot of snails. "We've tried everything to get rid of them," he offers, "but we never thought of a Frenchman."

IN THE HEAT OF THE NIGHT
1967

TYPE OF FILM: Police
STUDIO: United Artists
PRODUCER: Walter Mirisch
DIRECTOR: Norman Jewison
SCREENWRITER: Stirling Silliphant
SOURCE: *In the Heat of the Night*, novel by John Ball
RUNNING TIME: 109 minutes

PRINCIPAL PLAYERS:

Sidney Poitier . . . . .Virgil Tibbs
Rod Steiger . . . . .Bill Gillespie
Warren Oates . . . . .Sam Wood
Lee Grant . . . . .Mrs. Leslie Colbert
Scott Wilson . . . . .Harvey Obers
Larry Gates . . . . .Eric Endicott
James Patterson . . . . .Purdy
Quentin Dean . . . . .Delores Purdy
William Schallert . . . . .Webb Schubert
Beah Richards . . . . .Mrs. Bellamy/Mama Caleba

DID YOU KNOW? John Ball, the author of the book on which *In the Heat of the Night* was based, may have been one of the luckiest men who ever lived. He had an undistinguished career as a writer of various types of action novels when his first Virgil Tibbs book was submitted to Joan Kahn, the legendary editor at Harper & Row. Perhaps the finest mystery editor ever to have worked in the field, she made extensive notes and had the author rewrite over and over again, forcing him to follow her meticulously thought-out plot, character, and dialogue enhancements. The book went on to win the Edgar Allan Poe Award from the Mystery Writers of America, and film rights were acquired for a very large sum. Reviews of the novel were glowing, suggesting that Tibbs might be worthy of acceptance into the pantheon of Great Detectives. When the second novel was submitted, Kahn again suggested major changes and rewrites, only to have Ball refuse to do them. After all, he claimed, he'd already won an Edgar, had great reviews, and sold motion-picture rights for a ton of money, so he didn't really need her help. Needless to say, the second book, and the handful that followed, were critical and commercial failures, and Ball (and Tibbs) are remembered today only for that first book and the brilliant film made from it.

THE STORY: In the little cotton town of Sparta, Mississippi, Leslie Colbert, a wealthy industrialist who planned a big new factory employing a thousand people, half of them black, is found bludgeoned to death in an alley on a hot summer night. Virgil Tibbs is picked up at the train station for no reason except that he is a Negro. After Tibbs is hauled off to jail, sheriff Bill Gillespie discovers that Tibbs is a police officer from Philadelphia in town to visit his mother. As a homicide expert, Tibbs is asked by his boss to stay and help with the case, to the disgust of the sheriff. As the object of hatred of the mostly bigoted white town, Tibbs, who is equally prejudiced against whites, decides to return home but is tricked into staying by Gillespie, who taunts him by saying, "You're so damn smart . . . smarter than any white man . . . I don't think you could let an opportunity like that pass by."

A suspect has been hunted down and arrested for the murder because he has Colbert's wallet on him, but he protests that he merely picked it up from alongside the dead man's body, and Tibbs quickly proves him innocent. The dead man's widow uses her influence to ensure that Tibbs will stay on the case, and he becomes convinced that the true murderer is Eric Endicott, the wealthiest man in town. Angered by Tibbs's questioning, he slaps the policeman, and Tibbs slaps him back. Soon thereafter, gangs of rednecks chase Tibbs, ready to beat him to get him out of town.

Next to be arrested for the murder is Sam Wood, Gillespie's deputy, who has been accused of getting the town's sixteen-year-old tease pregnant. Tibbs visits the local abortionist, Mama Caleba, and encounters the girl and the true father, the counter man at the diner, who finally confesses that he murdered Colbert for the money to pay for the abortion.

With the case solved, Gillespie takes Tibbs to the train station, even carrying his suitcase for him, and the men shake hands in mutual respect.

* * *

In 1967, just as the civil-rights movement was gaining steam, this was the perfect film for the time. A handsome, confident, articulate black man is surrounded by stupid, loutish rednecks who use racial epithets and violence at every opportunity, while he maintains composure and proves to be their intellectual and moral superior. Regarded as a milestone in liberal media, it was bound to be a success, and it was, grossing nearly $11,000,000 (back in the time when that was considered real money in Hollywood).

The great success of *In the Heat of the Night* spawned two sequels, *They Call Me* Mister *Tibbs!* (1970) and *The Organization* (1971), both of which again starred Sidney Poitier as the perfect man. The former had terrible reviews but did pretty well at the box office, the latter had better reviews but sold fewer tickets.

Some years later, NBC aired a two-hour remake of *In the Heat of the Night*, with Howard E. Rollins as Tibbs and Carroll O'Connor as Gillespie. Critics wondered why anyone thought this was needed, but it was successful enough to foster a one-hour television series that enjoyed success.

Academy Awards went to the film for Best Picture, Rod Steiger for Best Actor, and Sterling Silliphant for Best Adapted Screenplay. Awards were also won for editing and sound. Norman Jewison was nominated for Best Director. Sterling Silliphant also received the Edgar Allan Poe Award from the Mystery Writers of America for his screenplay.

BEST LINE: Tibbs and Gillespie have just left the home of Eric Endicott, the rich but bigoted cotton grower who pretty much owns the town of Sparta. With the merest hint of evidence, Tibbs is convinced that Endicott is the murderer and wants to prove it. He has been slapped and has slapped back, so Gillespie warns him he'll have to get out of town, but the furious Tibbs begs him to let him stay a day or two. "I can pull that fat cat down," he rages at the sheriff. "I can bring him right off this hill." Gillespie pauses and says, "Man, you're just like the rest of us, ain't ya?"

BONNIE AND CLYDE
1967

TYPE OF FILM: Crime

STUDIO: Warner Brothers—Seven Arts

PRODUCER: Warren Beatty

DIRECTOR: Arthur Penn

SCREENWRITERS: David Newman and Robert Benton

SOURCE: Original, based on real-life characters and events

RUNNING TIME: 111 minutes

PRINCIPAL PLAYERS:

Warren Beatty . . . . .Clyde Barrow
Faye Dunaway . . . . .Bonnie Parker
Michael J. Pollard . . . . .C. W. Moss
Gene Hackman . . . . .Buck Barrow
Estelle Parsons . . . . .Blanche Barrow
Gene Wilder . . . . .Eugene Grizzard
Dub Taylor . . . . .Ivan Moss
Denver Pyle . . . . .Captain Frank Hamer
Evans Evans . . . . .Velma Davis

DID YOU KNOW? There is less attention paid to actual historical fact in *Bonnie and Clyde* than there is in an Oliver Stone movie.

MOVIE: Bonnie Parker hooks up with Clyde Barrow when she catches him trying to steal her mother's car. *HISTORY:* She met him while working as a waitress in a greasy-spoon luncheonette where she slung hash when she wasn't working as a prostitute.

MOVIE: After their first robbery, Bonnie is so sexually aroused that she practically attacks Clyde, only to be rebuffed, as he appears to be impotent; the angry Bonnie clearly believes him to be homosexual. *HISTORY:* Barrow was bisexual, using several of his male gang members as sex partners.

MOVIE: At a bank robbery, Barrow asks a patron if some money belongs to him or the bank. When he says it's his, Barrow tells him to keep it. *HISTORY:* This gesture was actually made by John Dillinger.

MOVIE: When they capture a Texas Ranger, they take pictures with him, then handcuff him and set him adrift in a rowboat. *HISTORY:* They killed every police officer they could, without mercy. Bonnie once shot a traffic cop in the head for fun as they drove by and, on another occasion, killed a motorcycle cop on a whim, then drove their car back and forth over his dead body.

MOVIE: Broke and hungry, they stop at an encampment, where the poor Okies give them food and water. *HISTORY:* Bonnie, Clyde, and the whole gang were despised and feared by their families, neighbors, and acquaintances, as they routinely robbed and shot them. The real-life Robin Hood of that era was Pretty Boy Floyd.

THE STORY: In the Depression-era South, Bonnie Parker spots Clyde Barrow trying to steal her mother's car and, impressed with his manner and bored with her small-town life, decides to run away with him. They commit one amateur stickup after another with small takings and decide to add a driver to help them, picking up C. W. Moss, the somewhat dim mechanic at a gas station they happen to pull into. They finally connect with Clyde's brother, Buck, recently out of prison, and his wife, the nervous daughter of a preacher.

Escalating their robberies from grocery stores to banks and adding murder to their list of crimes, the gang becomes the object of a large cross-country manhunt. When they escape from a huge cadre of police who have surrounded their hideout, their legend grows and they announce who they are whenever they hold up a bank.

With a sense of impending doom, Bonnie insists they visit her mother, and the gang is surrounded by police again. This time Buck is killed, his wife is partially blinded, and Bonnie is wounded. They hide out with Moss's father, who turns in the gang in an attempt to make a good deal for his son. When Bonnie and Clyde see Moss's father's truck broken down, they stop to help and quickly realize they have been set up for an ambush by the police, who gun them down in a barrage of bullets.

* * *

Bonnie and Clyde was a highly controversial film when it was released, and it still is today. It was both excorciated for its excessive and graphic violence and applauded for its portrayal of these symbols of the alienation and dehumanization felt by many

150

Americans in the 1960s. Many viewers and some critics also found it distasteful to glorify and glamorize two of the most cold-blooded killers in American history.

The film helped to make huge stars of its two principals. Warren Beatty is reported to have gotten on his knees to beg Jack Warner to finance the picture after two studios turned it down. Faye Dunaway, after two failures (*The Happening* and *Hurry, Sundown*), returned $25,000 of her $60,000 fee in exchange for billing above the title.

Bonnie Parker's sister sued Warren Beatty and Warner Brothers for—get this—blackening Bonnie's memory and exposing her to hatred and ridicule.

In perhaps the most virulent review of his long and distinguished career, Bosley Crowther of *The New York Times* wrote: *It is a cheap piece of bald-faced slapstick that treats the hideous depredations of that sleazy, moronic pair as though they were as full of fun as the Jazz Age cutups in* Thoroughly Modern Millie.

Ten Academy Award nominations went to the film, including Best Picture, Best Director (Arthur Penn), Best Actor (Warren Beatty), Best Actress (Faye Dunaway), Best Supporting Actor (Gene Hackman), and others, winning only for Best Supporting Actress (Estelle Parsons) and Best Cinematography. After the film lost in virtually every category, Beatty mumbled, "We wuz robbed."

BEST LINE: Clyde Barrow has pulled into a gas station and attempts to recruit C. W. Moss to join him and Bonnie Parker. "I know you got the nerve to shortchange old ladies coming in for gas," he says to the mechanic. "But what I'm asking is, do you have what it takes to pull bank jobs with us?"

SCARFACE
1932

TYPE OF FILM:	Gangster
STUDIO:	United Artists
DIRECTOR:	Howard Hawks
SCREENWRITERS:	Ben Hecht (story), Seton I. Miller, John Lee Mahin, W. R. Burnett (Continuity and dialogue), and Fred Pasley (adaptation)
SOURCE:	*Scarface*, novel based on the life of Al Capone, by Armitage Trail
RUNNING TIME:	90 minutes

PRINCIPAL PLAYERS:

Paul Muni . . . . .Tony Camonte
Ann Dvorak . . . . .Cesca Camonte
George Raft . . . . .Guino Rinaldo
Boris Karloff . . . . .Gaffney
Karen Morley . . . . .Poppy
Vince Barnett . . . . .Angelo
Osgood Perkins . . . . .Johnny Lovo
C. Henry Gordon . . . . .Guarino
Parnell Pratt . . . . .publisher
Tully Marshall . . . . .managing editor

DID YOU KNOW? While director Howard Hawks was still in production on *Scarface*, which had been closely based on the life and crimes of Al Capone, several of the gangster's "associates" paid a visit to Hawks and asked to see the film. Hawks famously told them that when the picture came out, Capone could buy a ticket like everyone else. The ensuing conversation appears to be unreported, but Hawks was persuaded to change his mind and showed a rough cut to the film aficionados. They loved it and reported back to Capone.

THE STORY: Tony Camonte (the real-life Al Capone) shoots Italian mob boss Big Louie Costillo, initiating mob wars for control of the bootlegging business on Chicago's South Side. The am-

FBI Agent Clarice Starling (JODIE FOSTER) explores the mind of serial killer Dr. Hannibal Lecter (ANTHONY HOPKINS) in *The Silence of the Lambs*. (Copyright © 1990 Orion Pictures Corporation. Supplied by Photofest.)

Private eye Sam Spade (HUMPHREY BOGART) demands answers about *The Maltese Falcon* from Casper Gutman (SYDNEY GREENSTREET) while Joel Cairo (PETER LORRE) looks on. (Copyright © 1941 Warner Brothers, Inc. Supplied by Photofest.)

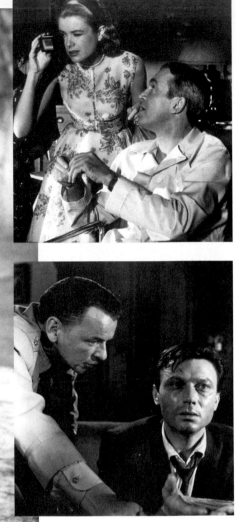

Injured photographer L. B. "Jeff" Jeffries (JAMES STEWART) and his girlfriend, Lisa Carol Freemont (GRACE KELLY) glance through the *Rear Window* to watch the events in other apartments. (Copyright © 1954 Paramount Pictures Corporation. Supplied by Photofest.) Bennett Marco (FRANK SINATRA) tries to determine the nature of the nightmares he's been having by questioning fellow Korean War veteran Raymond Shaw (LAURENCE HARVEY) in the screen adaptation of Richard Condon's novel *The Manchurian Candidate*. (Copyright © 1962 United Artists. Supplied by Photofest.) Black marketeer Harry Lime (ORSON WELLES) on the run from the law in *The Third Man*. (Copyright © 1949 London Films. Supplied by Photofest.)

Marion Crane (JANET LEIGH) discovers—much to her dismay—why the Bates Motel has so few guests in *Psycho*. (Copyright © 1960 Paramount Pictures Corporation. Supplied by Photofest.)

Ready for her close-up: Aging silent-film star Norma Desmond (GLORIA SWANSON) dramatically descends a staircase in the climax of *Sunset Boulevard*. (Copyright © 1950 Paramount Pictures Corporation. Supplied by Photofest.)

A portrait of *Laura*: New York City detective Mark McPherson (DANA ANDREWS) comes face-to-face with the object of his obsession (GENE TIERNEY) in the screen adaptation of Vera Caspary's novel. (Copyright © 1944 20th Century-Fox Film Corporation. Supplied by Photofest.)

"Mr. Pink" (STEVE BUSCEMI) and "Mr. White" (HARVEY KEITEL) come to a deadly disagreement in *Reservoir Dogs*. (Copyright © 1992 Miramax Films. Supplied by Photofest.)

Who is Keyser Soze? One of these men (l. to r., Todd Hockney [KEVIN POLLAK], Michael McManus [STEPHEN BALDWIN], Fred Fenster [BENICIO DEL TORO], Dean Keaton [GABRIEL BYRNE], and "Verbal" Kint [KEVIN SPACEY]) holds the answer to that question in *The Usual Suspects*. (Photo by Linda R. Chen. Copyright © 1995 Gramercy Pictures. Supplied by Photofest.)

Moments after the most exciting chase scene in film history, narcotics dealer Pierre Nicoli (MARCEL BOZZUFFI) is shot by NYPD Detective Jimmy "Popeye" Doyle (GENE HACKMAN) while trying to escape in *The French Connection*. (Copyright © 1971 20th Century-Fox Film Corporation. Supplied by Photofest.)

Making an offer he can't refuse: Don Vito Corleone (MARLON BRANDO) in *The Godfather*. (Copyright © 1972 Paramount Pictures Corporation. Supplied by Photofest.)

Despite finding out what happens to "nosy fellows," private eye J. J. "Jake" Gittes (JACK NICHOLSON) continues his investigation into the secrets of *Chinatown*. (Copyright © 1974 Long Road Productions. Supplied by Photofest.) They call him *Mr.* Tibbs: Homicide expert Virgil Tibbs (SIDNEY POITIER) examines a piece of evidence, to the consternation of Sparta, MS Police Chief Bill Gillespie (ROD STIEGER) in *In the Heat of the Night*. (Copyright © 1967 United Artists. Supplied by Photofest.) San Francisco detective Harry Callahan (CLINT EASTWOOD) takes aim at a sniper on the loose in *Dirty Harry*. (Copyright © 1971 Warner Brothers, Inc. Supplied by Photofest.)

Taxi Driver Travis Bickle (ROBERT DeNIRO) prepares for his date with destiny in the climax of the New York-set thriller. (Copyright © 1976 Columbia Pictures Industries, Inc. Supplied by Photofest.)

bitious Tony next kills the North Side boss as well, and takes control of all Chicago for his boss, Johnny Lovo. To solidify his position, Tony orders the St. Valentine's Day Massacre to eliminate rival gang leaders. Lovo is frightened of his ruthless right-hand man and sets him up to be killed, but Tony escapes and kills Lovo instead. By killing him, Tony becomes the supreme ruler of Chicago's underworld.

On a more personal level, Tony sees his sister Cesca dancing with a man in a nightclub and takes her home and beats her in a jealous rage. While Tony hides out in Florida after killing his boss, Cesca falls in love with Guino, Tony's best friend, and marries him. Tony returns to find them together and, again enraged with jealous passion for his beautiful sister, Tony kills Guino before Cesca can explain that they are married. The police come, surround the apartment, and start blasting. Cesca and Tony hold them off until she is shot dead and Tony, unable to stand the tear gas, surrenders. At the last moment, he changes his mind and decides to make a dash for freedom but falls in a hail of bullets.

* * *

One of the earliest and greatest of all gangster films, *Scarface* was a major project as well as a major problem for Howard Hughes, president of Caddo, his production company. The Hays Office, the censoring body for Hollywood films, had major concerns about gangster films in general and this one in particular. Anything that made the Al Capone character look heroic, or even human, had to be eliminated, and references to the obvious incestuous interest of the protagonist toward his sister had to be removed as well. Numerous changes were made to attempt to comply with the endless requests—at great cost to the production company—and delayed the film's release for nearly a year. Finally, Hughes refused to make further revisions and released the film, threatening to file a lawsuit in New York, where the most adamant censoring body opposed the film. Of the three versions of the film, the one that was finally released, and the one that may now be seen on video, is Hughes original version.

In preparation for the making of the film, director Howard Hawks and screenwriter Ben Hecht interviewed real gangsters, as well as Capone's biographer, Fred Pasley. Hecht claimed that he based his scripts on the Borgia family of the Italian Renaissance. It was also reported that Capone met with Hawks and, separately, George Raft, who had reputed connections to the underworld, particularly to Owney Madden. The famous gangster thought the film was terrific and loved the publicity it gave him— *Scarface* was in lights on theater marquees all over the country.

Paul Muni was outstanding as Tony, but another actor, a young song-and-dance man, had one of his most memorable roles ever. George Raft played Tony's bodyguard and best friend, Guino, and Hawks had the idea of having him flip a coin in the air and catch it. Raft practiced so hard that he could do it without looking, and it became a little acting trick that indelibly imprinted the character. The coin, incidentally, was a nickel, not a quarter as usually stated.

Scarface was remade in 1983 with Al Pacino in an over-the-top orgy of violence and excess, with mobsters transformed from Italians to Cubans.

BEST LINE: On his swift and ruthless rise to the top of gangland Chicago, Tony took as his motto the words from the Cook's Tour sign outside his window: THE WORLD IS YOURS. When he is gunned down trying to escape, he dies beneath the sign. The last words of Scarface are: "The world is yours."

GOLDFINGER
1964

TYPE OF FILM: Espionage/Crime

STUDIO: United Artists

PRODUCERS: Harry Saltzman and Albert R. Broccoli

DIRECTOR: Guy Hamilton

SCREENWRITERS: Richard Maibaum and Paul Dehn

SOURCE: *Goldfinger*, a novel by Ian Fleming

RUNNING TIME: 112 minutes

PRINCIPAL PLAYERS:

Sean Connery	James Bond
Gert Frobe	Auric Goldfinger
Honor Blackman	Pussy Galore
Tania Mallet	Tilly Masterson
Harold Sakata	Oddjob
Bernard Lee	M
Lois Maxwell	Miss Moneypenny
Shirley Eaton	Jill Masterson
Martin Benson	Solo
Cec Linder	Felix Leiter

DID YOU KNOW? Ian Fleming, the creator of James Bond, was himself a member of the British Secret Service for some years. He began writing the books about Secret Agent 007 in 1956 with *Casino Royale*, but the books had only modest success until President John F. Kennedy endorsed them. After that they became international best-sellers, and the movies inspired by them, beginning with *Dr. No* in 1962, became enormous box-office smashes.

THE STORY: Auric Goldfinger, who has loved gold since he was young, has amassed great wealth and bought as much gold privately as possible. Aided by his Korean henchman, Oddjob, whose innocuous, even comical bowler is a deadly weapon, he plots to infiltrate Fort Knox, the American depository of a vast gold reserve. Goldfinger doesn't plan to steal it but to cause it to be radioactive and therefore worthless, thereby enhancing the value of his own holdings to make him the richest man in the world.

As with all the Bond movies, there are no "whodunit" elements, and even the overall plot is merely a device for smaller bits of action. In the opening scene, Goldfinger, unable to resist the opportunity to cheat at cards, is taking a pigeon for a few thousand dollars as his blond girlfriend uses a telescope in a hotel window to see his opponent's cards and inform him via a miniature radio receiver in his ear. Bond sneaks in, forces Goldfinger to lose a larger amount than he had won, and seduces the girl. Goldfinger's bodyguard, Oddjob, sneaks into Bond's room at night and knocks him unconscious. When Bond awakes, he finds the girl-covered with gold paint, which has asphyxiated her.

Bond later meets another of Goldfinger's associates, a beautiful blonde of ambivalent sexuality. As he awakes from again having been knocked unconscious, she introduces herself: "I'm Pussy Galore." "I must be dreaming," he replies. Pussy and her flying circus of five gorgeous blondes spray nerve gas over Fort Knox in preparation for the planting of Goldfinger's bomb that will radioactivate the gold. After the plot has been foiled, Pussy and Bond meet again. Having once kissed him, of course Pussy turns enthusiastically heterosexual, and the movie ends with her wrapped in Bond's arms while they are both wrapped in the silk of a parachute.

* * *

This is the third of the James Bond movies, all of which starred Sean Connery, and is typical of the series. Though it may be the best, an argument could be made that *From Russia With Love* is its equal. The opening credits are exquisitely handled, especially with the title song sung by Shirley Bassey; the reassuringly familiar figures of M and Miss Moneypenny are like coming home to 221B Baker Street and finding Dr. Watson and Mrs. Hudson waiting; and then there are the gadgets.

Bond maintains a look of extreme nonchalance, if not boredom, as Q describes the new Aston Martin and its enhancements for him: bulletproof glass, of course, but also machine guns from the headlights, tracking devices, and—Bond's favorite—a top that comes off so that the ejector seat can do its job.

While some viewers decry the sex and violence of the Bond films, the almost cartoonlike savagery of the villains, the total absence of blood, and the witty insouciance of the hero make them the most entertaining series of the 1960s and indeed have sustained sufficient energy to keep them successful into the 1990s.

BEST LINE: The best line in all of the Sean Connery James Bond films is probably the same one: He introduces himself memorably as "Bond. James Bond." In this film, he learns that his foe is to be Auric Goldfinger. He responds, "Sounds like a French nail polish."

I AM A FUGITIVE FROM A CHAIN GANG

1932

TYPE OF FILM:	Gangster
STUDIO:	Warner Brothers
EXECUTIVE PRODUCER:	Hal B. Wallis
DIRECTOR:	Mervyn LeRoy
SCREENWRITERS:	Howard J. Green, Brown Holmes, and (uncredited) Sheridan Gibney
SOURCE:	*I Am a Fugitive from a Georgia Chain Gang!*, the autobiography of Robert E. Burns
RUNNING TIME:	93 minutes

PRINCIPAL PLAYERS:

Paul Muni . . . . .James Allen/Allen James
Glenda Farrell . . . . .Marie Woods
Helen Vinson . . . . .Helen
Noel Francis . . . . .Linda
Preston Foster . . . . .Pete
Edward Ellis . . . . .bomber
Allen Jenkins . . . . .Barney Sykes
Berton Churchill . . . . .judge
David Landan . . . . .warden

DID YOU KNOW? Robert E. Burns escaped from the Campbell County Prison Camp in Georgia and wrote his autobiography, which castigated the chain gang system as overly cruel. His story was serialized in *True Detective Mysteries* magazine in 1931 before its publication in book form in 1932. It was once rumored that while Burns was making a publicity appearance, he was recaptured and sent back to prison. However, the truth is that he settled in New Jersey as a tax consultant, and three governors refused to extradite him. In 1945, twenty-five years after his arrest, the governor of Georgia commuted his sentence to time served.

Burns had stolen $5.29. He died of cancer in 1955. The warden of the Campbell County Prison Camp sued Warner Brothers after the release of the film because of the manner in which he was depicted, but the suit was dismissed by the Fulton County Superior Court. The chain-gang system was not abolished until 1937—five years after the release of the movie.

THE STORY: James Allen returns from World War I and is unable to find work because of the scarcity of jobs. In a situation that he is unable to control, he participates in a robbery, during which the real crook is killed. He is captured and sentenced to serve ten years on a southern chain gang. The brutal conditions wear him down and he enlists the help of a fellow convict to remove his shackles and enable him to run away. He gets free and flees, with armed guards and dogs chasing him through the Georgia countryside. Allen escapes to Chicago and becomes a successful construction contractor, living a normal life until Marie, his landlady, discovers the truth about him and forces him to marry her. Later, he meets Helen and falls in love with her. When he asks Marie for a divorce, she refuses and, enraged, turns him in to the authorities. When the state of Illinois refuses to extradite him, the officials at the prison from which he escaped offer him a deal: If he turns himself in, he will receive a full pardon after ninety days. Eager to put the past behind him, he agrees but quickly learns that he was lied to. When his requests for parole are refused, he escapes again. As a wanted fugitive, he cannot return home and must live on the outskirts of society. He cautiously sees Helen one more time and, when she asks him how he lives, he tells her, "I steal."

* * *

Unlike the other movies about criminals made in the 1930s, this dark film is not about the rise and fall of a tough, ambitious psychopath but is the tragic story of a decent man caught in a web of circumstances that batter him at every turn. It is one of the purest examples of filmmaking that shows how American society can force a man into a life of crime and violence. As a result, it was one of only three American films that were permitted to be shown in the Soviet Union (*Cabin in the South* was one of the others because it "exploited oppression of poor whites in the South").

Paul Muni, fresh from playing the vicious titular character in

Scarface, here plays an entirely different role, a victim oppressed by the same system that Scarface used to gain a fortune. For his role as the hunted convict, Muni was nominated for an Academy Award as Best Actor (losing to Charles Laughton in *The Private Life of Henry VIII*). The film also received an Oscar nomination for Best Picture (losing to *Cavalcade*). It was named Best Picture of the Year by the National Board of Review.

Immediately after Muni delivered his famous and still shocking last line—"I steal,"—the electricity in the studio failed, knocking out the klieg light. The resulting slow fade at the end of the film was so effective that director Mervyn LeRoy decided not to reshoot it.

Burns's autobiography was remade for television as *The Man Who Broke 1,000 Chains*.

BEST LINE: James Allen, on the run after escaping from prison a second time, visits his girlfriend one last time before resuming his life in the shadows. "No friends, no rest, no peace," he says to her. "That all that's left for me." She asks, "Can't you tell me where you're going? Do you need money? How do you live?" He responds, "I steal."

THE MANCHURIAN CANDIDATE
1962

TYPE OF FILM: Espionage

STUDIO: United Artists

EXECUTIVE PRODUCER: Howard W. Koch

PRODUCERS: George Axelrod and John Frankenheimer

DIRECTOR: John Frankenheimer

SCREENWRITER: George Axelrod

SOURCE: *The Manchurian Candidate*, novel by Richard Condon

RUNNING TIME: 126 minutes

PRINCIPAL PLAYERS:

Frank Sinatra . . . . .Bennett Marco
Laurence Harvey . . . . .Raymond Shaw
Janet Leigh . . . . .Rosie
Angela Lansbury . . . . .Raymond Shaw's mother
Henry Silva . . . . .Chunjin
James Gregory . . . . .Senator John Iselin
John McGiver . . . . .Senator Thomas Jordan
Leslie Parrish . . . . .Jocie Jordan
Khigh Deigh . . . . .Yen Lo

DID YOU KNOW? The casting of Angela Lansbury in *The Manchurian Candidate* was at the same time a brilliant and puzzling move. She gave a memorable performance as the manipulative and dominating mother of Raymond Shaw, the brainwashed former Army sergeant who has been programmed to kill at the direction of his Communist puppet master—who happens to be his mother. The performance was remarkable enough to earn her an Academy Award nomination (she lost to Patty Duke in *The Miracle Worker*). But what is perhaps most remarkable is that she was only one year older than Laurence Harvey, who played her son.

THE STORY: During the Korean War, a patrol of U.S. soldiers is captured and sent to Manchuria, where the Chinese Communists brainwash them. Upon their return to the United States, Sergeant Raymond Shaw is given a Congressional Medal of Honor for his courageous action in battle, as attested by the other members of the patrol. In fact, the incident never occurred; they have all been brainwashed into thinking it did. Furthermore, Shaw has been instilled with triggered-response patterns, set off by the sight of the queen of diamonds, which command him to do the bidding of his superiors with no memory of his subsequent actions. When he kills he has no guilt, because he has no memory of committing the deed.

Shaw establishes himself as a journalist and is soon turned over to the head of a major Communist operation. The operative is his own ambitious mother, who plots to have her son assassinate a presidential nominee so that her husband, Senator Iselin, the vice-presidential nominee, will be in control of the United States after the assured election.

Another member of the patrol, Bennett Marco, has recurring nightmares of the time in Manchuria and begins to remember certain events and notices the strange behavior of Shaw when he sees the playing card. He discusses his dreams with the other men on patrol and they share his memories, leading to an Army investigation of Shaw. Shaw advances his mother's plan by killing his wife and his father-in-law, Thomas Jordan, a liberal senator who is the prime opponent for Iselin.

When Marco figures out the plot, he tries to convince Shaw that he no longer has control over his own mind, but the mindless robot follows his mother's orders and takes his rifle to the assassination point, only to have the hypnotic spell broken at the last moment. He kills his mother and stepfather, and then himself.

* * *

The Manchurian Candidate was made by staunch supporters of John F. Kennedy, who was himself a great fan of the Richard Condon novel on which the film was based. Their counterattack on Joseph McCarthy and his anti-Communist crusade was done in usual Hollywood fashion: the right-wing senator Iselin is portrayed as so moronic that he cannot remember a number when he speaks of the number of "card-carrying Communists" in the Defense Department, changing it every time the subject comes up and finally asking his manipulative and domineering wife to give him a nice easy number to remember. The liberal Senator

162

Jordan, on the other hand, is portrayed as kindly, gentle, and principled, as well as a good father of a sweet and lovely girl.

The overall politics of the film are confusing, however. Clearly the villains are the Communists in China and the Soviet Union, who commit unspeakably ruthless acts. The head of their operation in America is Raymond Shaw's mother, who is manipulating the election so that her fascist husband can be president. She is outraged that her Communist bosses have used her son as the weapon by which their plans will come to fruition. But is their plan to have a right-winger as president? Or is the plan Mrs. Iselin's own, electing her lunatic-right husband to the presidency as a rebuke to those who destroyed her son? Ultimately, the film seems to warn about extremists on both ends of the political spectrum, placing its faith in the American security system.

A corollary may be drawn between *The Manchurian Candidate* and *2001: A Space Odyssey*. In both films, humans create a perfect machine in which they are totally confident and dependent. In one case, it is an altered human who has been made into a robot. In the other, it is a machine made of metal and plastic. In both cases, the machines turn on their creators and destroy them. Is there a lesson here?

In the fight scene in which Frank Sinatra (as Bennett Marco) has it out with Henry Silva (as Chunjin), a lack of adequate rehearsal and practice proved to be a problem. In one bit of action, Silva moved the wrong way and Sinatra slammed his hand onto a tabletop. But it was not a fake table designed to splinter on impact. It was a real table, and Sinatra hit it hard enough to break the top—as well as the finger on his right hand.

BEST LINE: Raymond Shaw tells Bennett Marco: "It's a terrible thing to hate your mother. But I didn't always hate her. When I was a child, I only kind of disliked her."

MEAN STREETS
1973

TYPE OF FILM:	Crime
STUDIO:	Warner Brothers
EXECUTIVE PRODUCER:	E. Lee Perry
PRODUCER:	Jonathan T. Taplin
DIRECTOR:	Martin Scorsese
SCREENWRITERS:	Martin Scorsese and Mardik Martin
SOURCE:	Original screenplay
RUNNING TIME:	110 minutes

PRINCIPAL PLAYERS:

Robert De Niro . . . . .Johnny Boy
Harvey Keitel . . . . .Charlie
David Proval . . . . .Tony
Amy Robinson . . . . .Teresa
Richard Romanus . . . . .Michael
Cesare Danova . . . . .Giovanni
Victor Argo . . . . .Mario
George Memmoli . . . . .Joey
Martin Scorsese . . . . .man in the car

DID YOU KNOW? It is blindingly clear that none of the main characters in *Mean Streets* is Rhodes Scholarship material. The bloody battle in Joe Catucci's pool hall is caused by the insult of the word *mook* and it is likely that no one—not the audience, and not the characters in the movie—knows what it actually means. The fact is, it doesn't mean anything, except in some isolated Brooklyn neighborhoods. Director Martin Scorsese heard about a fight over the word in one of the neighborhoods and thought it was funny, so he used it in the film.

In Harvey Keitel's high school in Brooklyn, neighborhood kids developed a vernacular that did not travel far. A *Gropo* was a dope, and a *Mook* was even dimmer than a *Gropo*. A *Harvey*, in contrast, was someone to whom everything came easily. Lou Gossett, Jr., who also came from Keitel's neighborhood, invented the term *Harvey Mookie*—a person who is really good at being stupid. It has been heard in recent years on *NYPD Blue,* with the added connotation of dishonesty, so when Andy Sipowitz says he'll talk to the mook privately, he means he knows he has a moronic crook in custody and he's preparing to beat or frighten some truth out of him.

THE STORY: Johnny Boy and Tony are second-generation Italian punks living in Little Italy, where they survive on the fringes of the law by running numbers, loan sharking, and anything else that involves a few bucks.

Charlie is a natty dresser who still lives with his parents but is having an affair with Teresa, Johnny Boy's epileptic cousin. Johnny Boy is a volatile loner who is deeply in debt to Michael, the suave but dangerous neighborhood bookie. Tony runs a bar where the neighborhood hoods hang out.

When Johnny Boy demeans Michael in front of the others at the bar, his life is in danger. The bookie is already enraged because he can't collect Johnny Boy's debt, which grows rapidly because Johnny Boy isn't even trying to pay the vigorish (interest). Johnny Boy asks Charlie to intercede with his uncle, a Mafioso, but Charlie doesn't want to bother his powerful uncle with such a trivial matter and offers to hide his pal in Brooklyn instead. Tony borrows a car to take them where it will be safer, and Teresa joins them at the last moment.

As they pull away, they are followed by the murderous Michael and two gunmen, who open fire on the car with an endless torrent of bullets.

* * *

Much like *GoodFellas* and *The Godfather* films, this portrait of gangsterdom is not driven by a single narrative but by a series of vignettes that ultimately provide a picture of each of the characters, their surroundings, and the lives they lead. Unlike the Corleone family and its associates, these characters have no cultivation, no Machiavellian schemes, no brains, and no future. They are doomed from the outset—doomed to die or to continue to live as borderline survivors in the gutters and alleys of Little Italy.

The title *Mean Streets* is an ironic homage to Raymond Chandler, whose brilliant essay likening the honorable private detective to a knight famously bears the phrase, *Down these mean streets a man must go who is himself not mean. . . .*

The gunman in the back of Michael's car is Martin Scorsese in his Hitchcockian cameo. The director's other trademark is a brief scene for his mother, who is the woman who comes to Teresa's aid when she has an epileptic fit.

George Memmoli, who played Joey, the owner of the pool hall, had been a member of The Ace Trucking Company comedy ensemble. He dropped out of comedy and acting for a career in home renovation and died in 1985 due to complications connected to his obesity; he weighed more than 500 pounds.

BEST (REPEATABLE) LINE: Charlie, attempting to convey some of his philosophy: "You don't make up for your sins in church. You do it in the streets. You do it at home. The rest is bullshit and you know it."

DIRTY HARRY
1971

TYPE OF FILM: Police

STUDIO: Warner Brothers

PRODUCER: Don Siegel

DIRECTOR: Don Siegel

SCREENWRITERS: Harry Julian Fink, Rita M. Fink, and Dean Riesner

SOURCE: Unpublished story by Harry Julian Fink and Rita Fink

RUNNING TIME: 102 minutes

PRINCIPAL PLAYERS:

Clint Eastwood . . . . .Harry Callahan
Harry Guardino . . . . .Lieutenant Bressler
Reni Santoni . . . . .Chico Gonzalez
Andy Robinson . . . . .Scorpio
John Larch . . . . .Chief
John Mitchum . . . . .DeGeorgio
John Vernon . . . . .Mayor
Mae Mercer . . . . .Mrs. Russell
Lyn Edgington . . . . .Norma
Ruth Kobart . . . . .bus driver
Woodrow Parfrey . . . . .Mr. Jaffe

DID YOU KNOW? The role that made him a Hollywood superstar nearly didn't go to Clint Eastwood. The story of *Dirty Harry* had been planned for Paul Newman at Universal Pictures, but when that didn't work out it was taken on by Frank Sinatra. Irving Kirschner was hired to direct the motion picture, then titled *Dead Right*. When Sinatra suffered a hand injury, the role of Harry Callahan was offered to John Wayne, who turned it down. Clint Eastwood's production company, Malpaso Productions, then acquired the rights to the screenplay, and the rest is history. Although Eastwood had enjoyed a huge career boost and many happy paydays making westerns in Italy for Sergio Leone, he did not move into the elite of Hollywood's players until *Dirty Harry*.

THE STORY: A psychopathic sniper in San Francisco attempts to hold the city hostage unless his demands are met. At first, he demands $100,000 or he will shoot one citizen a day. When he isn't paid, he escalates the demand to $200,000 to reveal the location of a teenaged girl he kidnapped and buried alive. Unable to capture him in traditional ways, the mayor and police chief call in the experienced but unpredictable Harry Callahan to pay off the killer, who calls himself Scorpio.

Callahan and his new partner, a young Mexican named Chico, go to deliver the ransom. Scorpio surprises Callahan from behind and beats him viciously until Chico comes out of hiding, only to be machine-gunned by the killer. Callahan manages to stab him in the leg with a pocketknife, but he escapes. Callahan tracks him to a football stadium, torturing a confession and the location of the buried girl out of him, but when she is found she is already dead.

When the killer is brought in, the District Attorney reprimands Callahan for violating Scorpio's civil rights, and he is released. Chico, recuperating from his wounds, quits the police force in disgust. Scorpio hires a thug to have himself beat up so that he can go to the media with the story that "Dirty Harry" was responsible.

Scorpio strikes again, kidnapping a school bus and demanding a ransom plus an airplane for an escape. Callahan, now officially off the case, nonetheless goes after the killer, who crashes the bus and, as Callahan continues to chase him, takes a young boy hostage, holding a gun to his head and warning Callahan to drop his gun. Instead, the cop shoots Scorpio, wounding him as the gun falls to the ground and the boy escapes. Callahan gives him the choice of surrendering or reaching for the gun. It is possible, he tells the desperate killer, that he has used all six of his bullets. Scorpio goes for the gun and Callahan shoots him, then disgustedly throws his badge away.

* * *

The killer and the events were drawn from real life, with Scorpio loosely modeled on the notorious Zodiac killer who terrorized San Francisco.

Before the role of Scorpio was given to Andy Robinson (the son of Edward G. Robinson), Audie Murphy had been considered. Murphy, a World War II hero, had gone to Hollywood after his heroics and made several western and war movies, but he died in an airplane crash in May of 1971 and the role went to Robinson.

Dirty Harry was a seminal motion picture with its depiction of screen violence being committed by a policeman who was not also corrupt. While tough vigilante cops who are as violent as the criminals they chase have become a staple of television and movies since the release of *Dirty Harry*, it was shocking at the time, especially coming as it did in the very liberal climate of the early 1970s.

Paving the way for the even greater violence of *Death Wish* and its sequels, and indeed for the subsequent Harry Callahan movies, *Dirty Harry* was a favorite target of the liberal media, which deplored its police brutality and accused it of other social insensitivities.

After the brunt of media attacks at its release, it is amusing to read the reviews of its four sequels, which wax nostalgic about how brilliant *Dirty Harry* is but how far Eastwood and all those associated with the ensuing films have fallen.

Magnum Force (1973) was the first sequel, doing even bigger box-office business than the original picture, and it was followed by *The Enforcer* (1976), *Sudden Impact* (1983), and *The Dead Pool* (1988), all of which were extremely successful commercially, in spite of increasingly hostile (almost stridently so) reviews.

The Dirty Harry movies have enriched the language, putting some pretty good tough guy lines into Callahan's mouth. Both Eastwood and his director thought the most memorable lines from any of the five films would be his response when asked who would handle a situation and he replied that it would be just the three of them. The apparently solitary cop elaborated: "Me. Smith. And Wesson."

Far more frequently quoted, of course, is the plea that he makes as a punk starts to reach for a gun. "Go ahead," he says. "Make my day."

Beginning another tradition, which makes it patently clear that police departments take psychological profiles of cops to be certain that they can pair the most mismatched members of the force, the grizzled old reactionary, Harry Callahan, has a different partner in every film, including a young Mexican, a young woman, a black man, and an Asian-American.

BEST LINE: Although off duty, Harry Callahan notices a bank robbery in progress and is compelled to stop it, shooting the three robbers, killing two. The third is wounded and lying on the ground, his shotgun nearby. Callahan sees him considering whether he ought to make a grab for it and says, "I know what you're thinking. Did he fire six shots or only five? Well, to tell you the truth, in all the excitement, I kinda lost track myself. But being this is a .44 magnum, the most powerful handgun in the world, and would blow your head clear off, you've got to ask yourself one question . . . do I feel lucky today?"

LITTLE CAESAR
1930

TYPE OF FILM:	Gangster
STUDIO:	First National/Warner Brothers
PRODUCER:	Hal B. Wallis
DIRECTOR:	Mervyn LeRoy
SCREENWRITERS:	Francis Faragoh and Robert E. Lee (continuity)
SOURCE:	*Little Caesar,* novel by W. R. Burnett
RUNNING TIME:	80 minutes

PRINCIPAL PLAYERS:

Edward G. Robinson . . . . .Enrico Cesare Bandello
Douglas Fairbanks, Jr. .Joe Massara
Glenda Farrell . . . . .Olga Strassoff
Stanley Fields . . . . .Sam Vittori
Sidney Blackmer . . . . .Big Boy
William Collier, Jr. . . . . .Tony Passa
Ralph Ince . . . . .Diamond Pete Montana
George E. Stone . . . . .Otero
Thomas Jackson . . . . .Sergeant Flaherty
Maurice Black . . . . .Little Arnie Lorch

DID YOU KNOW? Clark Gable was supposed to·be in this movie. Rumor and revisionist memory are at odds, but it seems that director Mervyn LeRoy spotted Gable in the Los Angeles production of a stage play, *The Last Mile*, and decided he would make a perfect Joe Massara, going so far as to sign Gable to a $500 contract. But when Darryl F. Zanuck, head of production for the film, saw him he immediately got rid of him, outraged that LeRoy had considered such a homely actor for the part. His ears, he claimed, looked like wind socks. In Jack Warner's biography, he claimed that he had wanted Gable to play the part of Rico.

THE STORY: Enrico Cesare Bandello, known as Rico, leaves his small town with his friend Joe Massara to make his fortune in Chicago. Joe wants only to be a dancer, but Rico, captivated by the notion of the fame and wealth of the mobster Diamond Pete Montana, wants to be a gangster and joins Sam Vittori's gang, one of the two most powerful in town. Joe gets a job dancing in a nightclub owned by Little Arnie Lorch, head of the other big Chicago gang. During the fabulous New Year's Eve celebration at Lorch's club that Joe sets up, Rico commits a robbery. Using the daring heist as a stepping stone, Rico takes over the mob from Vittori, and when Lorch tries to kill him and fails, Rico forces him out as well. Joe, at the urging of his girlfriend and dance partner, Olga, wants to get out of the mob and confronts Rico, who threatens to kill Olga if Joe leaves. Fearful for his own life and Olga's, Joe decides to turn state's evidence against Rico. Rico learns of the plan, and he sets out to kill Joe but can't pull the trigger on his old friend. When Rico is forced into hiding, Sergeant Flaherty tries to get him to show himself by telling the newspapers that the little gangster is a coward. Rico belligerently calls the police, the call is traced to his hideout, and the police come en masse and shoot him dead.

* * *

While there had been a few gangster movies before *Little Caesar,* this thinly disguised portrait of Al Capone is conceded to have been the impetus for a flood of similar gangster epics that flourished in the early 1930s. This uniquely American movie genre had a short life, however, because the end of Prohibition changed America, essentially breaking the power of the mobs, whose major income source had been bootleg alcohol.

Edward G. Robinson had been a bit-part player and wanted the role of Rico Bandello. He had the advantage of looking somewhat like Capone but was not regarded as a big enough star for what was to be a major production. He was offered the role of Otero but went to a meeting with producer Hal B. Wallis in full gangster regalia: dark suit and tie, spats, homburg hat, and a big stogie stuffed in his mouth. He got the part, and this gentle, bookish art collector was typecast as a tough gangster for most of his career.

Robinson's major problem with acting wasn't the snarl or the trend-making elocution. His problem was that he blinked every time he fired his gun, which wasn't what tough guys were supposed to do. Unable to stop the actor from shutting his eyes, after several takes director Mervyn LeRoy had Robinson's eyelids taped open for scenes in which he had to fire a gun.

BEST LINE: Bandello, in a hail of bullets, is shocked to be hit. Clutching himself, he asks, "Mother of God, is this the end of Rico?"

THE BIG HEAT
1953

TYPE OF FILM: Detective/*Noir*

STUDIO: Columbia

PRODUCER: Robert Arthur

DIRECTOR: Fritz Lang

SCREENWRITER: Sydney Kiernan

SOURCE: *The Big Heat*, novel by William P. McGivern

RUNNING TIME: 90 minutes

PRINCIPAL PLAYERS:

Glenn Ford . . . . .Sergeant Dave Bannion
Gloria Grahame . . . . .Debby Marsh
Jocelyn Brando . . . . .Katie Bannion
Alexander Scourby . . . . .Mike Lagana
Lee Marvin . . . . .Vince Stone
Jeanette Nolan . . . . .Bertha Duncan
Peter Whitney . . . . .Tierney

DID YOU KNOW? *The Big Heat* is the last of the classic *noir* films, using all the genre's conventions and going as far as a first-rate film could go with them. In showing the corruption of an entire city and the efforts of a single man to restore order, it was, oddly, the last film under the wire before Senator Joseph McCarthy convinced Americans (and the film industry) that it was more important to look for villains outside the borders of America than inside them.

THE STORY: After a police officer commits suicide, his wife removes his confession note and uses it to blackmail Mike Lagana, the enormously wealthy and powerful gangster who essentially controls the city. Homicide detective Sergeant David Bannion is assigned to investigate the suicide and learns that the dead cop had been taking payoffs from crooks and corrupt officials. As Bannion digs deeper, he is ordered off the case, but when the dead cop's girlfriend gives him evidence, he becomes more determined than ever to uncover the corruption.

When the girl's tortured body is discovered, Bannion confronts Lagana, who retaliates by planting a bomb that accidentally kills Bannion's wife in the tough cop's car. His superiors remove Bannion from the police force, but he takes his gun with him and goes on a single-handed mission to bring down the underworld boss, his organization, and the corrupt officials who allow it to flourish.

Bannion enlists the help of Debby Marsh, the girlfriend of Lagana's hit man, Vince Stone, who is scarred when Stone, who suspects (rightly) that Debby is overly fond of the cop, flings coffee in her face. She determines that killing the blackmailing widow will release the suicide note and destroy the syndicate, so she shoots her. She then confronts Stone and flings her own scalding coffee at him and gets shot. Bannion arrives too late to save her but arrests Stone, resisting the temptation to kill him on the spot. Debby dies in his arms, but the corruption is uprooted and Bannion returns to the police force.

* * *

The Big Heat can be compared with the classic American literary and film archetype, the western, with its lone hero moving into a crime-ridden town and cleaning it up. Questions of due process and the legality of various actions seem out of place in such a context, when the forces of evil seem overwhelming and immutable. To attempt to maintain the use of the system, when the system has been preempted by the bad guys, seems foolish and hopeless, as western marshals and Dave Bannion understood.

The *noir* style was perfectly suited to the German-born director Fritz Lang, who had garnered worldwide praise for his grotesque postexpressionist filming of *Dr. Mabuse, King of Crime* and *M*.

Although Gloria Grahame had been nominated twice for Oscars as Best Supporting Actress (*Crossfire*, 1947, and *The Bad and the Beautiful*, 1952), her portrayal of the party girl Debby Marsh is generally recognized as her finest performance.

BEST LINE: Debby Marsh, as she enters Bannion's seedy motel room: "Hey, I like this. Early nothing."

AND THEN THERE WERE NONE
1945

TYPE OF FILM: Detective

STUDIO: Twentieth Century-Fox

PRODUCER: Harry J. Popkin

DIRECTOR: René Clair

SCREENWRITER: Dudley Nichols

SOURCE: *Ten Little Niggers*, novel by Agatha Christie

RUNNING TIME: 98 minutes

PRINCIPAL PLAYERS:

Barry Fitzgerald .... Judge Quincannon
Walter Huston .... Dr. Armstrong
Louis Hayward .... Philip Lombard
Roland Young .... Blore
C. Aubrey Smith .... General Mandrake
June Duprez .... Vera Claythorne
Judith Anderson .... Emily Brent
Mischa Auer .... Prince Nikki Starloff
Richard Haydn .... Rogers
Queenie Leonard .... Mrs. Rogers
Harry Thurston .... Fisherman

DID YOU KNOW? There were almost as many different titles and endings for *And Then There Were None* as there were victims. Agatha Christie's most famous book was originally titled *Ten Little Niggers* (1939) in England and *And Then There Were None* in the U.S. There were also alternate titles for the 1943 play version, called *Ten Little Niggers* in England but the title was changed to *Ten Little Indians* for the U.S. stage version. The working title for the film version was *Ten Little Indians*, but Christie retained control of that title for dramatic purposes, and so it was changed to *And Then There Were None*.

There were also several different endings. In the book, all ten characters are guilty of the crimes of which they have been accused, and at the end, Vera shoots Philip, after which she hangs herself and the judge commits suicide.

In the play, Vera and Philip are innocent, but Vera, convinced that Philip is guilty and that he plans to murder her, shoots at him but misses. Philip then kills the judge, who is trying to hang Vera.

In the original version of the screenplay, Vera and Philip are guilty of murder but survive, a situation that would not be tolerated by Hollywood censors, who also would not allow the judge to kill himself in order to evade prosecution. He was allowed to commit suicide only when it was clear that he did so to incriminate Vera.

THE STORY: Eight strangers arrive by boat on remote Indian Island, the guests of Mr. Owen, whom none of them has met. They are greeted by the butler and cook, Mr. and Mrs. Rogers, who admit that they, too, have not met their employer. At dinner, the guests notice a centerpiece of ten little Indians, causing them to recite the nursery rhyme in which all the little Indian boys die. After dinner, Rogers, the butler, plays a phonograph record, as he was instructed to do. A voice on the record recites the crimes of the guests, all of whom are accused of having caused the death of others while escaping punishment themselves. When the guests realize that Mr. U.N. Owen is really "unknown," they decide to leave the island but are informed that the next boat won't arrive for three days.

Soon after, Prince Starloff, having casually admitted to running down and killing two people while drunk, suddenly keels over—a victim of poison; meanwhile, one of the centerpiece Indians has been broken.

In the morning, Mrs. Rogers fails to awaken because of an overdose of sedatives. She and her husband have allegedly been responsible for "helping to end the suffering" of their former employer. Soon after Mrs. Rogers' death, the others find that a second Indian has been broken from the centerpiece.

The eight remaining people determine that the island is deserted and one of them must be responsible for the deaths. When they arrive back at the house for dinner, General Mandrake, who has been accused of causing the death of his wife's lover, is missing and later found stabbed in the back. As has happened before and will continue to happen, another Indian is smashed.

That evening, the drunken Rogers locks himself in the woodshed overnight and is found dead the next morning—killed with an axe. Miss Brent, who had sent her nephew to reform school, where he hanged himself, becomes the object of suspicion, but she is found murdered by a hypodermic needle.

Later on, after being drawn away from the dinner table, the group returns to find Judge Quincannon, who had allegedly sent an innocent man to the gallows to discredit the defense attorney, with a bullet hole in the head.

The next morning, Blore, a detective whose testimony sent an innocent man to prison, where he was killed, is searching for the missing Dr. Armstrong and spots something with binoculars. At that moment, a load of bricks falls onto him, crushing him to death. Vera and Lombard find Blore's crushed body, and later the doctor, who had admitted to operating while drunk and killing his patient, is found dead on the beach.

Only Vera—who had confessed to a crime committed by her sister—and the man called Philip Lombard remain alive. It turns out that Lombard is actually Charles Morley, who came in place of his friend Lombard, who had committed suicide when threatened by Mr. Owen. Neither believes the other to be guilty. Then, Lombard/Morley orders Vera to shoot at him, and he collapses as if hurt. When Vera returns to the house, Judge Quincannon is waiting for her to admit that he was the killer, seeking justice that had been denied earlier and explaining how he faked his death. Quincannon has prepared a hangman's noose for Vera, telling her that she will be found guilty and publicly hanged anyway, so she might as well hang herself privately. He swallows poison and dies, just as Morley enters the room. The fishing boat arrives and the two survivors happily board together.

* * *

While the novel is memorably suspenseful, the motion picture is much lighter, with many moments of comedy—notably from Rogers the butler—interspersed to lessen tension. The greatest suspense lies in waiting to see who will be murdered next and in what fashion.

An original plan for casting was to have as many members as possible from the Broadway stage production recreate their roles for the film. ZaSu Pitts had been signed, but the delay in making the film removed her from the cast. John Ireland, too, had been cast at one time.

There were three other film versions of Christie's novel and play. Curiously, all four pictures have different settings. After the remote island in the first and best version, future locales were: a lodge in the Swiss Alps with the guests arriving by cable car, a hotel in the middle of the desert in Iran with a helicopter delivering the guests, and finally (one hopes, since the quality of each succeeding film has deteriorated chillingly) an African safari camp. All three remakes were titled *Ten Little Indians*. The 1966 version starred Hugh O'Brian and Shirley Eaton, the 1975 remake (described by *The New York Times* as a "Global Disaster in Iran") had an international cast that starred Oliver Reed and Elke Sommer, and the 1989 regurgitation starred (if that is the correct word) Donald Pleasence, Frank Stallone, and Sarah Maur Thorp.

BEST LINE: Three people have been killed within twenty-four hours, and Rogers, preparing the evening's dinner, snidely inquires, "How many will you be for dinner tonight?"

DETECTIVE STORY
1951

TYPE OF FILM: Police
STUDIO: Paramount
PRODUCER: William Wyler
DIRECTOR: William Wyler
SCREENWRITERS: Philip Yordan and Robert Wyler
SOURCE: *Detective Story*, play by Sidney Kingsley
RUNNING TIME: 103 minutes

PRINCIPAL PLAYERS:

Kirk Douglas . . . . .Detective Jim McLeod
Eleanor Parker . . . . .Mary McLeod
Horace McMahon . . . . .Lieutenant Monaghan
William Bendix . . . . .Detective Lou Brady
Cathy O'Donnell . . . . .Susan Carmichael
George Macready . . . . .Dr. Karl Schneider
Gladys George . . . . .Miss Hatch
Joseph Wiseman . . . . .Charles Gennini, the burglar
Lee Grant . . . . .shoplifter
Gerald Mohr . . . . .Tami Giacoppetti

DID YOU KNOW? By 1951, the great detective fiction writer Dashiell Hammett had just about lost his touch. Years of alcoholism and frail health were exacerbated by the House Un-American Activities Committee, which investigated his political activities. Although he wasn't broke, his early books providing him with serious Hollywood money and royalties (his five novels have never been out of print since their original publications), he was offered work in the movie industry on a regular basis, partly for his talent and partly out of sympathy for his difficulties. Producer/director William Wyler offered Hammett $10,000 to do a simple adaptation of Sidney Kingsley's play, *Detective Story*, which he accepted. Wyler flew him to California from Martha's Vineyard in Massachusetts, got him a suite of rooms at the lush Beverly Wilshire Hotel, and dropped by every few days to see how things were going. He and Hammett had friendly visits, but

Hammett was evasive when conversation turned to specifics about the script. Finally, after three weeks, Hammett handed Wyler a check for the full amount he had been paid. "I just can't do it anymore," he said.

THE STORY: This is the story of a single day in the life of New York's Twenty-first Precinct and the policemen who come to work every day, particularly Detective Jim McLeod. McLeod is rigid and moralistic, becoming more vicious because of the pressures of the job and the heavy influence of his father, a criminal. "A one-man army against crime" is how he is described by his boss, Lt. Monaghan. He treats suspects roughly, especially an abortionist, Dr. Karl Schneider, whom he brutally beats during an arrest and interrogation.

Schneider's lawyer reveals that Mary, McLeod's wife, had had a brief affair during the war, got pregnant, and went to Schneider, claiming a miscarriage but obviously for an abortion. McLeod's inflexible moral code turns him against her, calling her a tramp and effectively dooming their marriage. Although they both work at keeping it together, it is clear to her that he has made the same intolerant judgment of her that he does of the criminals who have become his whole life. McLeod, more and more despondent and aware that he is incapable of change, deliberately steps into the line of fire when a criminal tries to escape from the precinct house, and he is killed.

* * *

Detective Story was a hugely successful Broadway play that opened in March of 1949 and ran for nearly two years. Among its all-star cast were Ralph Bellamy (as McLeod), Lee Grant, Joseph Wiseman, Horace McMahon, Alexander Scourby, Maureen Stapleton, and Robert Strauss, some of whom went on to reprise their roles for the screen.

The motion picture, too, was both successful and influential. For the first time, the members of a police department were portrayed as fully fleshed-out characters, with lives outside of the precinct: families, fears, weaknesses, problems, and a range of personalities. Later cop pictures would reflect this new, penetrating look at the way the job affected, even tortured, members of the police force, and the influence extended to other media, like the Eighty-seventh Precinct novels of Ed McBain and such television programs as *Hill Street Blues* and *NYPD Blue*.

Academy Award nominations went to William Wyler for Best Director, Eleanor Parker for Best Actress, Lee Grant for Best Supporting Actress, and Philip Yordan and Robert Wyler for Best Screenplay. Grant recreated her role from the stage production in this, her first film, after which she was blacklisted.

BEST LINE: Jim McLeod, becoming more despondent as the job wears him down: "If I went home to an empty flat, I wouldn't dare take my gun with me."

L.A. CONFIDENTIAL
1997

TYPE OF FILM:	Police/Crime
STUDIO:	Warner Brothers
EXECUTIVE PRODUCERS:	David L. Wolper and Dan Kolsrud
PRODUCERS:	Arnon Milchan, Curtis Hanson, and Michael Nathanson
DIRECTOR:	Curtis Hanson
SCREENWRITERS:	Brian Helgeland and Curtis Hanson
SOURCE:	*L.A. Confidential*, novel by James Ellroy
RUNNING TIME:	136 minutes

PRINCIPAL PLAYERS:

Kevin Spacey . . . . Jack Vincennes
Russell Crowe . . . . Bud White
Guy Pearce . . . . Ed Exley
James Cromwell . . . . Dudley Smith
David Strathairn . . . . Pierce Patchett
Kim Basinger . . . . Lynn Bracken
Danny De Vito . . . . Sid Hudgens
Ron Rifkin . . . . D.A. Ellis Loew
Brett Chase . . . . Matt McCoy
Paul Guilfoyle . . . . Mickey Cohen
Paolo Seganyi . . . . Johnny Stompanato
Amber Smith . . . . Susan Lefferts

DID YOU KNOW? James Ellroy, the author of the novel *L.A. Confidential*, on which the motion picture was based, believed his book was unfilmable. So did almost everyone who had ever read it. The cast of characters was too large, the complexity of their various relationships seemed impossible to simplify, the plot was so complex and had so many interconnected subplots that there seemed no way to eliminate any of it without unraveling the whole. There were nearly a hundred characters and eight fully realized plots, all intertwined. Ellroy wrote that his novel was *uncompressable, uncontainable, and unequivocally bereft of sympathetic characters. It was unsavory, unapologetically dark, untamable, and altogether untranslatable to the screen.* No one disagreed with him until Curtis Hanson and Brian Helgeland wrote an adaptation that impressed first Ellroy, then Warner Brothers, and ultimately members of the Academy of Motion Picture Arts and Sciences, who voted them an Oscar for their screenplay.

THE STORY: Bud White, a white knight for women who need to be protected, stops to help a woman who is being beaten on Christmas Eve. After the rescue, he goes to a liquor store to pick up a case of booze for the precinct Christmas party and meets Lynn Bracken, a Veronica Lake look-alike. At the station house, some Mexicans have been arrested for beating up some cops and the entire squad brawls with them. Ed Exley, the ambitious by-the-book son of a former police hero, recently has been put in charge as watch commander and testifies that White and his partner were the major culprits in the brawl, but Dudley Smith, captain of the precinct, saves White's job while throwing his partner to the wolves.

Exley, now promoted to lieutenant, answers a homicide call and goes to the Nite Owl Coffee Shop, where he finds a bloody massacre. Two of the victims are White's former partner and a Rita Hayworth look-alike named Sue Lefferts. Three young Negroes driving a maroon Mercury are suspects. While White is interviewing Pierce Patchett, a high-class pimp, and Bracken, who works for Patchett (as did Lefferts), Exley and Jack Vincennes, a cop working as advisor to the TV show *Badge of Honor,* capture the youths, who appear to be innocent of the crime (though guilty of many others). They briefly escape, only to be caught and shot to death by several cops, including the shotgun-toting Exley.

White, unconvinced that the Nite Owl killings have been solved correctly, keeps digging and becomes obsessed with Bracken, who has fallen in love with him.

The body count mounts as the corrupt Smith attempts to kill everyone who knows that he has been trying to take over the organized crime syndicate left by gangster Mickey Cohen when Cohen was jailed. Patchett is killed, and so is Vincennes and Sid Hudgens, the sleazy columnist and informant for *Hush-Hush* magazine, who knew of Smith's plan. In a final shootout, Smith and his cronies are killed by White and Exley—the last two men standing.

The motion-picture version of *L.A. Confidential*, as is usual with adaptations, differs in many elements from the novel, but certainly the spirit of the book was upheld. Ellroy mixed a great many actual historical figures into his fictional tour de force, such as Mickey Cohen, Lana Turner, and Johnny Stompanato, as well as such actual events as the famous "Bloody Christmas" massacre, the corruption surrounding the building of the freeway system, and even the plans for a disguised Disneyland many miles away. Some of this got into the movie and some didn't.

As totally American as the film is, note James Cromwell's Irish accent, and though you probably won't catch their native accents, both Russell Crowe (Bud White) and Guy Pearce (Ed Exley) are Australian.

As extraordinary as the picture is, there are a few minor slipups that can be observed if you pay *very* close attention.

In the scene in which Susan Lefferts's corpse lies naked on a gurney, she has goose bumps. Dead people don't feel the cold.

When Bud White leaves Lynn Bracken's house, his car leaves dust clouds although it is the middle of a rainstorm. The rainstorm continues while he has a fight with Ed Exley, but when they go to District Attorney Ellis Loew and hang him out the window, it is a perfectly clear day and there is no evidence of rain having fallen.

And when a kidnapped girl is rescued, she is taken from the house amid a gathering of police. A blue mailbox can be seen on the corner. In the 1950s, U.S. Post Office mailboxes were olive-drab.

Kim Basinger won an Academy Award for Best Actress, as did Brian Helgeland and Curtis Hanson for Best Adapted Screenplay. Nominations went to *L.A. Confidential* for Best Picture, Curtis Hanson for Best Director, and for several other categories in the year in which *Titanic* swept almost everything in sight.

BEST LINE: Ed Exley, who throughout most of the picture has been an irritant to everybody except the top brass, has gotten in the way of Bud White, saying the wrong thing at the wrong time, and White attacks him. Dudley Smith tells Exley, "Best to stay away from a man when his blood is up." "His blood is always up," Exley responds. Smith answers, "Perhaps you should stay away from him altogether."

THE DAY OF THE JACKAL
1973

TYPE OF FILM:	Suspense/Espionage
STUDIO:	Universal
PRODUCER:	John Woolf
DIRECTOR:	Fred Zinnemann
SCREENWRITER:	Kenneth Ross
SOURCE:	*The Day of the Jackal,* novel by Frederick Forsyth
RUNNING TIME:	141 minutes

PRINCIPAL PLAYERS:

Edward Fox . . . .The Jackal/Paul Oliver Duggan/Per Lundquist
Alan Badel . . . . .The Minister
Tony Britton . . . . .Inspector Thomas
Denis Carey . . . . .Casson
Cyril Cusack . . . . .The Gunsmith
Terence Alexander . . . . .Lloyd
Michael Auclair . . . . Colonel Rolland
Adrien Cayla-Legrand . . . . .The President
Maurice Denham .General Colbert
Vernon Dobtcheff .The Interrogator
Jacques Francois . . . . .Pascal
Olga Georges-Picot . . . . .Denise
Derek Jacobi . . . . .Caron
Michel Lonsdale . . . . .Lebel
Eric Porter . . . . .Colonel Rodin

DID YOU KNOW? To this day, there is speculation about how much of *The Day of the Jackal* is true and how much is fiction. There is an OAS (Organisation de l'Armée Secrète), and most of the characters in the book (and the film) were real, although most of the names were changed and even their physical descriptions altered to protect against libel suits. Forsyth has refused to confirm or deny that this plot to assassinate de Gaulle ever actually took place or that there was a leak in the top ranks of the Secret Service, though it is true that there were several attempts on de Gaulle's life in 1963, the year in which this thriller is set. Forsyth has admitted that the Jackal was real and that he met him, though he lacked the suave sophistication and intelligence of the fictional character.

THE STORY: Many Frenchmen, especially former soldiers, are outraged with Charles de Gaulle for having given independence to Algeria and they vow to kill him, forming an organization called the OAS. After several assassination attempts fail, the group decides that it needs a professional to carry out the job and hires an Englishman with the code name Jackal.

After the Jackal receives $250,000, the first half of his fee, he begins to make meticulous preparations for his assassination attempt, acquiring expertly forged papers and buying a rifle made to his own design.

While he is attending to the details of his job, a member of the OAS is captured and provides information to the authorities, and a secret but massive manhunt is begun. Led by the man described as the best detective in France, top members of the Surete and Scotland Yard go to work and learn the Jackal's identity, his description, and even the kind of car he drives. However, because a female member of the OAS has insinuated herself into the life of one of the ministers and pries information out of him, the Jackal is kept apprised of each step of the investigation.

The Jackal takes up with a beautiful and wealthy woman but kills her when she tells him the police have asked about him. He changes his disguise and his documents, assuming now the identity of a Danish schoolteacher.

As de Gaulle prepares to make a speech on August 25, Liberation Day, the Jackal makes his way into a house from which he will have a clear shot. Only the last-minute intervention by the detective, who shoots the Jackal, saves de Gaulle.

* * *

Frederick Forsyth claims to have written the entire novel in thirty-five days. It was rejected by several publishers before Hutchinson bought it, spurred on by the fact that the manuscript had been read and approved by Andre Malraux, de Gaulle's Minister of Culture.

It is difficult to imagine that a book or film in which the end is known could be a successful suspense story, but that is exactly what Frederick Forsyth, the author of the novel on which the film is based, and Fred Zinnemann, the director who translated the novel onto the screen, achieved. Everyone who remembers French history knows that General Charles de Gaulle did not die as a result of an assassin's bullet, yet the maintenance of suspense throughout the cat-and-mouse game played by the security forces on one hand and the cold-blooded contract killer on the other is remarkable.

In 1997, *The Jackal* was released. It was "officially" based on *The Day of the Jackal* but bore only the slightest superficial resemblance to the original. It starred Bruce Willis, Richard Gere, Sidney Poitier, and Diane Venora. While no match for the original, it was stylishly and expensively filmed and is worth seeing.

BEST LINE: The three heads of the OAS are contracting the Jackal to assassinate Charles de Gaulle. He says his fee will be a half-million dollars. "Are you mad?" one of them asks. "Considering you expect to get France in return," he replies, "I'd have thought it a reasonable price."

TO HAVE AND HAVE NOT
1944

TYPE OF FILM:	Crime/Espionage
STUDIO:	Warner Brothers—First National
EXECUTIVE PRODUCER:	Jack L. Warner
PRODUCER:	Howard Hawks
DIRECTOR:	Howard Hawks
SCREENWRITERS:	Jules Furthman and William Faulkner
SOURCE:	*To Have and Have Not*, novel by Ernest Hemingway
RUNNING TIME:	100 minutes

PRINCIPAL PLAYERS:

Humphrey Bogart . . . . .Harry Morgan
Walter Brennan . . . . .Eddie
Lauren Bacall . . . . .Marie "Slim" Browning
Hoagy Carmichael . . . . .Cricket
Dan Seymour . . . . .Captain Renard
Marcel Dalio . . . . .Gerard
Dolores Moran .Helene de Brusac
Sheldon Leonard .Lieutenant Coyo
Walter Molnar . . . . .Paul de Brusac
Walter Sande . . . . .Johnson
Aldo Nadi . . . . .Renard's bodyguard
Paul Marion . . . . .Beauclerc
Patricia Shay . . . . .Mrs. Beauclerc

DID YOU KNOW? Lauren Bacall made her screen debut in this film version of Ernest Hemingway's novel. She had been working as a successful model and was spotted on the cover of *Vogue* magazine by director Howard Hawks's wife, Nancy Raye Gross, a model whose nickname was "Slim." Bacall, whose real name was Betty Bacal (first changed to Lauren and with an "L" added to the last by Hawks, who signed her to a personal services contract), was nicknamed "Slim" in *To Have and Have Not*. Within three weeks of meeting, she and Humphrey Bogart fell in love, somewhat complicated by the fact that he was married at the time. Bacall was only nineteen when they met and uncomfortable with the notion of getting involved with a married man, so Bogart got a divorce and they were married within the year. They went on to star together in *The Big Sleep* (1946), *Dark Passage* (1947), and *Key Largo* (1948).

THE STORY: Harry Morgan is a professional fisherman who rents out his boat on Martinique, a French island in the Caribbean, in the days following the fall of France. He returns to his hotel after a disastrous trip with an American client who tries to cheat him out of his fee. Later, when he tries to collect, a stray shot in a Vichy raid on the hotel kills the client, all of whose funds are impounded.

Morgan, broke and hoping to help Marie—the singer at the hotel with whom he has begun a flirtation—buy a plane ticket back to America, agrees to use his boat for a risky mission. He will smuggle a leader of the French underground and his wife, Paul and Helene de Brusac, onto an island.

With Eddie, an old rummy he takes care of, aboard, Morgan picks up the French couple and encounters a Vichy patrol boat; Brusac gets wounded. When he brings his passengers to the hotel, Morgan finds that Marie has not used her ticket but remained at the hotel, waiting for Morgan to return. Guessing that the Vichy police will suspect him of the run that brought the resistance leader to the island, Morgan and Marie get ready to flee, when he learns that Eddie has been arrested. The police are confident that withholding liquor from him will force him to talk. Morgan suddenly turns violent when the police inform him of their plan, and he shoots one, beating two others until they call for Eddie's release. Handing the surviving policemen over to the de Gaullists, Harry and Marie board his ship to leave the island.

* * *

Although the story of *To Have and Have Not* was not an especially original one (more than one viewer has noticed its structural similarity to *Casablanca*), it became an enormous box-office hit, largely because of the extraordinary charisma of the two stars and the heat they generated whenever they were together on screen (to say nothing of the heat they generated when they were off screen).

In one of the more interesting little rumors that has entered cinematic mythology, it has been widely reported that the singing voice of Marie was not Lauren Bacall's but that it was dubbed by Andy Williams, the popular singer of the 1960s and '70s. The fourteen-year-old singer had indeed been used several times to dub actress's voices and was hired to do the same for this film. In her autobiography, Bacall maintained that she did her own singing. Williams had always maintained that his voice was used. In fact, Williams originally sang "How Little We Know," and Hawks heard Bacall singing along. He was so impressed with Bacall's singing that he reshot the scene, using her own singing voice throughout. She also sang her own song in *The Big Sleep* the following year.

To Have and Have Not was remade in 1950 as *The Breaking Point*, a first-rate film starring John Garfield and Patricia Neal. It was remade again in 1958 and shouldn't have been.

The memorable, if understated, sexiness of Bacall was in part the result of her posture and carriage. Her head was always down, so when she looked at Bogart, even if she was standing and he was seated, her eyes were looking upward at him in a coy manner. This was not her natural bearing. As a very young woman taking on a starring role in her first film, she was so nervous that she couldn't stop her head from shaking. In time, she learned that the only way she could stop it was to put her chin on her chest, which obviously kept her head down and eyes up.

BEST LINE: (Could it be anything else?) Marie "Slim" Browning is making an overtly flirtatious overture to Harry Morgan. "You know you don't have to act with me, Steve," she tells him. "You don't have to say anything and you don't have to do anything. Not a thing. Oh, maybe a whistle. You know how to whistle, don't you, Steve? You just put your lips together and blow."

BLADE RUNNER
1982

TYPE OF FILM: Detective

STUDIO: Warner Brothers

EXECUTIVE PRODUCERS: Brian Kelly, Hampton Francher

PRODUCER: Michael Delley, Ridley Scott

DIRECTOR: Ridley Scott

SCREENWRITERS: Hampton Francher and David Peoples

SOURCE: *Do Androids Dream of Electric Sheep?*, novel by Philip K. Dick

RUNNING TIME: 118 minutes

PRINCIPAL PLAYERS:

Harrison Ford ....Rick Deckard
Rutger Hauer ....Roy Batty
Sean Young ....Rachael
Edward James Olmos ....Gaff
M. Emmet Walsh ....Captain Bryant
Daryl Hannah ....Pris
William Sanderson ....J. F. Sebastian
Brion James ....Leon
Joe Turkel ....Dr. Eldon Tyrell
Joanna Cassidy ....Zhora

DID YOU KNOW? Although now regarded as a modern classic, both as a work of science fiction and as an old-fashioned noir private-eye film, complete with voice-over narration, *Blade Runner* was not an immediate success, costing $27,000,000 to make and earning only $14,000,000 on its initial release.

Critics, too, were tough on it, so much so that it was reedited more than once. In the original released version, Deckard and Rachael are reunited in his apartment, where he wonders how much time they will have together. The downbeat ending was changed for the second version, in which they head away from the filth of Los Angeles and drive into the country, where it seems they will have a better chance for happiness and a longer one, adding the notion that she did not have the usual four-year life span of other Replicants.

There was no voice-over in the first version. It was added to clarify some of the action in the rereleased second version, and it was eliminated from the director's cut (made in 1991 to celebrate the tenth anniversary of the film).

Finally, the director's cut placed greater emphasis on the romance between Deckard and Rachael and makes it more likely that Deckard, too, is a Replicant, which would be virtually impossible to comprehend from either of the first two versions, even with repeated viewing.

THE STORY: The Los Angeles of 2019 is a city of unrelenting rain and smog, with giant skyscrapers built on the ruins of what had once been there, populated by those who couldn't afford to move off-planet to a better, brighter place.

Rick Deckard, a former cop, former Blade Runner (a member of a police department unit with a license to kill), and former killer, is pressed into service against his will when some Replicants (highly intelligent robots that look exactly like humans), outlawed from Earth ever since a colony staged an uprising against its human slavemasters, have sneaked back to the planet. It is his assignment to find them and kill them.

The Replicants have come back to Earth to find their creator, Dr. Eldon Tyrell, in order to have him change the self-destruct mechanism that is activated after a four-year life. Deckard visits Tyrell and falls in love with Rachael, his "daughter," a special Replicant so advanced that no one has guessed that she is not human—not even herself, though she has begun to suspect it.

Deckard kills one of the Replicants, a woman, by shooting her in the back as she flees, and Leon, another of the superpowerful androids, nearly kills him, saying "Time to die." Rachael shoots Leon, saving Deckard's life.

The two surviving escaped Replicants—Roy Batty, the top-of-the-line leader with handsome features and exceptional physical abilities, and Pris, created as a prostitute—have managed to locate Dr. Tyrell. Batty kills him, crushing his skull, when he learns that termination dates cannot be altered and that he and Pris have only a very short time to live.

Deckard catches up with the rebels at the once-beautiful Bradbury Building and, after a fight with the powerful Pris, shoots her. When Batty finds her, he tenderly kisses her dead mouth while Deckard attempts to ambush him, but with extraordinarily fast reflexes, Batty eludes the gunfire.

They engage in a long and violent cat-and-mouse game until Deckard is trapped, hanging from a ledge near the roof. Desperately holding on but ultimately unable to save himself, his grip loosens and he begins to plunge to his death, when Batty grabs him and saves his life.

Deckard, puzzled at first, surmises that, at the very end, Batty saved his life just before he himself ran out of time and died, because "maybe in those last moments he loved life more than he ever had before. Not just his life, anybody's life, my life."

Deckard returns to his apartment to find Rachael asleep. As a Replicant and therefore illegal on Earth, she is supposed to be killed, but he leaves Los Angeles with her. As a special Replicant, the pet project of Dr. Tyrell, it is possible that she was not made with a termination date. "I didn't know how long we had together," Deckard muses. "Who does?"

* * *

When Deckard is hired, he is told that six Replicants, three male and three female, escaped and made it to Earth. One male was "fried" at the "electronic gate" at the Tyrell Corporation building; we never see this one. Zhora, the snake dancer, is killed by Deckard (that's two). Leon is shot and killed by Rachael (number three). Pris and Batty (four and five) die in the final confrontation with Deckard. The sixth rebel is never seen or mentioned again. However, Rachael is also a Replicant, though she was not one of the criminal Replicants being hunted and, indeed, was not known to be a Replicant by the police or Deckard until he did some tests at the behest of Dr. Tyrell, who tried to fool Deckard into thinking she was human.

The inability to count was not only the goof in the making of *Blade Runner.* The sheet music that Rachael apparently reads while playing the piano is for a different piece of music. Batty's shoes are blue when he climbs through the window in the final scene, yet they are black when he is on the roof. Earlier in the same scene, Batty clenches his hand and a nail can be seen to have been driven through it—an event that does not occur until later.

The original choice to play Rick Deckard was (yes, this is true) Dustin Hoffman.

BEST LINE: Rick Deckard has just ordered lunch—some raw fish over noodles—at an outdoor bar, and reminisces to himself, "Sushi, that's what my ex-wife called me. Cold fish."

GOODFELLAS
1990

TYPE OF FILM: Crime

STUDIO: Warner Brothers

PRODUCER: Irwin Winkler

DIRECTOR: Martin Scorsese

SCREENWRITERS: Nicholas Pileggi and Martin Scorsese

SOURCE: *Wiseguy*, biography by Nicholas Pileggi

RUNNING TIME: 146 minutes

PRINCIPAL PLAYERS:

Robert De Niro . . . . .James Conway
Ray Liotta . . . . .Henry Hill
Joe Pesci . . . . .Tommy DeVito
Lorraine Bracco . . . . .Karen Hill
Paul Sorvino . . . . .Paul Cicero
Frank Sivero . . . . .Frankie
Tony Darrow . . . . .Sonny

DID YOU KNOW? Crime did pay for Henry Hill, the real-life character at the center of *GoodFellas*, and so did ratting on his friends. When it became evident that he was about to be either killed by his gangster cronies or arrested for his activities by the police, Hill turned state's evidence and testified against his gangland associates in court. He was put into the Federal Witness Protection Program, where he remained safe from those he fingered. After the U.S. Supreme Court overturned New York State's "Son of Sam" law prohibiting criminals from profiting from their crimes, Hill also received $200,000 for the book and motion picture made from his experiences. He has also received substantial sums for appearing on talk shows (in disguise, of course) and as a consultant for television gangster shows.

THE STORY: Henry Hill, impressed with the cars and clothes of the neighborhood gangsters, decides to join the life by doing odd jobs for mob boss Paul Cicero and teaming up with two other thugs, Jimmy Conway and Tommy DeVito.

When Conway and DeVito kill a "made" member of the mob, Henry helps them bury the body. The three friends become wealthy and gain power in the mob, but their greed and stupidity, as well as the psychotic violence of DeVito, combine to undo them.

Henry, against the strict orders of his patron, Cicero, begins to traffic in drugs. DeVito is discovered to have murdered the "made" mobster, an uncondonable breach of mob rules, and is himself killed. Conway, helping to engineer a huge airport robbery, decides to eliminate partners so that he'll have more money for himself.

Henry, meanwhile, spots the narcs closing in on him and decides his only way out is to go into the Federal Witness Protection Program, testifying against his friends and former associates in court and sending them away for long prison terms while he mourns the life he has had to give up.

* * *

GoodFellas was successful both in commercial and critical terms, with reviewers often comparing it with *Mean Streets*, another Scorsese crime film which it closely resembles. It gives a close and accurate look at gangster life as the principals shared a single vision: to get married and raise a family, have a mistress on the side, spend a lot of time with male friends hanging out in bars, and do whatever is necessary to get money.

In addition to Henry Hill, the other characters are all based on genuine people. Jimmy Conway was based on James "Jimmy the Gent" Burke, whose nickname came from a film tough guy played by James Cagney in the movie of that title.

Events depicted in *GoodFellas* also actually transpired, most famously the airport robbery that was based on the heist of a Lufthansa plane at Kennedy Airport in 1978.

The motion picture undoubtedly would have been named *Wiseguy*, as was the book, since it is a better-known bit of gangster terminology for a hoodlum, but a popular television series with that title was airing at that time.

Joe Pesci won an Academy Award for Best Supporting Actor for his role as Tommy DeVito. Nominations also went to the film for Best Picture and to Martin Scorsese for Best Director.

BEST LINE: Henry Hill, having turned state's evidence, is not exactly contrite. "See, the hardest thing for me was leaving the life," he admits while on the stand. "I still love the life. We were treated like movie stars with muscle. We had it all just for the asking . . . Today everything is different. There's no action. I have to wait around like everyone else . . . I'm an average nobody. I get to live the rest of my life like a schnook."

THE UNTOUCHABLES
1987

TYPE OF FILM:	Crime
STUDIO:	Paramount
PRODUCER:	Art Linson
DIRECTOR:	Brian De Palma
SCREENWRITER:	David Mamet
SOURCE:	*The Untouchables* television series, which was based on *The Untouchables*, a true crime book by Oscar Fraley
RUNNING TIME:	119 minutes

PRINCIPAL PLAYERS:

Kevin Costner . . . . .Eliot Ness
Sean Connery . . . . James Malone
Charles Martin Smith . . . . .Oscar Wallace
Andy Garcia . . . . .George Stone
Robert De Niro . . . . .Al Capone
Richard Bradford . . . . .Mike
Jack Kehoe . . . . .Walter Payne
Brad Sullivan . . . . .George
Billy Drago . . . . .Frank Nitti
Patricia Clarkson . . . . .Catherine Ness

DID YOU KNOW? Purportedly based on real-life events, *The Untouchables* is three steps removed from reality. First, Oscar Fraley wrote a book called *The Untouchables*. It was written in collaboration with Eliot Ness, who made every effort to glamorize and glorify the role played by himself and his team in bringing the gangsters of Chicago to their knees. This was picked up and adapted for a television series, starring Robert Stack, which enjoyed great popularity from 1959 to 1963. In order to sustain a weekly series for five years, new exploits, new villains, and new acts of derring-do had to be invented. By the time the film was written (by David Mamet, who no one has ever accused of being a journalist), it became virtually impossible to know how many, if any, of the depicted adventures had ever actually taken place.

THE STORY: Chicago in 1930 is owned by Al Capone, who controls the mob and the liquor business and has stayed in power by having the police, judges, and powerful city officials on his payroll. A special U.S. Treasury agent, Eliot Ness, is assigned to bring down Capone and his gangsters. On his first big raid, cases of what were expected to be illicit liquor turn out to contain nothing of value, as the gangsters obviously had been warned by corrupt cops.

Ness builds his own small unit of men he can trust, beginning with Jim Malone, an elderly cop who continues to walk a beat because he won't be corrupted. They go together to the police academy and recruit its best sharpshooter, an Italian from the South Side who has renamed himself George Stone. When Oscar Wallace, an apparently meek bookkeeper, appears, confident that he can nail Capone for income-tax evasion, he, too, is added to the group, which the newspapers begin to call The Untouchables.

The special agents raid a large warehouse full of booze, infuriating Capone, who says he wants Ness and his entire family killed. On the next big job, they join with the Royal Canadian Mounted Police to capture ten trucks full of liquor coming across the border and the money that was to pay for it. More importantly, they seize a set of coded ledgers that list those on Capone's payroll and show large earnings for the gangster. After a shootout in which virtually all of the gangsters are killed, the agents try to get one of Capone's bookkeepers to decode the ledger, without success, until Malone, the wise old Irish cop, goes outside the cabin in which they have been meeting. He lifts one of the already slain gangsters against the window and yells at him to talk, putting a gun in his mouth and threatening to shoot if he won't. At the count of three, he pulls the trigger, inducing the terrified bookkeeper to offer to tell everything he knows. The Mountie, unaware that the gangster was already dead, tells Ness that he doesn't approve of his methods. "Well," Ness responds, "you're not from Chicago."

In a bold move at the police station, Capone's henchman, Frank Nitti, kills the captured bookkeeper and Oscar, causing Ness to confront Capone. They exchange threats. Nitti then goes after Malone at his apartment and kills him in a hail of machine-gun fire, but not before the dying cop lets Ness know where Capone's personal bookkeeper is to be rushed out of town by train. Ness and Stone capture him and bring him to court, where he has agreed to testify. Capone is unconcerned and Ness deduces that the jury has been bribed, so he coerces the judge to switch juries. Nitti, in the courtroom with a gun, is chased to the roof by Ness, where Nitti taunts the FBI agent by telling him that Malone squealed like a stuck pig when he died. Ness throws him from the roof, and as Nitti screams on his plunge, Ness yells after him, "Did he sound anything like that?" Capone is sentenced to eleven years. Outside the courtroom, a reporter informs Ness that Prohibition may be repealed and asks what he'll do then. He says, "I think I'll have a drink."

* * *

Kevin Costner, as stone-faced as Harrison Ford, is perfectly cast as the straight-arrow, grown-up Boy Scout who wants to do good, and Robert De Niro is compelling as a flamboyant Al Capone, but it is Sean Connery who steals the movie. No one can quibble with the fact that he's an old Irish cop who happens to have a Scottish accent, but one wonders how a cop consigned to a beat for so many years can know so much about Al Capone's business, where his secret warehouses of liquor are, why he is so intimate with the top brass in the department, and other stretches of imagination. However, his performance as a straightforward man of courage and action was good enough to earn him a deserved Academy Award for Best Supporting Actor.

If the film has a negative, it is the excessive amount of blood that Brian De Palma felt necessary. A single gunshot to the forehead had an entire side of an elevator covered (not splattered—*covered*) with blood, all the way to the ceiling. The violence with which Capone smashes the skull of one of his henchmen with a baseball bat (obviously lifted directly from *Party Girl*, a 1958 gangster movie made by Nicholas Ray) is so bloody that the other gangsters turn away in disgust!

BEST LINE: Jim Malone is in his apartment when one of Capone's thugs breaks in and sneaks up on him with a knife in his hand. Malone turns around with a large gun and smiles. "Isn't that just like a wop," he says. "Brings a knife to a gunfight."

REAR WINDOW
1954

TYPE OF FILM: Suspense

STUDIO: Paramount

PRODUCER: Alfred Hitchcock

DIRECTOR: Alfred Hitchcock

SCREENWRITER: John Michael Hayes

SOURCE: "It Had to Be Murder," short story by William Irish, pseudonym of Cornell Woolrich

RUNNING TIME: 112 minutes

PRINCIPAL PLAYERS:

James Stewart . . . . .L. B. "Jeff" Jeffries
Grace Kelly . . . . .Lisa Carol Fremont
Wendell Corey . . . . .Thomas J. Doyle
Thelma Ritter . . . . .Stella
Raymond Burr . . . . .Lars Thorwald
Judith Evelyn . . . . .Miss Lonelyhearts
Irene Winston . . . . .Mrs. Thorwald
Ross Bagdasarian . . . . .Composer
Georgine Darcy . . . . .Miss Torso
Jesslyn Fax . . . . .Miss Sculptress

DID YOU KNOW? Although the set of *Rear Window* seems so close as to be almost claustrophobic, the one-room set is perhaps the largest ever built on the Paramount lot. The apartment in which the wheelchair-bound Jimmy Stewart is restricted was, in fact, his own Greenwich Village apartment, but the apartment building across the way, into which he spies with binoculars, is a set. It required the construction of an apartment building with thirty-one separate apartments, twelve of which were fully furnished. It was Hitchcock's belief that it would have been impossible to properly light those apartments if they were genuine locations.

THE STORY: Photographer L. B. "Jeff" Jeffries broke his leg on an assignment and has been confined to his apartment for six weeks, his only amusement being to look into the apartments (and the lives) of the people who live across the courtyard.

While watching Miss Torso, the gorgeous dancer with countless suitors, and Miss Lonelyhearts, a lonely woman who prepares dinner for two but dines alone, a newlywed couple, a sculptress, and others, he notices the behavior of Lars Thorwald and becomes convinced that he has murdered his nagging wife.

After Jeff sees Thorwald make several trips out of the apartment with a suitcase late on a rainy night, he no longer sees the wife, who previously was always present. Later, he spots Thorwald wrapping a butcher knife and a saw in newspapers and watches as he ties up a large trunk to be hauled away.

Unable to get out of his wheelchair, Jeff enlists the help of his girlfriend, the beautiful model Lisa Carol Fremont, who wants to marry Jeff. Jeff feels she is too beautiful, too refined—too perfect—for him and tries to break up with her. She persists and helps him by slipping a note under Thorwald's door, asking the apparent murderer what he has done with his wife. Jeff follows with a telephone call to lure him out of his apartment, and Lisa climbs a fire-escape ladder and slips into his window, only to have Thorwald return unexpectedly and catch her. Jeff calls the police, but Lisa has found the vital clue—the murdered wife's wedding ring.

When Thorwald spots her signaling with the ring across the courtyard, he sees Jeff and comes after him, attempting to push him out the window while neighbors watch. Just as the police arrive, Jeff falls, breaking his other leg, and Thorwald confesses.

* * *

Rear Window is one of Hitchcock's greatest successes and may define his work better than any other single film, with the possible exception of *North by Northwest*. Here is suspense, but also humor (especially in the dialogue of the no-nonsense nurse, Stella). Here, too, is the gorgeous ice-blond heroine, played by the incomparable Grace Kelly. The leading man—laconic and charming, played by James Stewart, a production crew and writer with whom he often worked and felt comfortable, along with a MacGuffin (the dead woman's wedding ring) all combine to make the quintessential Alfred Hitchcock motion picture.

Cornell Woolrich, who wrote the story on which the film was based, was somewhat bitter about having been paid such a small amount for the story. It was one of eight stories in a collection

202

sold by his Hollywood agent, H. N. Swanson, in the 1940s for $5,000; it was not optioned—meaning that more money would be paid if a movie was actually produced—but sold outright, so the author would never be owed any further payments. Woolrich joked (bitterly) that Swanson sold everything for $5,000, hence was known as "Five Grand Swannie." His fee, therefore, was a little more than $600, but what angered Woolrich even more than the minuscule payment was that Hitchcock did not invite him to the premiere showing of the movie in New York, where Woolrich lived.

Alfred Hitchcock received an Academy Award nomination for Best Director, losing to Elia Kazan for *On the Waterfront*. John Michael Hayes won an Edgar Allan Poe Award from the Mystery Writers of America for his screenplay.

Grace Kelly had just been offered the female lead in *On the Waterfront* when Hitchcock called to tell her that she was expected for wardrobe fittings. Since she had not seen a script or been offered a contract, she was taken aback, but having enjoyed working with Hitchcock in *Dial M for Murder*, she agreed to take the part. Eva Marie Saint went on to win an Oscar for Best Supporting Actress, while Kelly won the Best Actress award—not for *Rear Window,* but for *The Country Girl.*

Hitchcock Alert: When you see a man winding a clock, that is Hitchcock.

BEST LINE: Stella, Jeff's nurse, telling him what an idiot he is for not marrying Lisa: "When a man and a woman see each other and like each other, they oughtta come together—*wham!*—like a coupla taxis on Broadway . . . not sit around analyzing each other like two specimens in a bottle."

CRISS CROSS
1949

TYPE OF FILM: *Noir*
STUDIO: Universal
PRODUCER: Michael Kraike
DIRECTOR: Robert Siodmak
SCREENWRITER: Daniel Ruchs
SOURCE: *Criss Cross*, novel by Don Tracy
RUNNING TIME: 87 minutes

PRINCIPAL PLAYERS:

Burt Lancaster . . . . .Steve Thompson
Yvonne De Carlo . . . . .Anna Dundee
Dan Duryea . . . . .Slim Dundee
Stephen McNally . . . . .Lt. Pete Ramirez
Tom Redi . . . . .Vincent
Percy Helton . . . . .Frank
Alan Napier . . . . .Finchley

DID YOU KNOW? Mark Hellinger, the gifted journalist and short story writer, went to Hollywood to write screenplays and produce movies, quickly becoming master of the *noir* film. He produced *The Killers* and had begun to put together the talent to make *Criss Cross*, based very loosely on Don Tracy's novel of the same name. Unexpectedly, Hellinger had a heart attack and died at the age of forty-four, cutting short what was destined to be a great career.

THE STORY: Armored-car guard Steve Thompson, once married to Anna, is still in love with her, though she's left him for Slim Dundee, a gangster and owner of Slim's, the nightclub where Steve and Anna had so many happy evenings. The fire apparently reignites for Anna as well, until they are caught together at Dundee's beach house. To explain his presence there with Slim's wife, Steve tells him of an elaborate robbery plan that he's been working on and was hoping to learn if Dundee wanted to be in. As Dundee questions Steve more intensely about the details of the planned robbery, Steve finds himself locked into a scheme that he had never wanted in the first place. No one is telling the truth. Steve plans to take all the money and run away with Anna. Slim plans to kill Steve during the robbery. Anna just wants the money.

Steve's partner is killed during the robbery, and he is wounded while killing two of Dundee's cohorts. Steve wakes up in a hospital, a hero for having killed two gangsters who tried to rob his armored car, while Anna has absconded with the money. One of Dundee's men takes him to Anna's hiding place, only to have Slim walk in on them and kill them both.

* * *

One of the greatest of all *noir* films, *Criss Cross* utilized every convention and brought all the perfect talent together to make it memorable. The sense of hopelessness is emphasized by a long flashback with its moody voice-over. Audiences recognize that flashback is useful in this dark universe only because there is no future. The beautiful woman who betrays the man (who is totally captivated by her) is another staple of the *noir* film, and Yvonne De Carlo fits right in with Veronica Lake, Ava Gardner, and Lizabeth Scott when it comes to turning strong men into mush. Burt Lancaster, of course, made a career out of going against type. A big and muscular man (who had been a trapeze artist), tough to the core, lost all his spine when it came to bad women. He starred in such *noir* classics and near-classics as *The Killers* (1946), *Desert Fury* (1947), *Brute Force* (1947), *I Walk Alone* (1947), *Sorry, Wrong Number* (1948), *Kiss the Blood Off My Hands* (1948), and *All My Sons* (1948). Lancaster, much like the other tough guys of *film noir* who gave up everything for the wrong woman (only Robert Mitchum ranks with Lancaster in the sucker category), could have as his epitaph the sad and frustrated line he speaks to De Carlo at the end of *Criss Cross*: "I never wanted the money," he tells her. "I only wanted you."

Robert Siodmak, the director, made so many memorable films noir in the brief period from 1944 to 1949 (*Phantom Lady, Christmas Holiday, The Suspect, The Dark Mirror, The Spiral Staircase, The Killers, Cry of the City* and *The File on Thelma Jordon,* as well as *Criss Cross*) that, as the genre became less popular, he found it difficult to find work in other forms and returned to his native Germany, his career largely over.

Tony Curtis (billed as James Curtis) made his screen debut as Yvonne De Carlo's dance partner.

Criss Cross was remade in 1995 as *The Underneath*, starring Peter Gallagher, Alison Elliott and William Fichtner in a stylish but slow-moving update.

BEST LINE: Lt. Pete Ramirez, speaking to his doomed friend, Steve Thompson: "I should have been a better friend. I should have stopped you. I should have grabbed you by the neck. I should have kicked your teeth in. I'm sorry, Steve."

THE SILENCE OF THE LAMBS
1991

TYPE OF FILM:	Detective/Suspense
STUDIO:	Orion
EXECUTIVE PRODUCER:	Gary Goetzman
PRODUCERS:	Edward Saxon, Kenneth Utt, Ron Bozman
DIRECTOR:	Jonathan Demme
SCREENWRITER:	Ted Tally
SOURCE:	*The Silence of the Lambs*, novel by Thomas Harris
RUNNING TIME:	118 minutes

PRINCIPAL PLAYERS:

Jodie Foster . . . . .Clarice Starling
Anthony Hopkins .Dr. Hannibal Lecter
Scott Glenn . . . . .Jack Crawford
Ted Levine . . . . .James Gumb
Anthony Heald .Dr. Frederick Chiltern
Brooke Smith . . . . .Catherine Martin
Diane Baker . . . . .Senator Ruth Martin
Kasi Lemmons . . . . .Ardelia Mapp
Charles Napier . . . . .Lieutenant Boyle

DID YOU KNOW? Hannibal "The Cannibal" Lecter, one of the most chilling villains in the history of literature and cinema, is loosely based on a real person. Ed Gein, a multiple murderer and eater of his victims, also served as the prototype for Norman Bates in Robert Bloch's *Psycho* (later filmed by Alfred Hitchcock) as well as inspiring *Deranged,* the 1974 motion picture directed by Jeff Gillen and starring Alan Ormsby, Roberts Blossom, and Cosette Lee. Finally, Gein influenced the making of the cult favorite, *The Texas Chainsaw Massacre* (1974), which is less violent than its title and reputation suggest and was directed by Tobe Hooper and starred Gunnar Hansen, Ed Neal and Marilyn Burns.

THE STORY: Clarice Starling, still a student at the FBI Academy, is recruited by the head of the behavioral science unit, Jack

Crawford, to seek help from the imprisoned Hannibal "The Cannibal" Lecter in capturing another serial killer, who removes the skins from his raped and murdered victims. Nicknamed "Buffalo Bill" by the press (because he skins his humps), he has murdered at least five young women, and the pressure to capture him escalates when he kidnaps the daughter of a senator from Tennessee.

Dr. Lecter, a brilliant psychopath who ate parts of his victims (he describes one incident to Starling in which he ate a man's liver, "with fava beans and a nice Chianti"), agrees to help the young FBI trainee if she will help him get a cell with a view. Starling comes back with an offer: He will be transferred to another prison and be given a week each year at a guarded beach in exchange for a profile of the serial killer.

Lecter and Starling exchange information—she about her childhood, he about the killer, including an explanation of why a moth's cocoon was found stuffed down a victim's throat. But Dr. Frederick Chiltern, the ambitious head of the facility housing Lecter, reveals to Lecter that the offer was bogus and makes him his own offer, for which he received approval from the senator. Lecter provides the name and physical description of the killer in a face-to-face meeting with the senator.

Lecter quickly escapes from a new facility: After killing his two guards, he changes into the uniform of one, smears himself unrecognizable in blood, and is rushed into an ambulance, after which he kills the doctor and drivers.

Meanwhile, Crawford and a large team of agents has gone off on a wild-goose chase to the believed residence of "Bill." Starling, alone, conducts interviews regarding an earlier victim and goes to the house of her acquaintance, only to discover that "Bill" now lives there and has imprisoned the senator's daughter in the basement. After nearly being killed herself, Starling shoots and kills the deranged killer.

At the graduation celebration at the FBI Academy, Starling receives a telephone call from the still-free Lecter, who wishes her well. As he spots Dr. Chiltern, Lecter says he'd like to chat longer, he says, but he's "having an old friend for dinner."

* * *

The Silence of the Lambs was an enormous best-seller by Thomas Harris and is one of the best serial-killer books ever written. It was a sequel to the even more suspenseful *Red Dragon*, which introduced "Hannibal the Cannibal" in a small role and which was filmed as *Manhunter* in 1986, written and directed by Michael Mann. It starred William L. Petersen as a somewhat imbalanced retired FBI agent who was called back to help track the ruthless genius; Brian Cox wonderfully played Lecter.

Just as *Psycho* brought on a wave of imitations by lesser talents who created the slasher movie with graphic depictions of violence, *The Silence of the Lambs* spawned an overwhelming flood of serial-killer books and movies, some of which have been excellent but many of which attempted to be more violent or outlandishly grisly than anything that had preceded them.

Academy Awards were given for Best Picture, to Demme for Best Director, to Foster for Best Actress, to Hopkins for Best Actor, and to Tally for Best Adapted Screenplay. The Mystery Writers of America gave an Edgar Allan Poe Award to Tally for his screenplay.

BEST LINE: Clarice Starling has come to visit Hannibal Lecter in his new prison, and a guard asks her, "Is it true what they're saying? He's some kind of vampire?" Starling replies, "They don't have a name for what he is."

MURDER, MY SWEET
1944

TYPE OF FILM:	Detective
STUDIO:	RKO
EXECUTIVE PRODUCER:	Sid Rogell
PRODUCER:	Adrian Scott
DIRECTOR:	Edward Dmytryk
SCREENWRITER:	John Paxton
SOURCE:	*Farewell, My Lovely*, novel by Raymond Chandler
RUNNING TIME:	93 minutes

PRINCIPAL PLAYERS:

Dick Powell . . . . .Philip Marlowe
Claire Trevor . . . . .Mrs. Grayle
Anne Shirley . . . . .Ann Riordan
Otto Kruger . . . . .Jules Amthor
Mike Mazurki . . . . .Moose Malloy
Miles Mander . . . . .Mr. Grayle
Douglas Walton . . . . .Marriott
Don Douglas . . . . .Lieutenant Randall

DID YOU KNOW? Moose Malloy, played by Mike Mazurki, had one overwhelming characteristic (apart from his devotion to his girlfriend, Velma): his huge size. Although Mazurki was six foot four, he failed to convey that gigantic presence, because Dick Powell was six two. To assure that Mazurki would tower over everyone else, Powell had to walk in a trench when paired with him in a scene, and he took off his shoes to stand barefoot while Mazurki stood on a box. Director Edward Dmytryk even created a ceiling slanted at an angle to the camera so that, as Mazurki moved closer to other cast members, he would appear to grow enormously as he approached.

THE STORY: Moose Malloy hires Marlowe to find Velma, the girlfriend he hasn't seen in eight years because of a jail sentence. When asked to describe her, he helpfully says, "She was as cute as lace pants." Meanwhile, Marlowe is also hired to retrieve a stolen necklace, and when the detective and his client show up to make the transaction, Marlowe is knocked out and the client murdered. Ann Riordan discovers the body and tells Marlowe that the necklace was once owned by Mrs. Grayle, who claims that a psychic, Jules Amthor, uses his racket to blackmail people. Marlowe visits Amthor with Moose, who joins forces with the psychic to beat up and imprison the detective. Marlowe escapes to learn that Moose has killed Amthor, and is on a gambling ship run by gangsters. Mrs. Grayle—who was actually Velma—is killed, as is her husband and Moose.

* * *

Murder, My Sweet was one of the first *noir* detective films, in which decent, honorable people are few and far between. Marlowe is a cynical detective who nonetheless has an optimistic view of the world and believes it is his role to be a white knight, protecting and helping those unable to defend themselves. He is a loner, relentless in his pursuit of justice, and uninterested in playing by the rules.

Casting Dick Powell as Philip Marlowe was risky, because he had a well-established career as a young singer and dancer and the change to a grizzled tough guy stretched his acting ability to the limit. Yet he was so successful that those became the roles he had for the rest of his career.

The film was initially released as *Farewell, My Lovely*, the title of Chandler's novel, but audiences were small. It turned out that the few who came to the cinema were expecting to see another Powell musical. The film was immediately withdrawn and retitled, becoming a box-office smash.

The director, Edward Dmytryk, had made only B movies until given the opportunity to shoot this film on a very healthy budget of $400,000; with his B background, he had no trouble bringing the film in on time and within the budget.

This is actually the second screen version of the story. The first was *The Falcon Takes Over* (1942), made as part of the series about "The Falcon" and starred George Sanders. RKO had paid Chandler only $2,000 for the screen rights, and when it made the big-budget Powell version, it already owned the rights and paid Chandler nothing.

It was made yet again in 1975 as *Farewell, My Lovely*, starring

Robert Mitchum; no one in the audience expected a musical this time.

BEST LINE: Marlowe (Powell) to a flirtatious Mrs. Grayle (Trevor): "Tell your husband I went home; tell him I got bored."

THE POSTMAN ALWAYS RINGS TWICE

1946

TYPE OF FILM:	*Noir*
STUDIO:	Metro-Goldwyn-Mayer
PRODUCER:	Carey Wilson
DIRECTOR:	Tay Garnett
SCREENWRITERS:	Harry Ruskin and Niven Busch
SOURCE:	*The Postman Always Rings Twice,* novel by James M. Cain
RUNNING TIME:	113 minutes

PRINCIPAL PLAYERS:

Lana Turner	Cora Smith
John Garfield	Frank Chambers
Cecil Kellaway	Nick Smith
Hume Cronyn	Arthur Keats
Audrey Totter	Madge Garland
Leon Ames	Kyle Sackett
Alan Reed	Ezra Liam Kennedy
Wally Cassell	Ben
Jeff York	Blair

DID YOU KNOW? It took twelve years to get James M. Cain's book filmed because of the powerful resistance of the Production Code Authority (PCA), the official censoring body of Hollywood that found everything about the book objectionable. Its tawdry sexuality, adultery, murder, and the dishonesty of the lawyers and insurance-company officials were all deemed unsuitable for audience sensibilities. The PCA felt so strongly about Cain's book that in February of 1934 it warned RKO, which wanted to make the motion picture, that they would never allow it to be released. Columbia and Warner Brothers, also interested in the rights, were also told that the film could never receive approval. Within two hours of Columbia's accepting the PCA verdict, MGM acquired the rights, convinced it could get a screenplay that would pass muster. But April of the same year, MGM, too, became convinced that it could not get approval and shelved it. Six years later, a script was submitted that removed the adultery, virtually all of the sex, and the murder attempts on Nick, who would die accidentally. Even then, the PCA judged that it was too sordid, and it was again abandoned. The enormous popularity of Cain's *Double Indemnity* revived interest in the earlier novel, and in May of 1945 a script was approved, restoring all but some of the more graphic sex to Cain's original version. Lana Turner, the ultrasexy star, initially turned down the role because of the steaminess of the subject but was finally persuaded to take the part.

THE STORY: Drifter Frank Chambers stops at a roadside diner, spots the luscious Cora, and takes a job offered by her older, alcoholic husband, Nick. Frank and Cora are immediately attracted to each other, begin an illicit affair, and they leave, but Cora changes her mind and they return to the diner. Wanting a better life with Frank, both financially and romantically, Cora convinces him to help her kill her husband so they can be together and collect his insurance money. Just as Cora smashes Nick's head with a bottle, planning to make his death look like a bathtub accident, their cat trips a power line, plunging the diner into darkness and foiling the plan.

Frank and Cora make a second attempt to kill Nick, getting him drunk and staging an automobile accident, and this time they are successful, though they have made District Attorney Kyle Sackett suspicious. Sackett tricks Frank into signing a document that states that Cora tried to kill him and Nick, which convinces Cora to sign a confession. An agreement is reached in which Cora pleads guilty to manslaughter. On probation, she and Frank do not see or speak to each other because of mutual distrust, but then they decide to marry and run the diner together.

When Cora visits her sick mother, Frank has an affair with a woman he meets at the train station, and Cora learns of it. She tells Frank that she is pregnant. Distrustful and disappointed with him, she decides to kill herself by going for a long swim in the ocean and, too exhausted to return to shore, drowning. When she tells Frank to swim back without her, they realize that they really do love each other and he manages to save her. On the drive home, he loses control of the car and she is killed.

Frank is arrested and convicted for murdering Cora. Although he got away with the murder of Nick, he now faces execution for a crime he did not commit.

* * *

Like *Double Indemnity* and so many other *noir* novels and films, *The Postman Always Rings Twice* is driven by the bad girl who becomes the object of sexual desire for a man who will do virtually anything to have her, usually including murder. The novel, written in 1934, paved the road for all the *noir* fiction and film that followed.

Some elements of *The Postman Always Rings Twice* sprang from real life, notably the infamous Ruth Snyder murder case, in which the defendant murdered her husband with the help of her lover, who she then tried to poison. Cora was modeled on a girl who pumped Cain's gas at a service station. She was kind of cheap, Cain acknowledged (more like the Cora of the novel than the Cora of the motion picture, who just seemed too classy to be working in a cheap roadside diner), but so sexy that she stuck in his memory.

As inappropriate as Lana Turner seemed for the role of Cora, surely the oddest bit of casting was having Cecil Kellaway as Nick, who in the novel was a rough, drunken boor who treated his wife very badly. It is stretching credulity to think that Lana Turner would ever have been married to Cecil Kellaway.

When the major studios were unable to get the motion picture past the censors, Cain adapted *The Postman Always Rings Twice* for the stage in 1936, hoping that a Broadway smash would grant it an aura of respectability. The play flopped, as did a French film version, *Le Dernier Tournant*, made in 1939, and an Italian version, *Ossessione*, made in 1942.

A commercially successful remake was released in 1981, starring Jack Nicholson as Frank and Jessica Lange as Cora. David Mamet's screenplay was far more faithful to the novel, but the heightened violence did not enhance the film.

John Garfield had been released from military service because of a bad heart. It was reported at the time that Turner and Garfield had even more chemistry off the set than on it but that Garfield decided to otherwise occupy his free time for fear that he would have a heart attack.

BEST LINE: Where have you heard this before? In a line used so frequently during the past half century that it is more self-parody than a cliché, Frank Chambers's line to Madge Garland, the girl he picks up at the train station, was used here first: "With my brains and your looks," he tells her, "we could go places."

THE BIG SLEEP
1946

TYPE OF FILM: Detective

STUDIO: Warner Brothers

PRODUCER: Howard Hawks

DIRECTOR: Howard Hawks

SCREENWRITERS: William Faulkner, Jules Furthman, and Leigh Brackett

SOURCE: *The Big Sleep*, novel by Raymond Chandler

RUNNING TIME: 114 minutes

PRINCIPAL PLAYERS:

Humphrey Bogart . . . . .Philip Marlowe
Lauren Bacall . . . . .Vivian Sternwood Rutledge
John Ridgely . . . . .Eddie Mars
Martha Vickers . . . . .Carmen Sternwood
Dorothy Malone .bookshop proprietress
Peggy Knudsen . . . . .Mrs. Eddie Mars
Regis Toomey . . . . .Bernie Ohls
Charles Waldron . . . . .General Sternwood

DID YOU KNOW? One of the most complicated plots in mystery fiction is that of *The Big Sleep*, both in novel form and in the film version. Playing Marlowe, Bogart asked director Howard Hawks who had murdered Owen Taylor, the Sternwood chauffeur whose car is being pulled out of the water. Hawks admitted that he didn't know but that he'd ask William Faulkner, who had worked on that sequence. Faulkner, too, said he didn't actually know, so Hawks wired Chandler, who immediately fired back, "The butler did it."

THE STORY: The wealthy and dying General Sternwood summons Philip Marlowe to his home to stop the blackmailer who has pornographic pictures of his daughter, the very young Carmen Sternwood. After the family chauffeur murders the blackmailer, he, too, is found dead. The photos fall into the hands of the blackmailer's boss, who tries to sell them to Carmen's sister,

Vivian, and he, too, is killed. Further murders, double crosses, and general bad behavior abound in a plot too convoluted for Chandler to write, for Faulkner to adapt, and for anyone to adequately summarize.

* * *

Humphrey Bogart again plays a tough private eye in *The Big Sleep*, just as he had in *The Maltese Falcon*, doing for Chandler what he had done for Hammett: He immortalized a fictional character while also making it very much his own, bearing small resemblance to the character in either book. The viewer is not watching a Philip Marlowe movie, he is watching a Bogart movie, which appears to be just fine with all concerned.

It was reported that the on-screen chemistry of Bogart and Bacall in Howard Hawks's *To Have and Have Not* was so great that the public clearly wanted to see them together again, and Bacall was hired to play opposite Bogart. The film was completed in the beginning of 1945, but because the studio wanted more and more of Bogart and Bacall, there had to be additional shooting and editing, which held the release of the film for about a year and a half. The extra time given to Bacall resulted in a smaller and smaller role for Martha Vickers as the young, drug-using, nymphomaniacal sister of Bacall.

Chandler was so pleased to have Bogart play Marlowe (incredibly, a letter he wrote in 1939, before Bogart made *Casablanca* and *The Maltese Falcon* and hence before he was a star, suggested that he thought Bogart would be the perfect screen Marlowe) that he sold the motion-picture rights to *The Big Sleep* for $10,000, even though the studio had told Hawks he could pay up to $50,000 for the rights. Chandler was simply too happy about the deal to consider negotiating a higher fee.

The 1978 remake starring Robert Mitchum as an excellent, if too old, Marlowe was more true to the novel, but it was updated and ludicrously shot on location in London.

BEST LINE: Vivian Sternwood has rebuked Marlowe for his offensiveness. He replies, "I don't mind if you don't like my manners. I don't like them myself. They're pretty bad. I grieve over them on long winter evenings."

REBECCA
1940

TYPE OF FILM: Suspense

STUDIO: Selznick Studios

PRODUCER: David O. Selznick

DIRECTOR: Alfred Hitchcock

SCREENWRITERS: Robert E. Sherwood and Joan Harrison; adapted by Philip MacDonald and Michael Hogan

SOURCE: *Rebecca*, novel by Daphne du Maurier

RUNNING TIME: 130 minutes

PRINCIPAL PLAYERS:

Laurence Olivier . . . . .Maxim de Winter
Joan Fontaine . . . . .Mrs. de Winter
George Sanders . . . . .Jack Favell
Judith Anderson . . . . .Mrs. Danvers
Nigel Bruce . . . . .Giles Lacey
Reginald Denny . . . . .Frank Crawley
C. Aubrey Smith . . . . .Colonel Julyan
Gladys Cooper . . . . .Beatrice Lacey
Florence Bates . . . . .Mrs. Van Hopper

DID YOU KNOW? With both of the principal actors being nominated for Academy Awards, one would think that casting had been not only inspired, but simple. Nothing could be further from the truth. The director, Alfred Hitchcock, and the producer, David O. Selznick, both brilliant and stubborn moviemakers with excellent taste, disagreed on casting from the outset. Selznick bought rights to the Daphne du Maurier novel especially for Carol Lombard and planned to have Ronald Colman opposite her. Colman turned down the role because he did not want to play a murderer and he regarded the film as a "woman-starring" vehicle. Selznick's next two choices were William Powell and Laurence Olivier, with Leslie Howard and David Niven also considered. Olivier, as an emerging star after his outstanding performance in *Wuthering Heights*, was willing to work for $100,000 less than the already established Powell, and so he was given the role.

Selznick's first choice for the role of Mrs. de Winter, Lombard, also did not take the part. He then decided he would conduct a major search for the female lead, as he had done for *Gone With the Wind*, which had not yet finished filming when he began work on *Rebecca*. He wanted Olivia de Havilland, which presented numerous problems: She was under contract to Warner Brothers, which was reluctant to loan her out to other studios, she was committed to begin principal photography on *Raffles*, and she was not interested in competing for the role with her sister, Joan Fontaine, with whom she had a lifelong animosity. Olivier desperately wanted the role for his wife, Vivien Leigh, while Fontaine's agent was pushing his own wife, Margaret Sullavan. Selznick also considered Loretta Young, Anne Baxter, Anita Louise, and more than twenty others for the role, finally settling on Fontaine over the objections of Hitchcock and others at the studio who claimed she had not established herself as a star—not surprising since she was only twenty-two at the time.

THE STORY: The shy, young paid companion to a wealthy socialite meets the wealthy Maxim de Winter in Monte Carlo and is enchanted by his charm, sophistication, and good looks, happily accepting when he proposes marriage. Her joy is dramatically diminished when she arrives with her husband at his magnificent mansion, Manderley, whose housekeeper, Mrs. Danvers, does everything in her considerable power to make her feel unwelcome.

At every opportunity, Mrs. Danvers contrasts the demure second Mrs. de Winter with Rebecca, Maxim's first wife, who was more beautiful, more sophisticated, and more elegant. Implicit, too, is that Rebecca was more loved by Maxim and certainly more respected and admired by the housekeeper.

Soon after Mrs. de Winter settles into Manderley, a boat is wrecked near the shore, and during the rescue attempt, another sunken boat is discovered to contain the body of Rebecca. For the first time, Maxim tells his bride of his miserable marriage to Rebecca, who had flaunted her infidelities. When Rebecca told him that she was pregnant with another man's child, Maxim had struck her and she smashed her head when she fell. He put her body into a boat and sank it. A new inquest is held, and it appears that de Winter will be charged with murder, until Rebecca's doctor testifies that his patient had been dying of cancer and contemplated suicide.

Maxim and his bride are now freed of the specter of Rebecca, but Mrs. Danvers, still devoted to her former mistress and the house she loved so much, commits suicide by setting fire to Manderley.

* * *

While *Rebecca* was Hitchcock's first American film, it is difficult to tell, since virtually all the actors (Olivier, Fontaine, Sanders, Anderson, Bruce, Denny, Smith, and Cooper) are British, as is the setting and the author (du Maurier) of the novel on which the film was based.

In addition to the difficulties with casting, there were terrible script problems. The original treatment was written by Hitchcock, his wife, Alma, and Joan Harrison, with whom he worked longer than virtually anyone else. It was submitted to Selznick, who loathed it, returning it with a memo longer than the treatment itself. Hitchcock once said that he had finally finished reading it. He said it in 1969. Hitchcock had changed nearly everything from the book, and Selznick insisted that the script be started again. Selznick had promised Daphne du Maurier (to whom he had paid $5,000 for the rights) the film would remain faithful to the novel, after she expressed such disappointment in the film of *Jamaica Inn*, which Hitchcock had filmed and changed unrecognizably.

In spite of the endless problems incurred in making *Rebecca*, it was a huge box-office success and received eleven Academy Award nominations, winning only for Best Picture and Cinematography. Other nominations went to Hitchcock for Best Director, Olivier for Best Actor, Joan Fontaine for Best Actress, and Judith Anderson for Best Supporting Actress.

BEST LINE: The most memorable line is the first of the picture, "Last night I dreamt I went to Manderley again," but since it is also the opening line of Daphne du Maurier's novel, no credit goes to the screenwriter. For much of the film, the second Mrs. de Winter (unnamed in both the book and film) worries that her husband loves the dead Rebecca so much that he cannot love her. In a desperate moment, she begs for reassurance that they are, in fact, happily married. "We are happy, aren't we?" When Maxim does not respond, she asks why he won't answer. "How can I answer you," he finally replies, "when I don't know the answer myself. If you say we're happy, let's leave it at that. Happiness is something I know nothing about."

WITNESS FOR THE PROSECUTION
1957

TYPE OF FILM: Courtroom

STUDIO: United Artists

PRODUCER: Arthur Hornblow

DIRECTOR: Billy Wilder

SCREENWRITERS: Billy Wilder and Harry Kurnitz; adapted by Larry Marcus

SOURCE: *Witness for the Prosecution*, short story and play by Agatha Christie

RUNNING TIME: 114 minutes

PRINCIPAL PLAYERS:

Marlene Dietrich . . . . .Christine Vole
Tyrone Power . . . . .Leonard Vole
Charles Laughton . . . . .Sir Wilfrid Robarts
Elsa Lanchester . . . . .Miss Plimsoll
John Williams . . . . .Brogan-Moore
Henry Daniell . . . . .Mayhew
Una O'Connor . . . . .Janet McKenzie
Ian Wolfe . . . . .Carter
Torin Thatcher . . . . .Judge

DID YOU KNOW? Being too good an actress in *Witness for the Prosecution* probably cost Marlene Dietrich an Academy Award nomination. Although famous for her sultry singing voice and gorgeous legs, Dietrich never made anyone's top ten list for the best actress in Hollywood. She had always been offered a limited choice of roles—the femme fatale—and she yearned to prove she had a greater range than that, so she desperately wanted the part of Christine Vole. Director Bill Wilder obliged her. She and her film husband developed a plot in which it was vital that she wear a disguise good enough to fool their barrister. Dietrich played the part of a cockney tart to perfection, fooling both the film barrister and audiences. She played it so well, in fact, that critics and Hollywood insiders refused to believe that she was good enough to have actually played both roles. However, Elsa Lanchester, the nurse in the film and Charles Laughton's wife in real life, spoke freely about how often Dietrich showed up at the couple's house to borrow appropriate clothing and study a cockney accent with the accomplished Laughton. There are even production stills showing Dietrich, without makeup, rehearsing the role. When Academy Award time came, however, Dietrich was one of the few principals who did not receive a nomination. She was defeated on two fronts: First, the rumor that she did not play both parts persisted, casting enough doubt that members of the Academy were reluctant to vote for her. Second, an aura of secrecy about the film prevailed, with the studio's entire publicity campaign focused on asking viewers not to reveal the stunning twists in the plot. Therefore, Dietrich's dual role went unknown by all except those who had actually seen the picture.

THE STORY: Befriended by Emily French, a wealthy old woman, Leonard Vole grows very close to her, raising suspicion with Janet MacKenzie, her housekeeper. When Mrs. French is murdered and Leonard inherits 80,000 pounds, he is accused of murdering the elderly woman.

The great barrister, Sir Wilfrid Robarts, weakened by a heart condition, has been told to slow down and take only bland civil cases, but when he meets Leonard, he likes the challenge of what appears to be an open-and-shut case against him and agrees to defend him.

Leonard tells Sir Wilfrid that his only alibi is his wife, Christine. When Christine shows up at Sir Wilfrid's house to tell him that she is providing an alibi only because her husband wants her to, he becomes suspicious of her. She later admits that she and Leonard were never legally married, as she already had a husband when they met, fell in love, and married.

At the trial, after much legal thrusting and parrying, the prosecution shocks Sir Wilfrid by calling as a witness Christine Vole, who admits that she is not really married to Leonard and is therefore able to testify against him, which she does, telling the judge that she was forced to provide an alibi and that her husband had admitted the murder to her. Vole stands in the dock, shouting, "Lies!" in horror and disbelief.

Sir Wilfrid's only defense is to make Christine appear to be a liar, but it's a weak defense and his client seems doomed. As they await the verdict, the barrister receives a telephone call offering vital evidence for sale. He meets with a cockney slattern and buys love letters that Christine had written to a mysterious lover.

223

The next day, the trial is reopened and he confronts Christine with the letters, proving that she had lied to be rid of Leonard so she could be with another man. The jury returns a "not guilty" verdict, but Sir Wilfrid, uneasy about the case, realizes that it was all a sham when Christine walks up to him, alone in the court-room, and speaks to him in the same cockney accent. It was the only way to ensure her husband's acquittal, she tells him.

When Leonard also walks into the courtroom, he admits that he actually did kill the old lady but knows he is safe because he can-not be tried again under the rules of double jeopardy. He then shocks his wife by telling her he is leaving her for another woman, whereupon Christine grabs a knife and kills him. Sir Wil-frid then agrees to defend Christine.

* * *

Witness for the Prosecution began as a short story, published in 1933 in *The Hound of Death and Other Stories*. Agatha Christie rewrote and expanded it for a stage version in 1953; it was a sen-sation in London. It is this version that was then filmed, the only major change being to add Nurse Plimsoll for comic relief. Until *Murder On the Orient Express* (1974), this was the only motion pic-ture made from her works for which Christie had a kind word.

As the barrister is supposed to have a heart condition, an addi-tional element of suspense in the film is whether Sir Wilfrid will survive the rigors of a trial. Charles Laughton wasn't sure that he could successfully act the part of someone having a heart attack on screen so he tried it out at home, faking an attack in his swim-ming pool, almost giving his wife, Elsa Lanchester a heart attack.

Ironically, this was Tyrone Power's last completed film because, a few months after completion, he actually did die of a heart attack.

Academy Award nominations went to *Witness for the Prosecution* for Best Picture, Billy Wilder for Best Director, Charles Laughton for Best Actor, Elsa Lanchester for Best Supporting Actress, and in several technical categories.

A television adaptation was made for British television in 1982, seen later in the United States on the *Hallmark Hall of Fame*.

BEST LINE: Leonard Vole, afraid that he will be sent to prison for murder, says to his barrister, "But this is England, where I thought you never arrest, let alone convict, people for crimes they have not committed." Sir Wilfrid replies, "We try not to make a habit of it."

BODY HEAT
1981

TYPE OF FILM:	Noir
STUDIO:	Ladd Company/Warner Brothers
PRODUCER:	Fred T. Gallo
DIRECTOR:	Lawrence Kasdan
SCREENWRITER:	Lawrence Kasdan
SOURCE:	Original story
RUNNING TIME:	113 minutes

PRINCIPAL PLAYERS:

William Hurt . . . . .Ned Racine
Kathleen Turner . . . . .Matty Walker
Richard Crenna . . . . .Edmund Walker
Ted Danson . . . . .Peter Lowenstein
Mickey Rourke . . . . .Teddy Lewis
J. A. Preston . . . . .Oscar Grace
Kim Zimmer . . . . .Mary Ann Simpson
Jane Halleran . . . . .Stella

DID YOU KNOW? Kathleen Turner, the sexy black widow of *Body Heat*, makes her screen debut as the star of this very successful *noir* film. Amazingly, the superbly written and directed motion picture is also the first effort of Lawrence Kasdan, who fulfilled both roles. Kasdan's wife, Meg, also had a small role as a nurse.

THE STORY: Ned Racine, a notoriously incompetent lawyer and the town rake, spots the shapely Matty Walker and goes after her with nearly immediate success. They begin a torrid affair that culminates in a plan to murder her husband, which will enable them to be together always and also, not so incidentally, allow her to claim a fortune as his widow. Together they plan and carry out a near perfect crime, against the advice of Teddy Lewis, a small-time crook and expert bomb-maker, whom Racine once kept out of jail. Lewis tells him that fifty things can go wrong when you plan arson, and a genius can think of and avoid twenty-five of them. "And believe me," he tells the lawyer, "you're no genius."

225

Lewis is right, of course, and local cop Oscar Grace discovers small problems and oversights that point to Matty as the killer. However, all the missteps eventually lead Grace away from her and toward Ned.

When the ruthless Matty sends Ned to a booby-trapped boathouse, Racine realizes that he has been set up and double-crossed by his lover. He forces her to open the door that will explode the bomb, and as he waits in the darkness, she walks to the trap and sets off a huge explosion. He is arrested and, while lying awake one night, has an inspiration: She's alive!

BEST LINE: Racine flirts with Matty Walker, and she reminds him that she's married and not interested. He pursues her, refusing to take no for an answer. Finally, she says to him, "You're not too smart, are you? I like that in a man."

THE LADY VANISHES
1938

TYPE OF FILM:	Espionage
STUDIO:	Gaumont-British
PRODUCER:	Edward Black
DIRECTOR:	Alfred Hitchcock
SCREENWRITERS:	Sidney Gilliatt and Frank Launder; adaptation by Alma Reville
SOURCE:	*The Wheel Spins*, novel by Ethel Lina White
RUNNING TIME:	97 minutes

PRINCIPAL PLAYERS:

Margaret Lockwood . . . . .Iris Henderson
Michael Redgrave . . . . .Gilbert
Paul Lukas . . . . .Dr. Hartz
Dame May Whitty . . . . .Miss Froy
Googie Withers . . . . .Blanche
Cecil Parker . . . . .Mr. Todhunter
Linden Travers . . . . .Mrs. Todhunter
Naunton Wayne . . . . .Caldicott
Basil Radford . . . . .Charters

DID YOU KNOW? The concept of a person being seen by a large number of people, then disappearing, followed by everyone asserting that the person never existed, is a popular story, with a seed of truth in the Paris Exposition at the turn of the century. It seems that the person who "disappeared" there had contracted the plague, and in order to protect the enormous investment of the Exposition as well as to prevent public panic, the person was swept away to a hospital. Everyone with whom he or she had come in contact was sworn to secrecy. The same device was used by Cornell Woolrich in a story and was the basis for the film *So Long at the Fair* (1950).

THE STORY: Wealthy Iris Henderson is returning from a holiday in the Balkans and meets the septuagenarian Miss Froy

227

("rhymes with toy," she tells people) aboard the train. The lovable governess disappears during the course of the trip home. Henderson appears to be the only person interested in locating her, for virtually all the passengers deny ever seeing the old lady. Only Gilbert, a musicologist, believes the lovely young woman, or at least seems to, because he is even more interested in the young woman than the old one. Viewers eventually learn that the passengers are part of a vast spy ring and that Miss Froy, far from being the gentle and apparently scatterbrained old maid she conveys, is in fact a counterespionage agent.

* * *

The Lady Vanishes is one of Alfred Hitchcock's most entertaining and enduring films. Although ranking high on the suspense level, it is so witty that it might easily be viewed as a comedy. The performances of Naunton Wayne and Basil Radford as a pair of twits mainly concerned with getting back to England in order to see some of the cricket matches at Manchester, utterly unaware of the chaos of World War II looming inevitably, were so perfect that the pair went on to play similar characters in several other films. On a more serious level, they were used by Hitchcock to illustrate British noninterventionists, as exemplified by Prime Minister Neville Chamberlain. Hitchcock's political position was in deep contrast to that of the Academy of Motion Picture Arts and Sciences, which gave a Best Picture nomination to a foreign-language film for the first time. Jean Renoir's *Grand Illusion*, a manifesto for isolationism and pacifism, apparently captured the mood of the Academy as well as of President Franklin D. Roosevelt, who gave it an unsolicited endorsement.

Hitchcock won the New York Film Critics' Award for his direction of *The Lady Vanishes*. Having undergone one name change from the Ethel Lina White book, *The Wheel Spins*, *The Lady Vanishes* was also released as *Lost Lady*.

In one of those decisions Hollywood executives make that leave most viewers flabbergasted and disgusted, some geniuses decided that a remake of Hitchcock's masterpiece would be a good idea. This occurred in 1979 when the aptly named (in this case) Rank Organisation miscast Elliott Gould in a film so bad that you may regard yourself as fortunate indeed that you have never seen it. A good cast (Cybill Shepherd, Angela Lansbury,

Herbert Lom, etc.) reached their cinematic nadirs in this colossal blunder.

BEST LINE: Iris Henderson, returning to England from yet another holiday: "I've been everywhere, done everything. What is there for me but marriage?"

THE KILLERS
1946

TYPE OF FILM:	*Noir*
STUDIO:	Universal-International
PRODUCER:	Mark Hellinger
DIRECTOR:	Robert Siodmak
SCREENWRITERS:	Anthony Veiller and (uncredited) John Huston
SOURCE:	"The Killers," short story by Ernest Hemingway
RUNNING TIME:	105 minutes

PRINCIPAL PLAYERS:

Burt Lancaster . . . . .Ole "Swede" Anderson, also Peter Lund
Ava Gardner . . . . .Kitty Collins
Edmond O'Brien . . . . .Jim Reardon
Albert Dekker . . . . .Big Jim Colfax
Sam Levene . . . . .Det. Lt. Sam Levinsky
Charles McGraw . . . . .Al
William Conrad . . . . .Mak

DID YOU KNOW? When Mark Hellinger decided to make a movie from Ernest Hemingway's landmark short story, "The Killers," he hired John Huston to write the screenplay. The job was more than an adaptation, because Hemingway's story never lets the reader know why "the Swede" is being killed. The opening sequence, in a little diner in which two hit men thuggishly ask about their intended victim, is all that Hemingway wrote. All the rest—the robbery, the girl, the double and triple crosses—was created by Huston. When Hellinger and Huston, two of the most overblown egos in Hollywood, clashed, Hellinger removed Huston's name from the writing credits; only the name of Huston's collaborator, Anthony Veiller, appears on the motion picture.

THE STORY: Two tough guys, Al and Mak, enter a little diner in Brentwood looking for Ole "the Swede" Anderson. When he doesn't show up as expected, they go to hunt for him. A young man at the counter goes to warn the Swede that they're coming, but the Swede refuses to run, accepting the inevitability of his imminent death. He lies back in his squalid room until the killers walk in and shoot him.

Insurance investigator Jim Reardon tracks down the beneficiary of Anderson's life-insurance policy—a hotel maid—and begins to trace the life of the dead man, connecting him to a robbery at a hat factory that netted more than a quarter of a million dollars.

When Reardon locates Anderson's old friend police lieutenant Sam Levinsky, the early years of the ex-fighter come into focus as Levinsky's wife, once the Swede's girl, tells Reardon how he met Kitty Collins, the girlfriend of gangster Big Jim Colfax, and instantly fell for her.

Kitty and Anderson became an item, and when she was caught with stolen jewelry, he took the fall for her, going away for three years. After his release, Anderson found Kitty had gone back to Colfax while he was in jail, and when the gangster planned a big robbery, the Swede decided to participate. Kitty came to Anderson in the middle of the night to warn him that the gang planned to cheat him of his share, so he took vengeance by stealing the entire $250,000. As planned, he and Kitty went to an Atlantic City hotel, but, two days later she disappeared—with the money. When he discovered that she'd left him, he tried to commit suicide, but the chambermaid saved him.

Reardon, still tracking the money, finds Colfax, now a successful contractor, which leads him to a meeting with Kitty. He has clearly been set up when the two men who killed the Swede show up and try to kill him, but he and Levinsky turn the tables and shoot them while Kitty escapes.

At Big Jim Colfax's house, Reardon and the cop find him dying. Kitty arrives, and they learn that she left the Swede in Atlantic City to return to Colfax, who had planned the double cross in order to get the entire payroll for himself. As he takes his last breaths, Kitty begs him to tell the cops that she's innocent.

* * *

Both Ava Gardner and Burt Lancaster made their screen debuts in *The Killers*, remarkable for a major production. Lancaster, the big, rugged, handsome former circus performer with a chiseled body of steel, has, in the best noir tradition, totally succumbed to the charms of the wrong woman. He is so emasculated that, when he learns two hit men are coming to kill him, he doesn't even get out of bed to run or fight. When he's betrayed by Ava Gardner, who has fled with a quarter of a million dollars, he never thinks of the money but tries to jump out a window because he's lost the girl who cold-bloodedly double-crossed him. He plays the same beaten-down role in *Criss Cross*.

Gardner, the extraordinarily beautiful and sensual actress who could turn most men to jelly, did the same in real life. Married to three famous men (Mickey Rooney, Artie Shaw, and Frank Sinatra), she was well known to lead an active . . . uh, social life. Among her myriad affairs was one with the powerful Howard Hughes, who was more active in Hollywood in the 1940s than he was with his airplane company. It has been reported that Robert Mitchum actually telephoned Hughes to ask permission to sleep with the sultry actress. Hughes is said to have replied, "If you don't, they'll think you're a pansy."

Robert Siodmak was nominated for an Academy Award as Best Director.

The musical score by Miklos Rozsa introduced the memorable "dum da dum dum" theme made famous by the television series *Dragnet*.

The Killers was remade in 1964 with Lee Marvin, John Cassavetes, Angie Dickinson, and Ronald Reagan—in his last screen role—as the brutal gangster. Originally made for television, it was regarded as too violent and had theatrical release instead.

BEST LINE: Reardon has tracked down Big Jim Colfax, who denies any knowledge of knowing the Swede. As Reardon relates the history that Colfax already knows, the tale turns to Kitty and the Swede's relationship. "That guy, what's his name? The Swede?" asks Colfax. "Never had a chance, did he? You might say Kitty Collins signed his death warrant."

VERTIGO
1958

TYPE OF FILM:	Suspense
STUDIO:	Paramount
PRODUCER:	Alfred Hitchcock
DIRECTOR:	Alfred Hitchcock
SCREENWRITERS:	Alec Coppel and Samuel Taylor
SOURCE:	*The Living and the Dead* (translation of D'Entre Les Morts) by Pierre Boileau and Thomas Narcejac
RUNNING TIME:	128 minutes

PRINCIPAL PLAYERS:

James Stewart . . . . .John "Scottie" Ferguson
Kim Novak . . . . .Judy Barton/Madeleine Elster
Barbara Bel Geddes . . . . .Midge Wood
Tom Helmore . . . . .Gavin Elster
Henry Jones . . . . .judge
Konstantine Shayne . . . . .Pop Liebl

DID YOU KNOW? Unlike most of the ice blondes whom Hitchcock used in his films and with whom he was always slightly in love, Kim Novak was always held in low regard by the director. He had wanted Vera Miles for the lead in *Vertigo*, but when she became pregnant with her third child, he was forced to replace her with Novak, which was probably the reason for his instant and apparently baseless dislike. Novak had been promised a fee for being loaned to Warner Brothers by Paramount and refused to work until she received the check. By the time she had been paid, Miles had given birth and was available, but Hitchcock, angry with her for getting pregnant and ruining his plans to make her a star, proceeded with Novak. His great satisfaction, he admitted years later, occurred in the scene in which Madeleine fakes a suicide attempt by jumping into San Francisco Bay. Hitchcock called for multiple retakes, forcing Novak to repeatedly leap, fully clothed and made up, into the studio's large tank that replicated the bay. As she was pulled, drenched, out of the water,

Hitchcock would call for yet another retake, forcing her to be remade up, have her hair done, and change into fresh clothes, only to have to do it again.

THE STORY: John "Scottie" Ferguson is chasing a criminal across the rooftops of San Francisco when he is struck by an attack of acrophobia and its resultant vertigo, causing the death of a fellow policeman. He resigns from the police department and is asked by an old friend, Gavin Elster, to follow his wife, Madeleine, who he claims is haunted by the ghost of her mad great grandmother and is likely to commit suicide. She makes an attempt, leaping into San Francisco Bay, and Ferguson saves her, bringing her back to his apartment, undressing her, and putting her in his bed until she recovers. As he sees her more often, he falls in love with her, but she makes another attempt, this time leaping from a church bell tower, and because of his illness, he is unable to save her as he watches her body plummet past him to the ground below.

In pain and guilt-ridden, he has a nervous breakdown, but an old girlfriend, Midge, nurses him back until he encounters Judy Barton—a brunette who bears an uncanny resemblance to his dead love. She swears she has never heard of Madeleine, and he pursues her, forcing her to change clothing styles and even her hair color to make her look more like the woman he lost.

He eventually learns that Madeleine was not Elster's wife, but his mistress and they had meticulously planned the murder of his wife in such a way that Ferguson would swear he had witnessed Madeleine's suicide. Anxious to learn the entire truth, he forces Judy to the top of the bell tower, where she tells him again of her genuine love for him. Frightened by the approach of a shadowy stranger, she steps back and plunges from the roof, smashed on the pavement—this time dead for real.

* * *

Vertigo, one of Hitchcock's suspense masterpieces, was based on a novel by Pierre Boileau and Thomas Narcejac, *The Living and the Dead*, which had been translated from the French *D'Entre Les Morts*. The writers had specifically written this book so that Hitchcock would buy it and film it. They had written several other books with the same plan after they learned that Hitchcock had tried to acquire the rights to their novel *Les Diaboliques*. Had Hitchcock failed to acquire their book, they reasoned, they would have been able to sell it to a French director with little difficulty after the great success of *Les Diaboliques*.

Curiously, although Alfred Hitchcock was nominated for five Academy Awards as Best Director and *Vertigo* is called his masterpiece, the film received not a single nomination.

Hitchcock Alert: In one of his less creative appearances, the director can be seen crossing the street.

BEST LINE: Madeleine, on her way to the fatal bell tower, asks John, "Do you believe I love you?" "Yes," he replies. "Even if you lose me," she continues, "then you'll know I loved you and I wanted to go on loving you."

THE USUAL SUSPECTS
1995

TYPE OF FILM: Crime

STUDIO: PolyGram

PRODUCERS: Bryan Singer and Michael McDonnell

DIRECTOR: Bryan Singer

SCREENWRITER: Christopher McQuarrie

SOURCE: Original

RUNNING TIME: 105 minutes

PRINCIPAL PLAYERS:

Gabriel Byrne . . . . .Dean Keaton
Kevin Spacey . . . . .Ronald "Verbal" Kint
Stephen Baldwin . . . . .Michael McManus
Kevin Pollak . . . . .Todd Hockney
Chazz Palminteri . . . . .Dave Kujan
Pete Postlethwaite . . . . .Mr. Kobayashi
Suzy Amis . . . . .Edie Finneran
Benicio Del Toro . . . . .Fred Fenster
Giancarlo Esposito . . . . .Jack Baer

DID YOU KNOW? One of the most improbable and enigmatic figures in cinema history is Keyser Soze, the ultimate criminal who virtually no one living has seen, though mythology surrounds him to the point where he is described as "the devil himself." As the police attempt to learn his identity, audiences are given several clues, though they are admittedly abstruse. The role had always been intended for Kevin Spacey, who has the same initials as Keyser Soze. Soze is referred to in *The Usual Suspects* as being Turkish, and the Turkish word *soze* means to talk, an obvious clue that Soze may be Verbal Kint. (Well, obvious if you speak Turkish.)

Five different people played the part of Soze at various times in the film. Both Gabriel Byrne's and Kevin Spacey's faces are shown as Soze, though not very clearly; an unnamed actor whose long hair obscures his face plays him in the flashback sequence where he is seen murdering his wife and children; and producer/director Brian Singer filmed himself and a friend when Soze's feet were shown and when he lights a cigarette.

There was so much secrecy about the film, even on the set and among the principals, that Gabriel Byrne thought he was Soze until he actually saw the completed film.

THE STORY: A boat at a San Pedro pier explodes and the police discover $91,000,000, twenty-seven corpses, a frightened Hungarian terrorist, and a crippled two-bit crook named Roger "Verbal" (because he talks too much) Kint, who is brought in to explain what happened.

The events are all "the cops' fault," he explains, because five crooks—the usual suspects—had been brought together for a lineup involving a truck hijacking and then thrown into a cell while awaiting their lawyers to post bail. "You don't put guys like that in a room together," Kint points out.

One of the five is Verbal and another is Dean Keaton, a crooked cop who had been caught and indicted but who wants to go straight. He is talked into one more job with the other four, and they set out to make a killing that is bigger and more complicated—and more dangerous—than they had ever expected.

They are approached by a Mr. Kobayashi, a representative of Keyser Soze, a legendary crime lord so powerful and ruthless that those few who know of his existence are paralyzed with fear at the mere sound of his name.

The plot involves an enormous drug transaction and a showdown at a boat that will ultimately be destroyed, taking with it the entire gang with the exception of Verbal. When the police interrogation finally concludes, Verbal is released. As he walks a few blocks away from the police station, his limp disappears, just as Detective Dave Kujan spots trivial clues that suggest that Verbal had fabricated every word of the extraordinary story he had told.

* * *

Christopher McQuarrie won an Oscar for his very original and highly intelligent screenplay, in which he created one of the most challenging, creative, and witty mystery films of recent years—an old-fashioned puzzle story updated with contemporary characters, dialogue, and restrained violence, without a car chase in sight.

The name of the character played by Gabriel Byrne, Dean Keaton, is Byrne's real name.

The title of the motion picture is a reference to Casablanca, in which the French policeman Louis Renault (played by Claude Rains) listlessly tells his underlings to round up the usual suspects. The name of the production company, Blue Parrot/Bad Hat Harry Productions, is also a partial reference to *Casablanca*. The Blue Parrot was the name of the nightclub owned by Ferrari, the Sydney Greenstreet character. The other half of the name is a reference to *Jaws*, where one character on the beach greets another who is wearing a bathing cap, and says, "That's a bad hat, Harry."

Kevin Spacey won an Academy Award for Best Supporting Actor.

BEST LINE: When asked whether he believes Keyser Soze exists, Verbal Kint replies, "I believe in God, and the only thing that scares me is Keyser Soze."

SHADOW OF A DOUBT
1943

TYPE OF FILM: Suspense
STUDIO: Universal
PRODUCER: Jack H. Skirball
DIRECTOR: Alfred Hitchcock
SCREENWRITERS: Thornton Wilder, Alma Reville and Sally Benson
SOURCE: Original story by Gordon McDonnell
RUNNING TIME: 108 minutes

PRINCIPAL PLAYERS:

Teresa Wright . . . . .Charlie Newton
Joseph Cotten . . . . .Uncle Charlie Oakley
Macdonald Carey . . . . .Jack Graham
Patricia Collinge . . . . .Emma Newton
Henry Travers . . . . .Joe Newton
Wallace Ford . . . . .Fred Saunders
Edna May Wonacott . . . . .Ann Newton
Hume Cronyn . . . . .Herb Hawkins
Charles Bates . . . . .Roger Newton
Wallace Ford . . . . .Fred Saunders

DID YOU KNOW? *Shadow of a Doubt* was based on a true story. In 1938, a man who lived in New York went to a small California town named Hanford ostensibly to visit his sister and her family, but he was actually trying to go into hiding. His efforts failed when the law caught up with him, and he was arrested for the murder of several rich women on the East Coast. Gordon McDonnell, a playwright, read newspaper accounts of the incident and went to Hanford with the idea of writing a play. He was married to Margaret McDonnell, the head of Selznick Studio's story department, who told Hitchcock that her husband had a wonderful story idea that he hadn't yet written. Hitchcock and the couple had lunch together while McDonnell told the story, and Hitchcock told him to go home and write it. He did, producing a nine-page treatment that the director gave to Thornton Wilder to turn into a screenplay.

THE STORY: Charles Oakley travels from New York to Santa Rosa, California, to visit his sister and her family. Unbeknownst to his family, he is suspected of murdering three widows in the East and has come across the country to hide from the police. Especially thrilled to meet him is Charlie, the lovely niece who was named for him and with whom he seems to have a telepathic connection.

Charlie becomes utterly infatuated with her handsome uncle, who gives her an emerald ring inscribed with the initials *M.B.* When she begins to hum "The Merry Widow Waltz," it obviously upsets him.

Jack Graham, a detective claiming to be a poll taker, and his partner, masquerading as a photographer, come to the house, ostensibly to interview the family but really to take a picture of Oakley. Jack takes Charlie on a date and she guesses his real identity. Although outraged, she agrees not to tell her uncle. As soon as they separate, she rushes to the library to find the newspaper and spots an article her uncle had removed earlier that day, a story about "The Merry Widow Murderer," one of whose victims had the initials *M.B.* Charlie becomes even more convinced that her uncle is the killer when he talks with open hatred and contempt for widows, likening them to swine.

When Oakley forces Charlie into a bar to discuss her evidently changed attitude, he tells her she knows nothing of the world but, realizing that she knows the truth about him, he agrees to leave town. When another suspect is killed in the East, he assumes he is now safe and decides to stay in Santa Rosa. Still concerned that his niece knows too much, however, he attempts to kill her by sawing a wooden step, which nearly makes her fall, and again by trapping her in a garage as a car motor runs.

Charlie pointedly wears the emerald ring to a party, convincing Oakley to leave town. The family sees him off, and he traps Charlie on the train as it takes off and tries to push her out as it speeds along the track, but in the struggle he trips and falls in front of an oncoming train. As the town gives him a grand funeral, Charlie and Jack agree to keep secret the truth about her psychotic uncle.

* * *

Often described as one of Hitchcock's favorite films (although he denied it), *Shadow of a Doubt* is one of only two of his movies in which the central character is a villain. The other is *Psycho*, though an argument could be made that the unseen Rebecca de Winter dominates *Rebecca*.

There is a strong autobiographical element in *Shadow of a Doubt*, probably more than in any other of Hitchcock's films. The mother of the family is named Emma, just as Hitchcock's mother was. Uncle Charlie is described as "neat and fussy," as the director often was, and an accident Oakley has on a bicycle is precisely the same as one Hitchcock incurred in childhood. Before the accident, Uncle Charlie is described as "such a quiet boy, always reading," as was true of Hitchcock, who also shared the villain's nostalgic view that the world was once a better place. Hitchcock also identified with Herbie Hawkins, who lives with a sickly and demanding mother and who is devoted to crime stories, obsessively talking about ways of murdering people.

Hitchcock wanted to film on location in Santa Rosa but was initially thwarted when the town refused. Less than two decades earlier, it had been swindled out of $25,000 when a production company said it wanted to build a studio but instead sold worthless bonds and disappeared. The secretary of the Chamber of Commerce, however, managed to convince the residents that Universal was a legitimate company, and permission was granted.

Hume Cronyn made his screen debut as Herbie Hawkins.

Shadow of a Doubt was remade in 1958 as *Step Down to Terror*, a listless production that was only a whisper better than the 1991 television movie using the original title.

BEST LINE: At the funeral for Oakley, his niece tells detective Jack Graham that her uncle saw the world as a terrible place. "It's not quite as bad as that," he tells her. "Sometimes it needs a lot of watching. Things go crazy every now and then. Like your Uncle Charlie."

THE CONVERSATION
1974

TYPE OF FILM:	Crime
STUDIO:	Paramount
PRODUCER:	Francis Ford Coppola
DIRECTOR:	Francis Ford Coppola
SCREENWRITER:	Francis Ford Coppola
SOURCE:	Original
RUNNING TIME:	113 minutes

PRINCIPAL PLAYERS:

Gene Hackman . . . . .Harry Caul
John Cazale . . . . .Stan
Allen Garfield . . . . .Bernie Moran
Frederic Forrest . . . . .Mark
Cindy Williams . . . . .Ann
Harrison Ford . . . . .Martin Stett
Michael Higgins . . . . .Paul
Elizabeth MacRae . . . . .Meredith
Teri Garr . . . . .Amy

DID YOU KNOW? Although one of the most brilliantly conceived and executed crime stories ever to reach the screen, *The Conversation* was poorly promoted, and released as if it were protected by the Official Secrets Act, and so was not a big box-office success. The chosen few who actually got to see it became devotees because of its sophisticated demonstration of bugging and surveillance techniques that came just at the height of interest in the bungled Watergate break-in and Richard Nixon's secret tapes. While many people then assumed that the film was inspired by those events, in fact Francis Ford Coppola had written the screenplay many years earlier and production had already begun when the inept burglary took place. The film failed to earn back its cost.

THE STORY: Harry Caul is a professional industrial spy who sells his services to anyone who wants them. With the help of his hired hands, he tracks a young couple, Mark and Ann, and gets photographs and audio tapes of their clandestine meetings for a man he doesn't really know, "the Director" of a secretive company. The tapes, gathered using highly powerful shotgun microphones among other sophisticated techniques, are cleaned up and reveal a murder plot, with the assumed victims to be the young couple because the woman clearly has been guilty of marital infidelity.

Martin Stett, the Director's assistant, attempts to get the tapes from Harry, who refuses to give them to anyone but the man who hired him, even though Stett assures him that they are working together. When Harry still refuses, a sexy blonde named Meredith seduces him and he wakes up to find the tapes gone—obviously delivered to Stett.

This turn of events is particularly upsetting to Harry, a paranoid with three locks on his door, no listed telephone, and so protective of his privacy that he alienates those few he allows into his life even superficially, including his girlfriend, Amy, who doesn't know where he lives, what he does for a living, or how to reach him.

Usually distant, professional, and incurious, Harry becomes guilt-ridden with this job. He is haunted by the sound of the young woman's laugh and charmed by her innocent-looking face. Feeling sorry for and protective of her, he is convinced that she has been doomed because of the tapes he masterfully produced.

A murder is committed at the place and time anticipated in the lovers' conversation, but they are not the victims. As Harry replays the tapes in his mind at the scene of the murder, he realizes that the young couple had not been afraid for their own lives but had been plotting the murder of the young woman's husband, the Director.

Back in his apartment, Harry gets a telephone call from Stett, saying they know that he knows and to stay uninvolved. "We'll be listening," he says. Frantically tearing apart his sparse furniture and even breaking the plaster on the walls and ripping up the floorboards, using all the expertise he's gained in his career, Harry is still unable to find the bugging device. He finally picks up his saxophone and plays along to jazz records, totally alone and neurotically paralyzed into inaction by the notion that he is being spied on.

* * *

While there is remarkably little action and virtually no sex or violence in a film about those very subjects, *The Conversation*

243

moves swiftly in a remarkably suspenseful narrative. Produced, written, and directed by Coppola, it was his first film after *The Godfather*—an enormous departure from that blockbuster in terms of scope and size.

Robert Duvall as the Director plays an uncredited cameo.

Academy Awards nominations went to *The Conversation* for Best Picture and Francis Ford Coppola for Best Director. It was named the Best Film at the Cannes Film Festival.

BEST LINE: Late at night, Meredith, an aging but sexy model, stays at Harry's workshop after a small party. He is uneasy, racked with guilt about the girl he thinks he has sent to her death, troubled by how confused and frightened she sounds. Meredith tries to comfort him, telling him: "Forget it, Harry. It's only a trick. It's a job. You're not supposed to feel anything about it. You're just supposed to do it, that's all."

NORTH BY NORTHWEST
1959

TYPE OF FILM: Espionage

STUDIO: Metro-Goldwyn-Mayer

PRODUCER: Alfred Hitchcock

DIRECTOR: Alfred Hitchcock

SCREENWRITER: Ernest Lehman

SOURCE: Original screenplay

RUNNING TIME: 136 minutes

PRINCIPAL PLAYERS:

Cary Grant . . . . Roger Thornhill
Eva Marie Saint . . . . Eve Kendall
James Mason . . . . Phillip Vandamm
Leo G. Carroll . . . . .Professor
Martin Landau . . . . .Leonard
Jessie Royce Landis . . . . .Clara Thornhill
Philip Ober . . . . Lester Townsand
Adam Williams . . . . .Valerian
Josephine Hutchinson . . . . .handsome woman

DID YOU KNOW? As seems true of so many films, even the great ones, there were ideas that seemed good, during filming that never made it onto the screen. *North by Northwest* is no exception. Hitchcock had several elements that he wanted to incorporate into a film, and he got Ernest Lehman to write most of them, including the famous chase across Mount Rushmore and the notion of a man being mistaken for someone who didn't actually exist. What didn't make it is a scene in which a speaker at the United Nations refuses to continue his speech until one of the delegates, head down on his desk, is awakened, only to be discovered to have been murdered. Another scene was planned for Cary Grant to be in an automobile factory in Detroit. As he walks through it, a car was to be built on the assembly line just behind him. When the car rolls off the line, he opens the door to drive it away, only to find a dead body inside. The entire sequence was even shot, but the director and the screenwriter could never find a way to incorporate it into the film.

THE STORY: An advertising executive, Roger Thornhill, is abducted from the Plaza Hotel and brought to a mansion where he is bullied and threatened and nearly killed as he attempts to convince his kidnappers that he is not George Kaplan, the man they are after. The problem is that George Kaplan does not exist at all, being a useful device for the U.S. Secret Service in their pursuit of a gang of spies led by Phillip Vandamm, who are trying to steal government secrets.

After escaping, Thornhill tries to track down his abductor at the U.N., only the man he is talking to is stabbed to death. His proximity to the victim makes him appear to be guilty, and he flees to Chicago aboard the Twentieth Century Limited, where he encounters the lovely Eve Kendall, who seduces him. On the run from both the spy ring and the police, Thornhill trusts only Eve, who turns out to be the mistress of Vandamm, although Thornhill soon learns that she is also in the employ of the CIA.

When Vandamm and his henchmen realize that Eve is a traitor, they plan to kill her, chasing her and Thornhill across the huge presidential faces of Mount Rushmore.

* * *

There are plot holes galore in this stylish thriller, but the action moves so briskly and so elegantly that they are noticed only upon careful reflection. *North by Northwest* (a title taken from *Hamlet*, incidentally) has often (and accurately) been described as the single film that most uses all the elements known to Hitchcock aficionados: The famous ice blonde (Eva Marie Saint), the charming leading man (Cary Grant starred in four Hitchcock movies, as did James Stewart), episodic action filled with almost unbearable suspense, and, of course, the MacGuffin, the object that makes the film move forward, whether it is money, jewelry, documents, or, in this case, government secrets. Hitchcock always maintained that he didn't care what the MacGuffin was, so long as the characters thought it was important. In *North by Northwest*, no mention is ever made of what the secrets are, making them the ultimate Hitchcock MacGuffin—they are nothing!

Hitchcock's long-standing wish to film a chase sequence on Mount Rushmore was finally realized in this film, but through no help of the U.S. government or the Department of the Interior, which threw endless roadblocks in his path and drew up strict rules about what could and could not be done at the site and even in the studio. (Of course, none of the chase actually occurs on

Mount Rushmore, as it would have been far too dangerous; it was all shot in the MGM studio). As his revenge, Hitchcock removed the credit from the film that would have thanked the government for its cooperation.

The original working title for the film was *In a Northerly Direction*, which seemed cumbersome, so *Breathless* was suggested and seems unusually apt, considering the number of chases. Another suggestion was *The Man in Lincoln's Nose*, as Hitchcock planned a scene in which Grant is standing in the giant nose of Abe Lincoln and has a sneezing spell, but it was never filmed.

Grant had wanted Sophia Loren for his leading lady, having worked with her on two other films and being in love with her. They had nearly married, and he hoped that working together on another film might lure her away from Carlo Ponti.

BEST LINE: As Thornhill is trying to escape the police, he tries to buy a ticket for the Twentieth Century Limited at Grand Central Station. The ticket seller, who has seen his picture in the paper as a wanted murderer, questions him about the sunglasses he's wearing. "Something wrong with your eyes?" "Yes," Thornhill replies. "They're sensitive to questions."

TOUCH OF EVIL
1958

TYPE OF FILM:	*Noir*
STUDIO:	Universal-International
PRODUCER:	Albert Zugsmith
DIRECTOR:	Orson Welles
SCREENWRITER:	Orson Welles
SOURCE:	*Badge of Evil*, novel by Whit Masterson
RUNNING TIME:	108 minutes

PRINCIPAL PLAYERS:

Charlton Heston . . . . .Captain Miguel "Mike" Vargas
Janet Leigh . . . . .Susan Vargas
Orson Welles . . . . .Hank Quinlan
Joseph Calleia . . . . .Pete Menzies
Akim Tamiroff . . . ."Uncle" Joe Grandi
Joanna Moore . . . . .Marcia Linneker
Victor Millan . . . . .Manolo Sanchez
Marlene Dietrich . . . . .Madame Tana
Dennis Weaver . . . . .hotel clerk
Ray Collins . . . . .District Attorney Adair
Zsa Zsa Gabor . . . . .owner of strip joint

DID YOU KNOW? There are uncredited cameo appearances by Mercedes McCambridge, Joseph Cotten, and Keenan Wynn, all friends of Welles.

THE STORY: Los Robles is a small, rotting Mexican border town filled with corruption. When a Mexican narcotics detective, Captain Miguel ("Mike") Vargas, drives through on his honeymoon with Susie, he witnesses a car exploding and takes interest in the case because the car had also recently come over the Mexican border.

It quickly becomes evident to Vargas that Hank Quinlan, the dissolute 300-pound local Texas police captain, plans to frame a young Mexican, Sanchez, for the crime, so he stays in the worn-out hellhole to learn why. His investigations into the long career of Quinlan reveal that he never got over the murder of his wife

248

thirty years earlier and that he has sunk to excessive drinking and eating. When a former girlfriend, Madame Tana, sees him after some years, she says, "I didn't recognize you. You should lay off those candy bars." He runs the town, doing the dirty work for the district attorney and the police chief, both of whom fear him, and both of whom he finds contemptible because of their corruption. When Quinlan learns that Vargas is becoming a threat, he joins forces with "Uncle" Joe Grandi, the town drug lord, to bring down the incorruptible Mexican cop. Grandi terrorizes Vargas's wife, Susie, planting drugs in her room in an attempt to portray her as an addict, but Quinlan decides to go a step further and murders Grandi, planning to pin the crime on the "drug-crazed" girl.

When the vicious double cross is revealed to Quinlan's partner, Pete Menzies, it marks the beginning of the end for the bloated cop, as his old friend betrays him to Vargas.

* * *

This strange, dark, film was made as a B movie on a small budget, as a distrustful studio would allow Orson Welles very little freedom with its budget. Offered the role of Quinlan, Welles offered to write the screenplay and direct the film for no additional money, hoping it would be the beginning of a return to a filmmaking career in Hollywood. *Touch of Evil* was to be the last film he ever made in Hollywood. It is possible to draw a parallel with Welles's career and that of Quinlan's, both of whom were doomed by their arrogance. The last line of the movie, then a commercial failure but now regarded as one of the great films of all time, was spoken softly by the madame of the whorehouse in which Quinlan spent some time. "Adios." (Incidentally, though identified as "Tanya" in the screenplay, Dietrich is called "Tana" in the film). Although Welles came in only a few dollars over budget, his time in the editing room was moving along so slowly that the studio took away his right to edit the film as he wanted to, adding some scenes and removing others, sending Welles back to Europe (where he'd been in self-imposed exile for several years).

In 1998, *Touch of Evil* was reedited according to Orson Welles's fifty-eight-page memo, written just after he was removed from the film, bringing it as close as possible to his vision. One of the most famous opening shots in film history, a three-minute twenty-second tracking shot, was shown as intended, without superimposed titles and with various bits of local music instead of Henry Mancini's score.

BEST LINE: Hank Quinlan walks into a familiar sporting house and sees Madame Tana spreading a deck of tarot cards: "Come on, read my future for me." Tana says, "You haven't got any." Quinlan, taken aback, mumbles, "Huh? Whadda ya mean?" Tana: "Your future is all used up."

THE PUBLIC ENEMY
1931

TYPE OF FILM: Gangster

STUDIO: Warner Brothers

PRODUCER: Darryl F. Zanuck

DIRECTOR: William Wellman

SCREENWRITERS: Kubec Glasmon and John Bright; Harvey Thew (adaptation)

SOURCE: "Beer and Blood," story by John Bright

RUNNING TIME: 83 minutes

PRINCIPAL PLAYERS:

James Cagney . . . . .Tom Powers
Jean Harlow . . . . .Gwen Allen
Edward Woods . . . . .Matt Doyle
Beryl Mercer . . . . .Ma Powers
Donald Cook . . . . .Mike Powers
Joan Blondell . . . . .Mamie
Mae Clarke . . . . .Kitty
Leslie Fenton . . . . .Samuel "Nails" Nathan
Robert O'Connor . . . . .Paddy Ryan
Murray Kinnell . . . . .Putty Nose
Frankie Darro . . . . .Matt Doyle as a boy
Purnell Pratt . . . . .Officer Powers, Tom's father

DID YOU KNOW? The role of Tom Powers, which made James Cagney one of Hollywood's biggest stars, was originally cast with Edward Woods in the role. After a few days of shooting, director William A. Wellman recognized the power of Cagney, who was playing Matt Doyle, and had the two actors switch roles. Producer Darryl F. Zanuck was opposed to the switch because he believed that the diminutive Cagney didn't have the strength to play the vicious psychopath. Furthermore, Zanuck was afraid of making an enemy of Woods's mother-in-law, the hugely powerful Hollywood gossip columnist Louella Parsons. However, once Zanuck saw Cagney in the role, he relented, and the song-and-dance performer would be forever associated with the toughest of tough-guy roles.

THE STORY: Tom Powers and Matt Doyle, friends as teenagers in Chicago, engage in petty crime and commit a robbery set up for them by their fence, Putty Nose. Although he has promised to protect them, Putty Nose turns his back on them when it goes wrong. As adults, the two friends run a brewery during Prohibition for Paddy Ryan. They progress to working for the big boss, Nails Nathan, as strong-arm men forcing speakeasies to carry only Nathan's beer. Tom's ruthlessness is prized by Nathan and he gains power, but a horse riding accident kills Nathan (Tom later shoots the horse), beginning a gang war. Ryan tells his gang to hide out until things cool down but Tom refuses, and he and Matt are attacked by rival gang members, who kill Matt. Tom goes berserk and single-handedly takes on the gang, killing several of the thugs, but is wounded himself. Taken to a hospital, he survives, only to be kidnapped and killed by the gangsters. His dead body, swaddled in bandages, is dropped on the steps of his mother's house.

* * *

The Public Enemy was a tremendous success, breaking the box-office records set the previous year by *Little Caesar*. Cagney was so well-liked by audiences that they found themselves rooting for him against their will, even though the movie showed him to be an amoral psychopath.

While the story of Tom Powers follows the traditional gangster movie arc of a criminal's life—starting out poor, being ruthless and determined enough to rise, and ultimately being killed—it is somewhat different from *Little Caesar* and *Scarface* in that Powers never becomes the big boss; he remains a powerful and loyal soldier for the head of his gang.

Cagney, like George Raft, grew up in the Hell's Kitchen section of New York, so he learned a good deal about scuffling at the edges of the law as a kid, and a fair amount about the behavior of hoodlums as an adult.

After the success of *Little Caesar*, William Wellman wanted to make a gangster movie based on the life of the Irish mobster "Deanie" O'Bannion, but Zanuck initially turned him down, fearing that nothing new could be made in the genre after *Little Caesar*. When Wellman promised him a film that would be tougher, more violent, and more realistic, Zanuck relented but gave Wellman only $151,000 and twenty-six days to make the movie.

Failure is an orphan, but success has many fathers. In this case,

252

the notorious scene in which Cagney pushes a grapefruit into the startled face of Mae Clark (she really *was* startled—Cagney was supposed to fake it but actually smashed it into her face) has been claimed to be the idea of several people. In Wellman's autobiography, he wrote that during an argument with his wife he fantasized about doing it. Another source claims that mobster "Hymie" Weiss shoved an omelette into his girlfriend's face. Zanuck, too, claims to have conceived the scene. Whoever was responsible managed to produce one of the most iconic moments in the history of Hollywood and one of the most shockingly violent acts against a woman at a time when this was uncommon behavior.

The scene in which Tom shoots the horse is based on events surrounding the death of real-life gangster Samuel "Nails" Morton.

BEST LINE: Tom Powers, shot numerous times, stumbling toward his death, rasps, "I ain't so tough."

THE NIGHT OF THE HUNTER
1955

TYPE OF FILM:	Crime/Suspense
STUDIO:	United Artists
PRODUCER:	Paul Gregory
DIRECTOR:	Charles Laughton
SCREENWRITER:	James Agee
SOURCE:	*The Night of the Hunter*, novel by Davis Grubb
RUNNING TIME:	93 minutes

PRINCIPAL PLAYERS:

Robert Mitchum . . . . .Preacher Harry Powell
Shelley Winters . . . . .Willa Harper
Lillian Gish . . . . .Rachel Cooper
Evelyn Varden . . . . .Icey Spoon
Peter Graves . . . . .Ben Harper
James Gleason . . . . .Birdie Steptoe
Billy Chapin . . . . .John Harper
Don Beddoe . . . . .Walt Spoon
Sally Jane Bruce . . . . .Pearl Harper
Gloria Castilo . . . . .Ruby

DID YOU KNOW? Although generally regarded as one of the great American films, *The Night of the Hunter* was such a staggering failure at the box office that Charles Laughton's first directorial effort was also his last. He was never again allowed to work behind the camera, so he resumed his position in front of it as one of filmdom's greatest actors. Laughton, using decidedly European stylistic techniques, most notably German Expressionism, with one film became a tremendous influence on some of today's most successful directors, including Martin Scorsese, just as Laughton in turn had been strongly influenced by Fritz Lang and Josef von Sternberg.

THE STORY: Unable to provide for his family in the Depression-era Midwest, Ben Harper commits a bank robbery and kills two people. Before the police can arrest him, he hides the $10,000 he stole in his daughter Pearl's rag doll, swearing her and his son, John, to secrecy about the hiding place.

A preacher, Harry Powell is arrested for stealing a car and is sent to prison. As Ben's cellmate, he overhears him talking in his sleep about the money. Ben is executed. When Powell is released, he sets out to find Ben's widow, Willa, and the stolen loot. When he arrives in town, he first ingratiates himself with Icey and Walt Spoon, proprietors of the diner and friends of Willa. He easily sweet-talks Willa into marriage, much to the displeasure of John, who distrusts him.

On their wedding night, Willa pretties herself with a negligee, but, when she comes to bed, he rebuffs her and preaches to her about her sinful lust. Powell asks Willa where the money is, but she truthfully swears she doesn't know. He repeatedly attempts to get the children to tell him, especially impressionable little Pearl, but John holds her to the promise they made to their father. As Powell becomes more and more frustrated with his inability to find the stolen money, he kills Willa and chases the children, who barely manage to escape his violent attacks. They get to a little rowboat in the river just ahead of Powell's grasp and float away while he steals a horse and slowly stalks them.

After a lengthy journey, the boat drifts ashore and the children are awakened by Rachel, who tells them to follow her home, where the kindly spinster has already taken in other stray children. The next day, Powell shows up at Rachel's cottage, telling her that he is a preacher and the children's father, but John says he isn't their father, and Rachel adds that he's no preacher either. When friendly smiles and charm fail to convince Rachel to give him the children, he angrily demands that she turn them over, but Rachel pulls out a shotgun and shoots at him. Screaming wildly, he takes refuge in the barn, so Rachel calls the police, telling them that she has "something trapped in my barn." The police arrive and drag him out of the barn, and John suddenly feels sorry for him, grabbing the doll from his sister's hands and wildly battering Powell with it as the bills fly all around. In town, a lynch mob gathers to string up the preacher, the loudest of the mob being Icey and Walt Spoon.

* * *

This unrelievedly dark and suspenseful tale may have been the finest performance of Robert Mitchum's long career, but he grew to hate it. The character was so unredeemably evil that it haunted Mitchum, and he grew increasingly uncomfortable being identified with it.

Director Charles Laughton had believed (probably correctly) that no other actor could so powerfully portray the psychopathic preacher who had LOVE tattooed on one hand and HATE on the other. When Laughton called Mitchum to play the role, he explained that he would play "a diabolical crud," and Mitchum replied, "Present!"

Mitchum not only played one of the most searing film roles of all time, he helped Laughton with a task that the director despised and was unable to manage: the directing of the children. Laughton apparently loathed the two principal child actors and was unable to communicate with them, while Mitchum, laid-back as always, had fun with them and got them to do whatever was needed.

James Agee was paid $30,000 to write the screenplay and died soon after he completed it. However, the script he turned in was more than twice as long as was filmable, so Laughton rewrote the entire motion picture, without any screen credit. This is attested to in the autobiography of Elsa Lanchester, Laughton's wife.

The film was made on a very modest budget, so most of it needed to be shot in the studio. One of the most memorable images was of Preacher Powell riding his horse on a ridge against the night sky. To make the silhouette appear to be in the distance of a deserted country setting within the confines of a small studio, Laughton miniaturized the horse and rider. It wasn't Robert Mitchum riding a horse, it was a midget riding a pony.

In spite of now being regarded as a classic of American cinema, *The Night of the Hunter* was not nominated for a single Academy Award.

BEST LINE: Icey Spoon, Willa Harper's busybody neighbor, talking to a group of women about Ben Harper's death and the sense of loss felt by his widow and their obviously earthy relationship: "She's mooning about Ben Harper. That wasn't love. That was just flapdoodle. . . . When you've been married to a man forty years, you know all that don't amount to a hill of beans. I've been married to my Walt that long, and I swear in all that time I just lied there thinking about my canning."

SUNSET BOULEVARD
1950

TYPE OF FILM:	*Noir*
STUDIO:	Paramount
PRODUCER:	Charles Brackett
DIRECTOR:	Billy Wilder
SCREENWRITERS:	Charles Brackett, Billy Wilder, and D. M. Marshman, Jr.
SOURCE:	Original
RUNNING TIME:	110 minutes

PRINCIPAL PLAYERS:

William Holden . . . . .Joe Gillis
Gloria Swanson . . . . .Norma Desmond
Erich von Stroheim . . . . .Max Von Mayerling
Nancy Olson . . . . .Betty Schaefer
Fred Clark . . . . .Sheldrake
Jack Webb . . . . .Artie Green
Lloyd Gough . . . . .Morino
Franklin Farnum . . . . .undertaker

DID YOU KNOW? *Sunset Boulevard* opened the door to a large number of dark films about Tinseltown itself. There was a rash of *mea culpas* in Hollywood in the early and mid fifties with the release of *In a Lonely Place, The Big Knife, A Star Is Born, The Bad and the Beautiful,* and *The Barefoot Contessa,* the best known of the exposés of Hollywood. Never before had an industry worked so hard to show itself in the worst possible light. Perhaps the attempts at self-immolation were a result of the investigations of the House Un-American Activities Committee; perhaps it was the breakup of the studio system that kept actors and writers under long-term contracts; perhaps it was the government-forced divestment of studio-owned theaters; or perhaps it was the rise of television's popularity; but whatever the reason, the bright lights and glamour of Hollywood would never again be as appealing to mass audiences.

THE STORY: Out-of-work screenwriter Joe Gillis, broke and on the run from repo men who want to take his car for nonpayment, pulls into the driveway of a huge but desiccated mansion owned by former silent-screen star Norma Desmond. He is brought to Desmond by the butler, Max Von Mayerling, who also happens to be her former husband. After a brief conversation, she hires him to write the screenplay that will be her vehicle back to the top of Hollywood stardom. She insists that he move into her house, where he falls uncomfortably into the role of gigolo. He tries to get away from her possessive clutches, but when a New Year's Eve party she has thrown just for him goes awry, she tries to kill herself, bringing him back. While working on her comeback movie, Gillis meets another young screenwriter, Betty Schaefer, and, inspired again, begins a new screenplay that he believes will be his best work to date. They fall in love and Desmond becomes enraged with jealousy. She calls Betty to tell her that Gillis lives off her, in the clothes she buys for him, in her house. When Betty comes to the old mansion to see for herself, Gillis cruelly admits exactly what he is, sending her off to the man she used to love. He then packs to leave, and Desmond breaks down and shoots him. As his corpse is pulled out of the swimming pool, the police and media swarm over the estate. As news cameras roll, Desmond, believing them to be movie cameras, regally descends her staircase and, chin held high, announces, "All right, Mr. DeMille. I'm ready for my closeup."

* * *

Famously, the film opens with the star, William Holden, floating dead in the swimming pool. With voice-over narration, the entire story unfolds in flashback.

Film historians have often described the great era of noir films as being bracketed by two of Billy Wilder's motion pictures, starting with *Double Indemnity* (1944) and concluding with *Sunset Boulevard* six years later. There are exceptions, of course, notably *Touch of Evil* (1958), but the time in which every studio had two or three dark crime dramas a year in production had largely ended with this Gothic masterpiece.

The grand old mansion in which most of the film was shot belonged to the Getty family, and Wilder thought it would be perfect as a location. Unfortunately, it did not have a swimming pool—clearly a necessity—so the studio built one for the movie and removed it after the film was completed.

Academy Award nominations went to the film for Best Picture, to Wilder for Best Director, to Holden for Best Actor, to Swanson for Best Actress, to Von Stroheim for Best Supporting Actor, and to Olson for Best Supporting Actress. All lost. Altogether, the film had eleven nominations and won three, including Best Story and Screenplay to Charles Brackett, Billy Wilder, and D. M. Marshman, Jr.

Billy Wilder initially had offered the role of Norma Desmond to Mae West, who turned it down. He then considered Mary Pickford but decided she would be wrong after all. He then offered it to Pola Negri, who also turned it down. He finally settled on Swanson, who got an Oscar nomination.

Cecil B. DeMille played himself, and there were cameos by Hedda Hopper, Buster Keaton, Anna Q. Nilsson, H. B. Warner, Ray Evans, and Jay Livingston, all of whom played themselves.

BEST LINE: Screenwriter Joe Gillis recognizes the silent-film star: "You're Norma Desmond. You used to be in silent pictures. You used to be big." "I am still big," she replies. "It's the pictures that got small."

WHO FRAMED ROGER RABBIT?
1988

TYPE OF FILM: Detective/Comedy

STUDIO: Touchstone-Amblin Silver Screen

EXECUTIVE PRODUCERS: Steven Spielberg and Kathleen Kennedy

PRODUCERS: Robert Watts and Frank Marshall

DIRECTOR: Robert Zemeckis

SCREENWRITERS: Jeffrey Price and Peter S. Seaman

SOURCE: *Who Censored Roger Rabbit?*, novel by Gary K. Wolf

RUNNING TIME: 103 minutes

PRINCIPAL PLAYERS:

Bob Hoskins . . . . Eddie Valiant
Christopher Lloyd . . . . Judge Doom
Joanna Cassidy . . . . Dolores
Stubby Kaye . . . . Marvin Acme
Alan Tilvern . . . . R. K. Maroon
Charles Fleischer . . . Voices of Roger Rabbit, Benny the Cab, and others
Lou Hirsch . . . . Voice of Baby Herman
Mel Blanc . . . . . . Voices of Daffy Duck, Tweety Bird, and others

DID YOU KNOW? Actor Bob Hoskins managed perhaps the most difficult achievement of his applaudable career by acting and interacting with empty space. As most of those playing opposite him are cartoon characters who were drawn into the frames after the live acting was completed, Hoskins had to pretend that he was speaking to someone, fighting with someone, engaged in a tug-of-war, etc., while in fact he was going it solo. To help prepare for the part, he watched his young daughter so that he could learn to act with imaginary characters. His son, meanwhile, was angry with him for failing to bring his cartoon costars home with him so that they could be introduced to, and play with, the young boy. Hoskins later had problems with frequent and believable hallucinations.

THE STORY: In 1947 Los Angeles, Roger Rabbit is a "Toon," a derogatory term for the characters who can perform many extraordinary things and suffer great violence without suffering serious injury but are despised by humans for their free-spirited, fun-loving ways. They are permitted to work in Hollywood with humans but then must return to Toontown, segregated from the rest of society.

When Roger seems to lack focus in his films, the owner of Maroon Cartoons guesses that he must be having marital problems, so he hires Eddie Valiant, a two-bit private detective, to check up on Roger's sexy wife, Jessica Rabbit. Valiant hates Toons, whom he believes murdered his brother, a cop, by dropping a safe on his head.

Valiant spots Jessica backstage at the nightclub where she sings, playing patty-cake (literally) with Marvin Acme, a prop supplier, and provides photographs to Roger. The next day, Acme is found murdered, a safe having been dropped on his head, and Roger is suspected.

Acme's death is a severe blow to the Toons because he owned the land on which Toontown was built and he had always acted kindly toward them. Roger swears he is innocent and hires the reluctant Valiant to find evidence that will clear him.

Judge Doom, a Toon-hating human, is eager to catch Roger and kill him with his invention, "The Dip," which is the only certain way to kill a Toon—it erases them. Doom wants Roger out of the way because he has a plan to use the land for an off-ramp for a massive highway network that will replace the clean, efficient, and inexpensive trolley system currently in use.

Valiant traces the murder to Judge Doom, and a battle between the detective and the villain ensues, with the lives of Roger and Jessica, and all of Toontown, at stake. A giant steamroller, brought to Toontown to spray "The Dip" all over it and wipe out everyone and everything, runs over Judge Doom during the battle. When he immediately pops up, alive and unhurt, he reveals that he is a Toon himself, finally melting and being erased by his own mixture of death, saving the Rabbits, who love each other, and Toontown and its residents.

Who Framed Roger Rabbit?, in addition to being one of the most entertaining films of modern times, is also one of the most innovative. It combines human and animation figures so realistically that audiences suspend disbelief after a few scenes and are as concerned with Toon characters as they would be with human actors.

This was not the first time that animation was mixed with real-life actors, with Disney having done it in *Song of the South* (1946) and again in *Mary Poppins* (1964), and Warner Brothers doing it briefly in a 1940 cartoon by Fritz Freleng, *You Ought to Be in Pictures*, in which Porky Pig and Daffy Duck demand better treatment from the real-life animation-department head Leon Schlesinger.

Although it was not the first, *Who Framed Roger Rabbit?* displays by far the most accomplished and ambitious use of this difficult technique, making the interaction between cartoon and real-life characters utterly convincing. The near-miraculous achievement of Steven Spielberg's Industrial Light and Magic Company, the director of animation, Richard Williams, and literally hundreds of animators cannot be praised too highly.

Perhaps equally miraculous is that all the major film studios cooperated in the production, an unheard of agreement in the highly competitive and protective world of Hollywood, where copyrights and trademarks are the fountain from which countless dollars flow. Disney permitted the use of Mickey Mouse and Donald Duck, Warner Brothers allowed Bugs Bunny and Daffy Duck to appear, Paramount gave permission for Betty Boop, Universal agreed to let Woody Woodpecker make an appearance, and virtually every other well-known cartoon character has at least a cameo role.

Kathleen Turner supplied the speaking voice of the sexy Jessica Rabbit but was uncredited; Amy Irving supplied her singing voice.

BEST LINE: Jessica Rabbit, who looks like an incredibly sexy human, is uncomfortable with her voluptuous figure, and tells Eddie Valiant, "You don't know what it's like being a woman looking the way I do." Valiant replies, "You don't know what it's like being a man looking at a woman looking the way you do." Later, Jessica says, "I'm not bad. I'm just drawn that way."

DOUBLE INDEMNITY
1944

TYPE OF FILM: *Noir*

STUDIO: Paramount

PRODUCER: Joseph Sistrom

DIRECTOR: Billy Wilder

SCREENWRITERS: Billy Wilder and Raymond Chandler

SOURCE: *Double Indemnity*, novella by James M. Cain

RUNNING TIME: 107 minutes

PRINCIPAL PLAYERS:

Barbara Stanwyck . . . . .Phyllis Dietrichson
Fred MacMurray . . . . .Walter Neff
Edward G. Robinson . . . . .Barton Keyes
Porter Hall . . . . Mr. Jackson
Jean Heather . . . . .Lola Dietrichson
Tom Powers . . . . .Mr. Dietrichson
Byron Barr . . . . .Nino Zachette
Richard Gaines . . . . .Mr. Norton

DID YOU KNOW? Billy Wilder, the director, cowriter, and driving force in bringing James M. Cain's novella to the screen, had a terrible time getting people to work with him on it. His usual collaborator on screenplays, Charles Brackett, reportedly found the story so repugnant that he refused to have anything to do with it. Barbara Stanwyck agreed to star because she wanted to broaden her image from the usual "good girl" roles she'd had, but virtually every male lead walked away from the project, including George Raft, who made a career of walking away from one great film after another (*The Maltese Falcon* and *Casablanca*, to name two, had both been offered to him). Finally, Fred MacMurray, who had previously played lighthearted song-and-dance men, went against type and took the role that made him a star.

THE STORY: Insurance salesman Walter Neff calls on a policyholder, Mr. Dietrichson, to sell him a life-insurance policy, only to run into his sexy young wife. He is instantly drawn to her, and they engage in sexual double entendre conversation that makes it clear they are attracted to each other. Phyllis Dietrichson convinces Neff that they could be married if Dietrichson had a fatal accident, which would pay her double the $50,000 indemnity on the insurance policy. After they plot to murder her husband, Neff conceives the plan that will make the crime look like an accident and then carries it out. Barton Keyes, an investigator at Neff's insurance company, is assigned to look into the case and becomes convinced that Dietrichson was murdered. As Keyes moves closer and closer to a solution, Neff realizes that Phyllis has used him only to get the money, and he plans to kill her. When the confrontation between the two takes place, she beats him to the punch and shoots him once but, realizing that she truly does love him, she can't finish him off. Neff then shoots her twice, killing her. Having confessed the entire story to Keyes on a recording, Neff dies of his wounds.

* * *

This hugely important film not only defined the noir genre, it was a milestone for Hollywood motion pictures in general. For the first time, audiences saw a murder planned and carried out as the two protagonists risked everything for greed and lust. The whopping sum of $25,000 had been paid to Cain for the novella, which had run in *Liberty* magazine, even though the Production Code Administration, Hollywood's censoring body, had warned that it would never get on the screen.

Wilder brought in Raymond Chandler, who had never before written a screenplay, to turn the amoral Cain story into a screenplay. Changing the overt sex into innuendo turned the trick and it was filmed.

Wilder and Chandler took an instant dislike to each other while working on the film. Chandler was quiet and dignified, reticent and shy, and married to a woman twenty years older than he (he was fifty-five at the time). Wilder was loud, arrogant, uncouth, and dated several beautiful young women at the same time. But Chandler learned from Wilder how to write a screenplay (getting two Oscar nominations within four years), and Wilder recognized the extraordinary talent of an author whose work mainly had been published in pulp magazines.

Oscar nominations went to the film for Best Picture, Billy Wilder for Best Director, Barbara Stanwyck for Best Actress, and Raymond Chandler for Best Screenplay. All lost.

The original ending had Neff going to the gas chamber and showed his execution in full detail. Wilder decided this scene was unnecessary.

A television version of *Double Indemnity* was produced in 1973, adapted by Steven Bochco and starring Samantha Eggar, Richard Crenna, and Lee J. Cobb.

BEST LINE: Neff has just met the sexy and scantily clad wife of the man to whom he's selling a large life insurance policy. The man's not in, so she suggests that he return to speak to her husband. "Mr. Neff, why don't you drop by tomorrow evening around eight-thirty. He'll be in then." "Who?" Neff asks. "My husband," she replies. "You were anxious to talk to him, weren't you?" "Yeah, I was," Neff responds, "but I'm sort of getting over the idea, if you know what I mean."

THE STING
1973

TYPE OF FILM: Crime/Comedy
STUDIO: Universal
PRODUCERS: Tony Bill, Michael and Julia Phillips
DIRECTOR: George Roy Hill
SCREENWRITER: David S. Ward
SOURCE: Original
RUNNING TIME: 129 minutes

PRINCIPAL PLAYERS:

Paul Newman . . . . .Henry Gondorff
Robert Redford . . . . .Johnny Hooker
Robert Shaw . . . . .Doyle Lonnegan
Charles Durning . . . . .Lt. William Snyder
Ray Walston . . . . .J. J. Singleton
Eileen Brennan . . . . .Billie
John Heffernan . . . . .Eddie Niles
Harold Gould . . . . .Kid Twist
Dana Elcar . . . . .F.B.I. Agent Polk
Robert Earl James . . . . .Luther Coleman

DID YOU KNOW? When *The Sting* was first planned, Paul Newman was not scheduled to have any part in it. Robert Redford had teamed with Paul Newman four years earlier in *Butch Cassidy and the Sundance Kid,* and their charisma, combined with director George Roy Hill's skill as a story-teller, had made the film one of the biggest box-office smashes of 1969. Redford was winding up his work on *The Way We Were* and preparing to star in *The Great Waldo Pepper* when he read the script for *The Sting,* an original screenplay by David S. Ward, who was set to direct it as well. Redford saw the great possibilities of the old-fashioned comic caper film as a vehicle for himself but was reluctant to trust a first-time director and talked with Hill about it. When the studio decided to use Hill as the director, Redford committed to it, and when Newman heard of it, he was not pleased with Hill, believing there should be a part for him so that the successful trio could be reunited. Hill reconsidered the part of Henry Gondorff, which had been dramatically smaller and portrayed the con man as a crude slob. There was a fair amount of rewriting to accommodate the two stars, who received a healthy (in 1973) half million dollars each; Newman also got a share of the gross, and *The Sting* became an enormous box-office hit.

THE STORY: In 1936, in Joliet, Illinois, Johnny Hooker and his partner, Luther Coleman, swindle a gangster courier out of a large cash delivery, so his boss, Doyle Lonnegan, orders them killed. Corrupt police lieutenant William Snyder learns of Hooker's haul and shakes him down for half the take, most of which Hooker has already lost in a gambling den. He, too, threatens to kill Hooker if he doesn't come up with more money. Coleman, ready to retire after his big score, is killed by Lonnegan's men, and Hooker promises to avenge his friend's murder by swindling the big-time gangster out of a fortune.

Hooker goes to Chicago to team up with Harry Gondorff, described as "the greatest con artist of them all," and they agree to do a "big con" on Lonnegan. They set up a classy but bogus gambling parlor and are offered the assistance of any con men they need, as all are eager to get revenge on the swaggering Lonnegan.

The con begins with Newman outcheating Lonnegan in a big poker game and Hooker telling their mark all about it, acting as the ambitious right-hand man who wants to take over his employer's rackets. He explains to Lonnegan that he has a system for beating Gondorff by "past-posting" him on horse races—i.e., placing bets after the results are already known to him but not to the betting parlor. After several tests and payoffs, Lonnegan trusts the system and Hooker.

Meanwhile, the FBI has entered the case, and Snyder is told to bring Hooker in, where he is forced to turn on Gondorff by informing agent Polk about the time and location of the "sting" that is to be perpetrated. When the moment arrives, Lonnegan hands over a suitcase with $500,000 to bet on a horse. As the result comes in, so does the FBI, and Gondorff recognizes that he has been betrayed by Hooker and shoots him, whereupon Polk shoots Gondorff. Lt. Synder hustles Lonnegan out of the betting parlor to protect him from involvement, leaving the suitcase full of cash behind. When the crook and the cop are out of sight of the gambling joint, Hooker and Gondorff get up from their faked deaths and everyone, including the phony FBI agent, celebrates the successful sting.

* * *

The fast-moving action, razzle-dazzle sets and costumes, great cast of character actors, best pairing of stars since Hepburn and Tracy, and a brilliant twisting plot combine to make this one of the most satisfying and watchable films ever made. The nostalgia oozes from sets that are a little too perfect and clean, costumes that are simply too original and enchanting, an unbelievable Redford as a two-bit lowlife, and the entire criminal element, which is a little too Runyanesque to be taken seriously. Realism is not what this picture is about, and if you seek it in this film, you were born without a sense of humor or the ability to enjoy magic.

Marvin Hamlisch adapted the ragtime music of Scott Joplin so wonderfully that he won an Oscar for Best Adapted Score and helped the nation rediscover the joys of old-time ragtime. In the same year, he won the Oscar for Best Original Dramatic Score for *The Way We Were*.

When Henry Gondorff, played by Paul Newman, is introduced to Doyle Lonnegan played by Robert Shaw, Gondorff is introduced as "Mr. Shaw."

The Sting was nominated for ten Academy Awards, winning seven, including Best Picture, Best Director (George Roy Hill), and Best Original Screenplay (David S. Ward).

At the Academy Awards ceremony, the big moment is always the presentation of the Oscar for Best Picture, which was to be presented by Elizabeth Taylor. As David Niven was introducing her, a genius by the name of Robert Opal streaked in front of the live audience and untold millions around the world. Comic singer and songwriter Ray Stevens was inspired to write "The Streak," which became the number-one record in America. Six years later, Opal was found murdered in his sex shop in San Francisco.

As good as *The Sting* is, it couldn't sustain a sequel. *The Sting II* (1983), incredibly also written by David S. Ward, who should have quit while he was ahead, starred Jackie Gleason and Mac Davis in the roles created by Newman and Redford, hard as that might be to comprehend.

BEST LINE: Johnny Hooker sees Doyle Lonnegan for the first time and says, "He's not as tough as he thinks." Henry Gondorff replies, "Neither are we."

PSYCHO
1960

TYPE OF FILM:	Suspense
STUDIO:	Paramount
PRODUCER:	Alfred Hitchcock
DIRECTOR:	Alfred Hitchcock
SCREENWRITER:	Joseph Stefano
SOURCE:	*Psycho*, novel by Robert Bloch
RUNNING TIME:	109 minutes

PRINCIPAL PLAYERS:

Anthony Perkins . . . . .Norman Bates
Janet Leigh . . . . .Marion Crane
Vera Miles . . . . .Lila Crane
John Gavin . . . . .Sam Loomis
Martin Balsam . . . . .Arbogast
John McIntire . . . . .Al Chambers
Simon Oakland . . . . .psychiatrist
John Anderson . . . ."California Charlie"
Lurene Tuttle . . . . .Mrs. Chambers
Frank Albertson . . . . .Cassidy
Pat Hitchcock . . . . .Caroline

DID YOU KNOW? Perhaps the most famous scene in cinematic history, the violent shower murder—which has been analyzed, written about, imitated, parodied, and remained in viewers' memories four decades after it was made—barely involved the film's principals. Janet Leigh, whose naked body is attacked by the killer's huge knife, was actually used only for her hands and face, the rest of her body being replaced by a nude model. Anthony Perkins, the psychopathic schizophrenic, was in New York, preparing for a play, and another actor was dressed up in his costume and makeup. Even the director, Alfred Hitchcock, had turned over the meticulous laying out of the scene, virtually frame by frame, to Saul Bass, the art director who designed the titles (as he also did for *Vertigo* and *North by Northwest*). Hitchcock himself added only two shots: the knife actually entering the abdomen, and the blood mixing with the water as it is washed down the drain. Apart from that, the storyboard created by Bass was followed precisely.

THE STORY: Marion Crane meets her lover, recently divorced Sam Loomis, in a hotel room for a liaison on her lunch hour. Wanting to be married to Sam, who is unable to afford it, she steals $40,000 from her real estate firm when her employer asks her to deposit the cash, taking off in her car instead. That night, she stops at a run-down motel and chats with Norman Bates, the friendly owner, who tells her that he lives in the nearby house with his aged and apparently demanding mother.

As Marion undresses for a shower, Bates watches her through a small hole in the wall. While in the shower, she suddenly sees a shadow and is viciously attacked and killed by an old woman wielding a huge knife. Bates, apparently irritated at his mother for the violent act, nonetheless cleans up the bathroom, puts Marion in the trunk of her car, and sinks it in a nearby swamp.

Sam, aided by Marion's sister, Lila, sets out to find the missing girl, as does an insurance detective, Arbogast, who is intent on retrieving the stolen money. The detective traces Marion to the Bates Motel and becomes suspicious when Bates is caught in lies and refuses to let him see his mother. He telephones Lila and Sam to inform them of his progress and sneaks back to the house to try to question the old woman. Just as he reaches the top of the stairs, he is attacked by the knife-wielding old woman, his already dead body toppling back down the stairs.

Lila and Sam talk to the local sheriff and learn that, in fact, Bates's mother has been dead for ten years. They go to the house, and Lila is attacked but escapes serious harm. In the fight that ensues, it is revealed that Norman is a schizophrenic, a friendly young man who becomes a violent maniac when he takes on his mother's personality.

* * *

Psycho was a tremendously influential film that, for all its brilliance, caused a terrible decline in horror and suspense films as less-talented writers and directors now felt free to show more and more graphic screen violence. Slasher films, unknown until then, have since become a staple of summer cinema, and the entire notion of subtlety appears to have died with Hitchcock.

Of all the successes enjoyed by Hitchcock, this was by far the most financially rewarding. Made for a preposterously little

270

$800,000, it earned Hitchcock a check for $2,000,000 within six months of its release and an additional $20,000,000 before his death.

It was cheaply made for several reasons—mainly because the actors were paid very modestly. Perkins, who had top billing, owed Paramount a picture and so had little negotiating position. In addition, he was eager to work with Hitchcock, as was Janet Leigh. Gavin and Miles were contract players who were being paid weekly salaries anyway. Already very active in his weekly television series, Hitchcock decided to save even more money by using his own TV studio and crew.

Years later, MCA became a huge conglomerate, as well as the parent company of Universal Pictures. Hitchcock left Paramount to go to Universal, where he exchanged his rights to *Psycho* and to his television programs in exchange for MCA stock, becoming its third-largest shareholder.

Oscar nominations went to Hitchcock for Best Director and Janet Leigh for Best Supporting Actress. An Edgar Allan Poe Award was given by the Mystery Writers of America to Joseph Stefano for his screenplay, and the organization also presented a special scroll to Robert Bloch, author of the novel that was followed closely for the film version. Anthony Perkins, in one of the most memorable screen performances of all time, was passed over.

Hitchcock Alert: That's the director standing on the sidewalk, wearing a large Texas hat.

BEST LINE: A rich braggart in her real estate office tells Marion that he is buying his daughter a house as a wedding present. "Forty thousand dollars," he asserts, "all cash." Caroline, the girl at the next desk, gasps, "I declare!" "I don't," the boor says. "That's how I get to keep it."

THE FRENCH CONNECTION
1971

TYPE OF FILM: Detective

STUDIO: Twentieth Century-Fox

PRODUCER: Philip D'Antoni

DIRECTOR: William Friedkin

SCREENWRITER: Ernest Tidyman

SOURCE: *The French Connection*, book by Robin Moore

RUNNING TIME: 104 minutes

PRINCIPAL PLAYERS:

Gene Hackman . . . . .Jimmy "Popeye" Doyle
Fernando Rey . . . . .Alain Charnier
Roy Scheider . . . . .Buddy Russo
Tony LoBianco . . . . .Sal Boca
Marcel Bozzuffi . . . . .Pierre Nicoli
Frederic De Pasquale . . . . .Devereaux
Bill Hickman . . . . .Mulderig
Ann Rebbot . . . . .Marie Charnier
Eddie Egan . . . . .Walter Simonson
Sonny Grosso . . . . .Klein

DID YOU KNOW? Because of his involvement with *The French Connection*, Eddie Egan, the real-life New York Police Department detective on whom Jimmy "Popeye" Doyle was based, was fired from his job only seven hours before his retirement papers were due to be signed.

Egan, one of the top cops of the NYPD, had, with his partner Sonny Grosso (the inspiration for Buddy Russo), cracked one of the biggest drug cases in New York City history, nabbing heroin worth $32,000,000 on the street. This case formed the basis for Robin Moore's book, subsequently made into *The French Connection*.

Hired to work on the film as a consultant along with a small role (as Walter Simonson), Egan was pleased with Gene Hackman's portrayal of him and was proud of the film. The NYPD, however, was not at all pleased to see its cops portrayed as vicious thugs who beat up suspects as brutally as criminals did. The image of rogue cops, ignoring the rules of the job as well as repeatedly breaking the laws they were sworn to uphold, enraged the department. Egan went on to do other film and television work, including small acting roles and consulting jobs, notably on *Prime Cut* (1972), which starred Lee Marvin and Gene Hackman; *The Seven-Ups* (1973), with Roy Scheider and Tony LoBianco; and *Report to the Commissioner* (1975), with Michael Moriarty.

THE STORY: Doyle and Russo spot a group of drug-involved crooks at a bar, and Doyle talks Russo into following the one they don't know, Sal Boca, "just for fun." They soon learn that they have stumbled onto one of the biggest drug deals ever to go down in New York, as 120 pounds of heroin are being smuggled into the United States from France in an automobile belonging to a French TV actor, Devereaux, who has no idea that he is smuggling drugs.

A major surveillance effort ensues, with the FBI being called in to work with the NYPD, and the principal suspects are followed. However, Alain Charnier (referred to by Doyle as "Frog One") spots Doyle's tail and loses him in the subway. With Doyle clearly their major problem, Charnier's associate, Pierre Nicoli, tries to shoot Doyle, accidentally killing a woman passing by. Doyle chases him to a rooftop and then to an elevated train, which Nicoli commandeers as the cop pursues him by car. When the train races out of control and crashes, Nicoli leaps out and Doyle shoots him.

The police realize that the drugs have been hidden in Devereaux's car, but they find it clean when they search. Doyle refuses to let the car go, knowing that the drugs must be there, and the car is virtually disassembled before they find the bags of powder in the rockers. The car is put back together and returned with apologies to the actor, who has been told that the car was stolen and recovered, and the police follow as he drives it to some ramshackle buildings on Ward's Island in New York's East River.

Just as the drug deal is about to be transacted, the police and FBI men, having surrounded the buildings, order the culprits to surrender, but the gangsters open fire and a full-scale gun battle ensues, during which Doyle accidentally shoots an FBI agent. When the roundup is concluded, Charnier has escaped, the remaining criminals are given relatively light sentences, and Doyle and Russo, because of their flouting of police-department rules, are transferred as punishment.

* * *

Director William Friedkin was only thirty-two years old when he made *The French Connection*. The chase scene, in which Popeye is in a car and his quarry is in an elevated train, is without question the most exciting chase scene in movie history. It has been emulated often, of course, but never bested.

Gene Hackman had been Friedkin's seventh choice to play "Popeye" Doyle. His first choice had been Steve McQueen, followed by a string of others, including Jackie Gleason and even columnist Jimmy Breslin. It was Hackman's first starring role, though he had made a good splash in *Bonnie and Clyde* (1967), for which he was nominated for an Academy Award. He had been eager to take the role. "When I first read the part," he has been quoted as saying, "it seemed like a chance to do all those things I watched Jimmy Cagney do as a kid."

Although not as good as the original, the sequel, *French Connection II*, made four years later, is also a first-rate drama, with Gene Hackman turning in another outstanding performance as "Popeye" Doyle and the elusive Alain Charnier again being well played by Fernando Rey. A much less successful effort was *Popeye Doyle*, a 1986 television movie.

Eight Academy Award nominations went to *The French Connection*. The film won for: Best Picture, Best Director (William Friedkin), Best Actor (Gene Hackman), Best Adapted Screenplay (Ernest Tidyman), and Best Editing (Jerry Greenberg). Tidyman also won the Edgar Allan Poe Award from the Mystery Writers of America for his screenplay, and Hackman was named Best Actor by the New York Film Critics. Friedkin also received the Best Director award from the Directors Guild. In recognition of the memorable chase scene as well as the superb moment when "Frog One" escapes Doyle's tail on the subway, Jerry Greenberg, thanked the New York City subway system when he picked up his Oscar for Editing.

BEST LINE: Doyle and Russo have just caught a junkie and are trying to get him to talk. Russo asks him to name his supplier, without much luck, when the apparently insane Doyle asks him: "When's the last time you picked your feet? Have you ever been to Poughkeepsie? You've been there, right? . . . You've sat on the edge of the bed, didn't you? You took off your shoes and put your fingers between your toes and picked your feet, didn't you? . . . I'm gonna nail you for picking your feet in Poughkeepsie." Don't worry if you don't get it. No one does.

WHITE HEAT
1949

TYPE OF FILM: Gangster

STUDIO: Warner Brothers

PRODUCER: Louis F. Edelman

DIRECTOR: Raoul Walsh

SCREENWRITERS: Ivan Goff and Ben Roberts

SOURCE: Original story by Virginia Kellogg

RUNNING TIME: 114 minutes

PRINCIPAL PLAYERS:

James Cagney . . . . .Arthur Cody Jarrett
Virginia Mayo . . . . .Verna Jarrett
Edmond O'Brien . . . . .Hank Fallon/Vic Pardo
Margaret Wycherly . . . . .Ma Jarrett
Steve Cochran . . . . .Big Ed Somers
John Archer . . . . .Philip Evans

DID YOU KNOW? In one of the most famous scenes in cinema history, Cody Jarrett, the gangster played by James Cagney, is in the prison mess hall when he learns that his mother, on whom he has a pathological fixation, is dead. He goes berserk, screaming and whimpering as he walks and crawls across the crowded tables, slugging prison guards in a nearly balletic sequence. While a young boy, Cagney had visited the famous mental institution on Ward's Island in New York's East River. The pathetic screams of the insane stayed in his memory, and he replicated them in this scene. Although the scene required the use of hundreds of extras, with numerous camera angles, it was shot in a single morning.

THE STORY: After a robbery of a mail train nets $300,000, Cody Jarrett and his gang, including his wife, Verna, and his mother, hide out in an isolated cabin. Big Ed Somers, one of the gang members, thinks Cody is crazy and hates the idea of having all that money while freezing in the middle of nowhere. Under stress, Cody has one of his more and more frequent headaches, which he describes as "like having a red-hot buzz saw inside my head." As he recovers, his ma hands him a drink and tells him, "Top of the world, son."

One of the gang members, badly burned during the robbery, is left behind when the gang changes hideouts, and fingerprints discovered by the Treasury Department point to the Jarrett gang as the robbers. When the T-men close in, Jarrett turns himself in for a minor robbery committed at the same time as the train heist, which left four dead, and he is sentenced to one-to-three years in prison. The Feds facilitate this so they can have one of their own, Hank Fallon, pose as convict Vic Pardo to share a cell with Cody and thereby learn the identity of the man who fences the stolen money.

Cody's mother visits him in jail to tell him that Big Ed and Verna have taken off together but that her son will soon be out and "on top of the world." Cody tells her he'll take care of Ed when he gets out, but his mother doesn't want Ed to live that long; she says she'll take care of him.

Cody later learns that his mother is dead and goes insane in the prison mess hall. Soon after he escapes with Pardo. He finds Big Ed and Verna and, with his wife's connivance, kills the dismal Ed. The gang then plans a big robbery at a gas plant, using a large tanker to sneak in. The police and T-men surround the plant, and the gang is wiped out. Cody, laughing hysterically, climbs to the top of one of the gas tanks, where marksman Fallon shoots him several times, finally firing into the gas tank. As it explodes, Cody looks skyward and yells, "Made it, Ma. Top of the world." On the ground, Fallon says, "Cody Jarrett. Finally made it to the top of the world, and it blew right up in his face."

* * *

Raoul Walsh had worked with Cagney before (*The Roaring Twenties*, 1939) and understood good action sequences (he himself had ridden with Pancho Villa while a young man). But he also trusted Cagney to bring something more to the motion picture than action and allowed the actor to make suggestions about Cody Jarrett's relationship with his mother. It was Cagney who suggested that Jarrett be comforted in her lap after one of his headaches—one of the most memorable scenes in any gangster movie.

Cody Jarrett was one of Cagney's greatest screen roles in a career with many. The film may have produced the two scenes for which he is most remembered: going crazy when he learns of his mother's death and his roaring demise atop the gas tank as he screams, "Top of the world." His career had been suffering since

277

the megahit, *Yankee Doodle Dandy* (1942), in which he played song-and-dance man George M. Cohan. The subject of the deranged outlaw seemed a sure hit, and it was, but Cagney came to hate it, frustrated that he would be most remembered for his role as an insane, Oedipal loser.

BEST LINE: Cody's wife, Verna, trying to convince him to keep all of the gang's money and spend it on her: "I'd look good in a mink coat, honey," she says. Cody replies, "Mm. You'd look good in a shower curtain."

OUT OF THE PAST
1947

TYPE OF FILM: *Noir*

STUDIO: RKO

EXECUTIVE PRODUCER: Robert Sparks

PRODUCER: Warren Duff

DIRECTOR: Jacques Tourneur

SCREENWRITER: Geoffrey Homes (pseudonym of Daniel Mainwaring)

SOURCE: *Build My Gallows High*, novel by Geoffrey Homes

RUNNING TIME: 97 minutes

PRINCIPAL PLAYERS:

Robert Mitchum . . . . .Jeff Markham/Bailey
Jane Greer . . . . .Kathie Moffett
Kirk Douglas . . . . .Whit Sterling
Rhonda Fleming . . . . .Meta Carson
Richard Webb . . . . .Jim
Steve Brodie . . . . .Jack Fisher
Virginia Huston . . . . .Ann
Paul Valentine . . . . .Joe Stefanos
Dickie Moore . . . . .deaf-mute boy
Ken Niles . . . . .Els

DID YOU KNOW? Robert Mitchum became RKO's biggest male star with his role as the laconic private eye in *Out of the Past*, but he almost didn't get the part. It had been offered to Humphrey Bogart, the actor who Daniel Mainwaring, the screenwriter, had in mind while adapting his book for the screen. But Bogart, who was enthusiastic about the film, was under contract to Warner Brothers, who wouldn't agree to loan him out to RKO. The role was next offered to John Garfield, who turned it down, as did Dick Powell, whose career was on the rise after he switched from singing and dancing to becoming a tough guy in *Murder, My Sweet* (1944). Mitchum, under contract to RKO, had played only supporting roles, notably in *The Story of G.I. Joe*, for which he received an Academy Award nomination, and another *noir* classic, *Crossfire* (1947), but this, his first starring role, catapulted him to stardom.

THE STORY: Private detective Jeff Markham is hired by gangster Whit Sterling to find his girlfriend, Kathie Moffett, who has fled, taking $40,000 of his money with her. Jeff tracks her down in Mexico and falls for her. While he sends telegrams to Whit informing him that he can't find her, he and Kathie begin a torrid affair and he believes her when she swears she didn't steal the money. They leave for San Francisco to begin a new life, but they have the bad luck to be spotted at a racetrack by his former partner in the detective agency, now hunting him and Kathie for Whit.

They try to shake Fisher, the detective, but he follows Kathie to a mountain cabin and attempts to blackmail them for a cut of the $40,000. Kathie icily and needlessly shoots him, fleeing to leave the corpse and the blame on her lover.

Jeff moves to a small town and opens a gas station under the assumed name of Bailey and gets engaged to a schoolteacher, Ann. One of Whit's henchmen finds him and summons him to meet the boss. As Ann drives him to the meeting, he tells her the sordid tale of his past and vows to put it all behind him and come back to her.

When he arrives at Whit's place, Kathie is there and Whit gives Jeff the chance to make up for his double dealing. Steal some tax records from Whit's former accountant, who has threatened to go to the Feds, and they'll be square, Whit assures him. Jeff senses a double cross and learns that Kathie has signed an affidavit pinning the murder of Fisher on him. He steals the tax papers, finding the accountant dead as he is set up for the murder, but he gets away and offers to trade the incriminating documents for the affidavit. When Jeff shows up for the switch, he finds Whit dead, shot by Kathie. "You can't make deals with a dead man, Jeff," she tells him. "Don't you see, you've only me to make deals with now." "Then build my gallows high, baby," he replies. As they drive away together, a police roadblock confronts them and Kathie realizes that Jeff has turned her in. She shoots him, and a hail of police machine gun fire kills her as the car crashes through the roadblock.

* * *

If any one film could be said to epitomize the term *film noir*, *Out of the Past* would be it. The tough hero who is doomed for love of the wrong woman; the treacherous femme fatale who double-crosses every man she meets; the inevitability of the past resurfacing to assure violent death; the night, when everything seems to happen so commonly that daylight seems an intrusion; gangsters; nightclubs; jazz; bright lights; deep shadows;a good woman lost; dialogue that sounds like pulp poetry—all of it and more can be found in *Out of the Past*.

The author of the screenplay, Daniel Mainwaring, using the pseudonym Geoffrey Homes, adapted his own novel, *Build My Gallows High* (the title under which the film was released in England), and little was changed except the ending, in which Whit's henchmen do the killing. After the first draft had been completed, Mainwaring went on to another project and the producer decided to spiff up the script and gave the rewrite job to James M. Cain, who was paid $20,000 or $30,000 for his work. Instead of doing a rewrite, however, he threw out the entire script and wrote a different story entirely. Mainwaring was then called back to polish the initial script.

Jane Greer, the worst bad girl in all of *film noir*, was known as the girl with the Mona Lisa smile, because her face was set in a perpetual gentle smile—the result of a bout with Bell's palsy when she was young.

The scene to watch is set in Mexico, as Mitchum sits in a little cantina, and Greer strides in out of the sunlight, through shadows. She is wearing an off-white dress and a big straw hat to match. Mitchum sees her, and he (and the viewer) knows he is doomed.

The 1984 remake was titled *Against All Odds*, starring Jeff Bridges and Rachel Ward, which was more explicitly steamy than the original. As remakes go, it was pretty good, though without the very sexy Ward it probably would have been a flop.

BEST LINE: Jeff/Bailey, speaking to Kathie Moffett, the girl who has inevitably caused his doom: "You're like a leaf that the wind blows from one gutter to another."

THE THIN MAN
1934

TYPE OF FILM: Detective/Comedy

STUDIO: Metro-Goldwyn-Mayer

PRODUCER: Hunt Stromberg

DIRECTOR: W. S. Van Dyke

SCREENWRITERS: Frances Goodrich and Albert Hackett

SOURCE: *The Thin Man*, novel by Dashiell Hammett

RUNNING TIME: 91 minutes

PRINCIPAL PLAYERS:

William Powell . . . . .Nick Charles
Myrna Loy . . . . .Nora Charles
Maureen O'Sullivan .Dorothy Wynant
Nat Pendleton . . . . .Lt. John Guild
Minna Gombell . . . . .Mimi Wynant
Cesar Romero . . . . .Chris Jorgenson
Natalie Moorhead . . . . .Julia Wolf
Edward Ellis . . . . .Clyde Wynant
Porter Hall . . . . .MacCauley
Henry Wadsworth . . . . .Tommy
William Henry . . . . .Gilbert Wynant
Harold Huber . . . . .Nunheim

DID YOU KNOW? The on-screen chemistry between Powell and Loy was so good that many people thought they were married in real life as well. On one awkward occasion, a San Francisco hotel had them booked into a single room as "Mr. & Mrs. Powell." Powell, meanwhile, was dating Jean Harlow, who had traveled to San Francisco to be with Powell while the film was being shot. The awkward situation was resolved by Loy and Harlow sharing one room, while Powell took the single room he had booked for Harlow.

THE STORY: Former private detective Nick Charles travels to New York for the Christmas season with his wealthy wife, Nora. When the successful inventor Clyde Wynant disappears shortly before his daughter's wedding, she asks Nick to find him. Although Nick is interested exclusively in drinking, partying, and watching over his wife's finances, Nora persuades him to help the young woman. He learns that Wynant had ruined his marriage by taking up with a young girlfriend, who had another lover and stole $50,000 from Wynant just before his disappearance. When the young mistress is murdered, suspicion falls on her lover until he, too, turns up dead. In a classic denouement scene, Nick brings all the remaining suspects together and identifies the surprise culprit.

Based on Dashiell Hammett's 1934 novel, *The Thin Man* became a tremendously successful film (one of the ten top-grossing films of 1934) and spurred five additional films about the hard-drinking and fun-loving Nick and Nora. The second *Thin Man* movie, *After the Thin Man*, was every bit the equal of the first, and while the last four did not quite measure up, they remained popular with audiences and continued to provide witty and sophisticated dialogue.

* * *

Lillian Hellman famously repeated often that she was the model for Nora, but she also claimed to be the real-life prototype of the best-friend character in the "biographical" movie *Julia*. The very existence of this saintly titular character is suspect, and it stretches the imagination to think of the humorless Hellman as having any connection to the very lovable Nora.

Asta, the hugely popular wire-haired terrier who played in all six *Thin Man* films, was played by Skippy, and no one except his trainers was permitted to interact with him while off camera. When Loy disobeyed the order and went to pet Skippy, the dog bit her.

In one scene, a thug visits Nick and Nora in the middle of the night, and the police come and capture him. After questioning Nick, they decide to search the apartment. Nora spots one of them in her room and exclaims, "What's that man doing in my drawers?" causing Nick to spit out his drink (and hundreds of theater operators to censor the line).

After the second film, it was reported that Powell would not continue in the role because of illness, and Melvyn Douglas and Reginald Gardiner were considered as his replacement. Happily, Powell recovered.

As has been noted on numerous occasions, the original Thin

Man was the gaunt Wynant; however, audiences so much associated Powell with the title of the first film that he then assumed the sobriquet.

Academy Award nominations went to *The Thin Man* for Best Picture, Powell for Best Actor, Van Dyke for Best Director, and Goodrich and Hackett for Best Adapted Screenplay.

BEST LINE: When the police discover a handgun in the Charles's apartment, a cop asks Nick if he has a permit, which he doesn't. "Ever hear of the Sullivan Act?" the cop asks. "Oh, that's all right," replies Nora. "We're married."

LAURA
1944

TYPE OF FILM: Detective/*Noir*

STUDIO: Twentieth Century-Fox

PRODUCER: Otto Preminger

DIRECTOR: Otto Preminger (although begun by Rouben Mamoulian)

SCREENWRITERS: Jay Dratler, Samuel Hoffenstein, and Betty Reinhardt

SOURCE: *Laura*, novel by Vera Caspary

RUNNING TIME: 85 minutes

PRINCIPAL PLAYERS:

Gene Tierney . . . . Laura Hunt
Dana Andrews . . . . Mark McPherson
Clifton Webb . . . . Waldo Lydecker
Vincent Price . . . . Shelby Carpenter
Judith Anderson . . . . Ann Treadwell
Dorothy Adams . . . . Bessie

DID YOU KNOW? Although Preminger got an Oscar nomination as Best Director, he was merely a replacement for the first director, Rouben Mamoulian, who had been forced on producer Preminger by Darryl Zanuck. Zanuck, the head of Twentieth Century-Fox, hated the arrogant Preminger. The first rushes were dreadful enough to cause Zanuck to fire Mamoulian and replace him with Preminger.

THE STORY: A hard-boiled New York City detective, Mark McPherson, attempts to solve the apparent murder of Laura Hunt, whose face has been blown away by a shotgun blast in her beautiful Upper East Side apartment. The suspects are wealthy snobs who find McPherson as abrasive as he finds them. Occupying center stage is snippy gossip columnist Waldo Lydecker, given to such remarks as, "In my case, self-absorption is completely justified. I have never found any other subject quite so worthy of my attention," and "It's lavish, but I call it home." Laura's fiancé, Shelby Carpenter, an unctuous Southern playboy, comes under suspicion, as does Ann Treadwell, who has set her cap for Carpenter and was fiercely jealous of the beautiful Laura, her niece.

McPherson becomes mildly obsessed with the exquisite portrait of Laura that hangs in her apartment and secretly arranges to purchase it. When Laura returns, alive and well, from a quiet few days in the country, McPherson has to learn the true identity of the corpse while competing for Laura's affection with Waldo, who is wittier, and Shelby, who is richer.

* * *

Although generally categorized as a *noir* film, *Laura* is more a mixture of romance and detective story in structure. Gene Tierney is heartbreakingly beautiful, but she is not the *noir* film's stereotypical bad girl who uses her lover, only to abandon him when he has fallen hopelessly in love. Nor is there the bleak vision of hopelessness so essential an element in the true *noir* film.

Neither of the two most memorable elements of *Laura*—the painting and the music—are human. The sentimentalized portrait of Laura is so romantic that McPherson falls in love with the subject even though she is presumed to be dead. When she returns, the real-life Laura is less adored than her image. The haunting theme music by David Raksin made it equally possible for every man in the cinema to fall in love with the image of the ravishing Tierney, and that music remains a staple of late-night piano bars and supper clubs.

Often described as everybody's favorite mystery movie, *Laura* had a few slightly odd subtexts. Although all the men in the movie seem to be in love with Laura, Lydecker's interest appears to be more as Pygmalion, and the rather fey journalist gives a more meaningful look to the handsome McPherson when they first meet than he ever does to Laura. Shelby, too, seems to walk on his toes a wee bit. And for all her sexy beauty, Laura does not project very much heat, except perhaps unintentionally.

Academy Award nominations went to Otto Preminger (Best Director) and Clifton Webb (Best Supporting Actor). Astonishingly, the memorable theme music and still much-loved song, "Laura," did not get a statue.

The success that Clifton Webb had in this role clearly had an impact on him, as he played a similar feisty and sharp-tongued character for the rest of his career. The tightly controlled Dana Andrews turned to alcohol with greater and greater reliance in later films, and within a decade, he was infamous for being continuously drunk on the set of every film he was in. Gene Tierney slipped into paranoia and was suicidal for some years, requiring institutionalization to save her. She ultimately took a job as a clerk in a Topeka dress shop and, happily, married a millionaire.

BEST LINE: Waldo Lydecker, clearly infatuated with Laura, asks tough cop Mark McPherson, "Have you ever been in love, detective?" The laconic McPherson replies, "A dame in Washington Heights once got a fox fur out of me."

THE GODFATHER, PART II
1974

TYPE OF FILM: Crime

STUDIO: Paramount

PRODUCER: Francis Ford Coppola

DIRECTOR: Francis Ford Coppola

SCREENWRITERS: Francis Ford Coppola and Mario Puzo

SOURCE: Inspired by characters from *The Godfather*, novel by Mario Puzo

RUNNING TIME: 200 minutes

PRINCIPAL PLAYERS:

Al Pacino . . . . .Michael Corleone
Robert Duvall . . . . .Tom Hagen
Diane Keaton . . . . .Kay Adams Corleone
Robert De Niro . . . . .Don Vito Corleone
John Cazale . . . . .Fredo Corleone
Talia Shire . . . . .Connie Corleone
Lee Strasberg . . . . .Hyman Roth
Michael V. Gazzo . . . . .Frankie Pentangeli
G. D. Spradlin . . . . .Senator Pat Geary
Richard Bright . . . . .Al Nevi
Gaston Moschin . . . . .Fanucci

DID YOU KNOW? The sequel to *The Godfather* is the most successful sequel in the history of motion pictures. Although it was not quite the financial success of its predecessor, costing twice as much and earning less than half, it nonetheless was one of the biggest box-office successes of the year. In addition, and equally important to many of those involved in the making of both films, it was an even greater critical success, frequently described as being superior to the original and having some tangible evidence of this in the form of awards. While *The Godfather* was nominated for ten Oscars and won three, *The Godfather, Part II* was nominated for eleven Oscars and won six, including Best Picture (the only time in the history of Hollywood that two films in a series have both won that award); Francis Ford Coppola for Best Director; Robert De Niro for Best Supporting Actor (defeating Michael V. Gazzo and Lee Strasberg, who both appeared in the film as well); and Mario Puzo and Francis Ford Coppola for Best Adapted Screenplay, repeating their triumph of two years earlier.

THE STORY: In 1918 Italy, young Vito Corleone sees his family murdered and moves to New York City. Married and working in a small shop, he loses his job when a gangster forces his boss to hire his nephew. Desperate for money, he joins forces with a couple of small-time hoodlums and they become successful gangsters, finally taking over an olive oil importing firm. Although still a crook, he becomes a dignified and respected member of the community and rises to head a mob family.

Vito's son Michael takes over the responsibility of head of the family and is threatened by a powerful and corrupt U.S. senator who wants to extort money from him. When Michael refuses, he becomes targeted for assassination. The attempt fails and Michael gathers ample evidence against the senator, assuring him that he will be left alone.

Having successfully entered the casino-gambling business in Las Vegas, Michael sees an equally huge opportunity in Havana, Cuba, and meets with Jewish gangster Hyman Roth to set up operations there, only to have his plans thwarted by the overthrow of the Batista government, which had been cooperative in hopes of making Havana an even greater tourist attraction.

When Michael returns to America, he learns that his wife, Kay, tired of a life inseparable from crime, is about to leave him just as he becomes the prime target of a massive government investigation of organized crime.

* * *

When Francis Ford Coppola made *Part II*, he reasoned that it would be successful only if audiences felt that it needed to be made in order to round out and complete the saga of the Corleone family. Because of the unimaginable success of the first movie, he was given virtually total control of the film and was able to do whatever he wanted to in a creative sense. He immediately signed Mario Puzo to again work on the screenplay, feeling (correctly) that no one knew these characters better than he did.

Al Pacino recommended Lee Strasberg for the role of Hyman Roth. Although the world's most famous acting teacher, Strasberg never had appeared before a camera.

In the scene in which Michael (played by Al Pacino) learns that his brother Fredo (played by John Cazale) has betrayed the family, he shows signs of tremendous stress. Some of this wasn't acting—Pacino was rushed to the hospital with pneumonia immediately after shooting of the scene concluded.

The Godfather and *The Godfather, Part II* were combined to make *The Godfather Saga* for television in 1977, with NBC airing it for nine hours over a four-day period, reaching a huge audience. The films were heavily edited, and previously unseen footage was added, eliminating the flashbacks to produce a linear chronology of the Corleone family's history. Also eliminated was much of the sex, obscenity, and violence, all of which were restored for the videotape, which ran 388 minutes and was titled *The Godfather: The Complete Epic*.

Even before *The Godfather* was released, plans were under way to make a sequel. Various titles under consideration were *The Son of Don Corleone, Michael Corleone,* and *Don Michael.*

The Godfather, Part III was released in 1990 but did not enjoy much success. Puzo and Coppola again wrote the script, which lacked the fire of the first two films, but the casting of Coppola's daughter Sofia, essentially an amateur, in the key role of Mary Corleone was the film's biggest problem. Coppola is still often asked if there will be a fourth film in the series, and he has never given a definite no.

BEST LINE: Michael Corleone, noting words of wisdom from his father, Don Vito: "Keep your friends close, but your enemies closer."

THE GODFATHER
1972

TYPE OF FILM:	Crime
STUDIO:	Paramount
PRODUCER:	Albert S. Ruddy
DIRECTOR:	Francis Ford Coppola
SCREENWRITERS:	Francis Ford Coppola and Mario Puzo
SOURCE:	*The Godfather*, novel by Mario Puzo
RUNNING TIME:	175 minutes

PRINCIPAL PLAYERS:

Marlon Brando	Don Vito Corleone
Al Pacino	Michael Corleone
James Caan	Sonny Corleone
Richard Castellano	Peter Clemenza
Sterling Hayden	McCluskey
Diane Keaton	Kay Adams
Talia Shire	Connie Corleone Rizzi
Robert Duvall	Tom Hagen
John Marley	Jack Woltz
Richard Conte	Barzini
Al Lettieri	Sollozzo
Abe Vigoda	Sal Tessio
Gianni Russo	Carlo Rizzi
John Cazale	Fredo Corleone
Rudy Bond	Cuneo
Al Martino	Johnny Fontane
Morgana King	Mama Carmella Corleone

DID YOU KNOW? The most important and successful casting decision for *The Godfather* was for the central figure of Don Vito Corleone. Mario Puzo, the author of the novel, had always envisioned Marlon Brando for this pivotal role, and both the producer and director agreed that Brando had the talent, the charisma, and the sheer gravitas to play the head of the powerful family. But several things weighed against this choice with the executives at Paramount. First, Brando's films had been commercial failures for more than a decade, and, equally important, he was regarded as one of the most difficult actors in Hollywood to work with. Stanley Jaffe is reputed to have said, "As long as I'm president of the studio, Marlon Brando will not be in this picture, and I will no longer allow you to discuss it." He further is reported to have said, "If Marlon Brando is in the picture, it will gross five million less than if no one is in it." When Coppola finally persuaded Jaffe to change his mind, it was under the most insulting conditions ever handed down to an actor of Brando's stature. He would have to submit to a screen test, accept far less money than the actor's usual minimum, and to assume personal financial responsibility for any delays in production caused by his actions. Incredibly, Brando accepted the terms and went on to win an Oscar for his performance.

THE STORY: At the wedding reception of Vito Corleone's daughter, Connie, his godson, Johnny Fontane, asks the don for help in getting a movie role that will revive his career. Corleone sends his adopted son and counselor, Tom Hagen, to Hollywood to convince the film's producer that, in spite of his previous rejection, he ought to cast Fontane in the coveted role. When the producer again refuses, he awakens to find the head of his prize racehorse in bed with him, causing him to change his mind.

When Vito's son Michael, who has tried to stay away from an involvement with crime, visits his father, who has been gunned down, in the hospital, he sees that the police guard has been sent away by Captain McCluskey, a corrupt cop, and saves Vito from a second attempt on his life. Michael's love for his father draws him into the family business, and at a meeting called to settle differences among the various crime factions, Michael kills both Sollozzo and his hireling, McCluskey. He then escapes to Sicily to be protected by friends and relatives of the Corleone family, leaving his fiancée, Kay Adams, behind.

War breaks out among the various crime families and results in the murder of Sonny, Don Vito's son, causing the Don to negotiate a truce with the other families and agree to become involved with the despised but lucrative drug trade that began the battles.

Michael, still in Sicily, has fallen in love with Apollonia and married her, only to see her killed when a car bomb intended for him explodes. He returns to America and Kay to become the head of the Corleone crime empire.

Planning to expand the family's influence in Las Vegas, he tries to buy a casino but is rebuffed by Moe Greene, who has the protection of another crime family. Michael plots revenge for various acts against himself and his family, especially the murder of Sonny. As his nephew is baptized, all his principal enemies are gunned down and his position is secured as the new Don Corleone.

* * *

The significance of *The Godfather* and its sequels cannot be overstated. Mario Puzo's long novel created a world that never existed as he shows it. His book added words and phrases to the language, including *godfather* in the context of the Mafia (which is never mentioned in the book and only rarely in the three *Godfather* movies) and *swimming with the fishes* which connotes a murdered body thrown into the river or ocean. Puzo and Francis Ford Coppola's vision of the largely Italian underworld seems so real and so complete that readers and viewers come away feeling that *this* is what it's really like.

When Paramount acquired film rights to *The Godfather*, it was expected to be a huge blockbuster, with a large budget and sprawling canvas. Then the studio released *The Brotherhood*, another "Mafia" picture, with Kirk Douglas, which proved unsuccessful, forcing Paramount executives to rethink the wisdom of making another gangster film. Backing away from its initial grandiose plans, they budgeted the film at $2,000,000, hired the relatively unknown Francis Ford Coppola to direct it when every other director they approached turned it down, and got Albert S. Ruddy to produce it. As the producer of one television show and three failed motion pictures, the only reason he was hired is that Paramount knew he could make the film cheaply. It was finished well over the original budget, costing $6,500,000.

In perhaps the most famous scene in *The Godfather*, movie producer Jack Woltz is persuaded to hire Johnny Fontane by waking up to find the bloody head of his prize racehorse in bed with him. The head was real. The studio prop looked nothing like what Coppola wanted, so someone was sent to a slaughterhouse to find a head. It was frozen and used in several takes.

The Godfather was nominated for ten Academy Awards, including Best Picture, Best Director (Coppola), Best Actor (Brando), Best Supporting Actor (James Caan, Robert Duvall, and Al Pacino), and Best Adapted Screenplay. It won only three (Best Picture, Actor, and Screenplay) as *Cabaret* won eight Oscars. The presenter for Best Picture was Clint Eastwood, who substituted for Charlton Heston, who got stuck in traffic. The producer, Albert S. Ruddy, an old friend of Eastwood's, had jokingly asked him earlier to read his name when he opened the envelope, no matter what name was on the card, and then quickly eat the card. When Eastwood named him the winner, Ruddy actually believed for a moment that Eastwood had done as he had been asked.

BEST LINE: Nearly washed-up singer Johnny Fontane has asked Don Corleone for help in getting an important film role. "I'll handle it," he tells the singer. When asked how he will manage it, the don famously responds, "I'm gonna make him an offer he can't refuse."

CHINATOWN
1974

TYPE OF FILM: Detective
STUDIO: Paramount
PRODUCER: Robert Evans
DIRECTOR: Roman Polanski
SCREENWRITER: Robert Towne
SOURCE: Original
RUNNING TIME: 131 minutes

PRINCIPAL PLAYERS:

Jack Nicholson . . . . .J. J. "Jake" Gittes
Faye Dunaway . . . . .Evelyn Mulwray
John Huston . . . . .Noah Cross
Perry Lopez . . . . .Escobar
John Hillerman . . . . .Yelburton
Darrell Zwerling . . . . .Hollis Mulwray
Roman Polanski . . . . .hood with knife
Dick Bakalyan . . . . .Loach
Diane Ladd . . . . .Ida Sessions
Roy Jenson . . . . .Mulvihill
Joe Mantell . . . . .Walsh
Bruce Glover . . . . .Duffy

DID YOU KNOW? This superb detective film was actually based on a true scandal of early twentieth-century Los Angeles. Then a modest-size western city filled with farmers, Mexican day laborers, Chinese immigrants, and adventurers seeking their fortunes in the west, it was also a hot, subtropical region that relied for its existence and well-being on a plentiful supply of water. A scheme had been hatched by a group of wealthy landowners to buy huge tracts on the outskirts of the sprawling city and then use their political power to have that arid, nearly useless acreage incorporated into the city of Los Angeles, giving them legal access to the water supply paid for by the taxpayers. Some of the most staggering fortunes of the time, many still in place (such as the heirs to *L.A. Times-Mirror* estate), were created in this manner. While the tactics employed to amass this wealth may have been corrupt, they were technically legal.

THE STORY: J. J. "Jake" Gittes (whose name is pronounced differently by virtually everyone with whom he comes in contact) is a former Los Angeles policeman who worked in Chinatown but now is a private detective handling mainly divorce cases in Hollywood. He is hired ostensibly to find evidence against a philandering water commissioner, Hollis Mulwray, by a woman claiming to be Mulwray's wife. While working on that case, he is also hired by the wealthy Noah Cross to find his daughter and granddaughter. Gittes comes to believe that he has been used as a pawn to set up Cross in the murder of Mulwray, who has discovered a scam to cheat the people of Los Angeles out of the water they need and for which they pay.

Gittes is warned off the case by a former cop and his partner, whom Gittes calls a midget. Feeling a verbal warning would not suffice, the tough holds a knife to Gittes's nose. "You're a very nosy fellow," he says to Gittes. "You know what happens to nosy fellows? Wanna guess? No? Okay. They lose their noses." He cuts through Gitte's nostril and adds, "Next time, you lose the whole thing. I'll cut it off and feed it to my goldfish."

Gittes persists and learns that Mulwray's wife, Evelyn, is Cross' daughter and that the woman who hired him was actually not Evelyn but her sister—and also her daughter, the result of an incestuous relationship with her father, Noah Cross.

Cross, already a multimillionaire, is the mastermind behind a scheme to buy arid, virtually worthless farms during a terrible drought and have the land irrigated by diverted water from nearby Los Angeles, guaranteeing the elderly tycoon even greater wealth and power. Gittes tries to protect Evelyn and her daughter from her ruthless father but is arrested. Powerless, Evelyn tries to escape, only to be shot by a policeman as her fifteen-year-old daughter, screaming in despair at the sight of her dead mother, is comforted by an almost leering Cross.

* * *

Chinatown is an original screenplay by Towne that started out at nearly 250 pages (twice as long as the film). Director Roman Polanski worked on the script for nearly two months, eliminating many characters and forming a more linear and coherent story line. He also wrote a new ending, about which he and Towne argued furiously. The final version had not been decided upon until after the picture was in production. In the original, Evelyn shoots Cross and goes off with Gittes and her daughter, but Polanski wanted the darker version that was eventually made. Towne never forgave the change and hated it.

Although a brilliant neo-*noir* film that paid open homage to Dashiell Hammett (Gittes bears numerous similarities to Sam Spade), James M. Cain (whose characters are rarely moral), Raymond Chandler (it is his Los Angeles in which the action transpires), and others, there is a major diversion from prototypical *noir* films: Evelyn Mulwray. Introduced and set up as the classic femme fatale for whom Gittes will fall, only to be betrayed by her greedy and cold heart, she instead turns out to be the victim whose life has been clouded by a terrible secret from which she can never escape.

Polanski may have been influenced in favor of his darker version of the story as he was still mourning the brutal murder of his pregnant wife, Sharon Tate, their unborn child, and several friends by members of the Charles Manson family. The brief but memorable scene in which Polanski uses a knife to slit open Nicholson's nose, forcing him to wear bandages for the rest of the film, reflects the brutal violence of the killings. Several years later, Polanski was arrested for the statutory rape of a thirteen-year-old girl and fled the United States to avoid prosecution.

Robert Towne was awarded an Oscar for Best Original Screenplay, while Academy Award nominations also went to the film for Best Picture, to Nicholson for Best Actor, to Dunaway for Best Actress, and Polanski for Best Director. Towne won the Edgar Allan Poe Award from the Mystery Writers of America for his screenplay.

Faye Dunaway, while glamorous and sexy, is not especially beautiful in this role. Director Polanski was more interested in making her seem subtly paranoid, sexually frustrated, and—reasonably—secretive. This effect is achieved by having her face overly powdered, with oddly thin eyebrows and deep red lipstick. Polanski filmed her by holding the camera very close to her face, which made even the experienced and talented actress unduly jumpy.

Given the tremendous critical and popular acclaim received by the film, there was a much discussed and anticipated sequel, *The Two Jakes* (1990), which was, predictably, a disappointment. It was directed by its star, Jack Nicholson, in a beautiful but ultimately incomprehensible and overly talky narrative that also starred Harvey Keitel (as the other Jake) and Meg Tilly as a philandering wife. Faye Dunaway has a nice cameo.

BEST LINE: Policeman to Jake Gittes: "You must really think I'm stupid, don't you, Gittes?" "I don't think about it that much," the detective replies, "but give me a day or two and I'll get back to you."

THE MALTESE FALCON
1941

TYPE OF FILM:	Detective
STUDIO:	Warner Brothers
EXECUTIVE PRODUCER:	Henry Blanke
PRODUCER:	Hal B. Wallis
DIRECTOR:	John Huston
SCREENWRITER:	John Huston
SOURCE:	*The Maltese Falcon*, novel by Dashiell Hammett
RUNNING TIME:	100 minutes

PRINCIPAL PLAYERS:

Humphrey Bogart . . . . .Sam Spade
Mary Astor . . . . .Ruth Wonderley/Brigid O'Shaughnessy
Peter Lorre . . . . .Joel Cairo
Sydney Greenstreet . . . . .Casper Gutman—The Fat Man
Ward Bond . . . . .Detective Sergeant Tom Polhaus
Gladys George . . . . .Iva Archer
Barton MacLane . . . . .Detective Lieutenant Dundy
Elisha Cook, Jr. . . . . .Wilmer Cook
Lee Patrick . . . . .Effie Perine
Jerome Cowan . . . . .Miles Archer

DID YOU KNOW? John Huston, one of the top writers at Warner Brothers, made his directorial debut with this, the third film version of Dashiell Hammett's detective novel. Because he was a first-time director, and because the film was a remake, Huston's first choice for the role of Sam Spade, George Raft, turned it down. Humphrey Bogart, who had been playing villains in B movies, accepted the role and became a huge star.

THE STORY: Ruth Wonderley comes to the office of Spade & Archer for an ambiguous reason and hires Spade. She soon admits that her real name is Brigid O'Shaughnessy and that she hadn't told the truth about her plight. Bogart reassures her, saying that he hadn't believed *her*—he had believed her two hundred dollars. Archer is later shot and killed in an alley, and Spade, although he hates his partner and is having an affair with his wife, vows to find the killer. He is successful, saying, "When a man's partner is killed, he's supposed to do something about it."

Spade learns that the lovely O'Shaughnessy is involved with a gang of strange and shady characters led by Casper Gutman, a fat man who has spent the last seventeen years of his life in pursuit of a legendary artifact worth a fortune: a statue of a falcon encrusted with jewels. His employees are the effeminate Joel Cairo and the nervous Wilmer Cook.

When a mortally wounded sea captain carrying a parcel falls through Spade's door, Spade unexpectedly has possession of the treasure, which he persists in calling the "dingus." Spade, under suspicion by the police for the murder of Archer, must prove his innocence while hunting for the real killer and working out a deal with the unflappable Gutman for a share of the fortune.

* * *

The Maltese Falcon is the most famous American detective novel, and it may be the greatest American detective film. The 1941 version remains the perfect film more than a half century after it was made, and the cast stays fixed in the memory forever once it's been seen.

Interestingly, Hammett had worked as a Pinkerton detective, and all the supporting cast were based on real-life characters he'd encountered as a private operative. Gutman's original was suspected of being a German spy, and after Hammett followed him for many days, he said, "I never remember shadowing a man who bored me so much." He'd picked up the Cairo character on a forgery charge. The prototype for Effie, the good-girl secretary, suggested that he go into the narcotics-smuggling business with her. Wilmer, the gunsel, was a twenty-one-year-old with a smooth face and quiet manner, who took pride in being called "The Midget Bandit" by the newspapers.

The famed actor Walter Huston agreed to do a small scene for his son John, the director, and played the murdered sea captain, Jacobi. As a joke, John Huston forced his father to do retake after retake, falling down again and again, getting more and more bruised after each take.

The first film version of *The Maltese Falcon* (1931) was a well-made film starring Ricardo Cortez as Spade and Bebe Daniels as Ruth Wonderley/Brigid O'Shaughnessy. A second version, titled

Satan Met a Lady (1936), was a disaster, with Bette Davis in the Casper Gutman role and Warren William (as Ted Shayne).

Oscar nominations went to the film for Best Picture and to Sydney Greenstreet (in his first film) for Best Supporting Actor.

BEST LINE: When all the suspects have been gathered and arrested, Lt. Polhaus picks up the falcon and asks Spade what it is. The detective replies, "The stuff that dreams are made of."

THE THIRD MAN
1949

TYPE OF FILM: Suspense/Espionage
STUDIO: London Films
PRODUCER: Carol Reed
DIRECTOR: Carol Reed
SCREENWRITER: Graham Greene
SOURCE: *The Third Man*, novella by Graham Greene
RUNNING TIME: 104 minutes

PRINCIPAL PLAYERS:

Orson Welles . . . . Harry Lime
Joseph Cotten . . . . .Holly Martins
(Alida) Valli . . . . .Anna Schmidt
Trevor Howard . . . . .Major Calloway
Bernard Lee . . . . .Sergeant Paine
Paul Hoerbiger . . . . .Porter
Wilfrid Hyde-White . . . . .Crabbin
Ernst Deutsch . . . ."Baron" Kurtz
Sigfried Breuer . . . . .Popescu
Erich Ponto . . . . .Dr. Winkel

DID YOU KNOW? Graham Greene based the villainous Harry Lime on Kim Philby, the infamous British double agent. Greene had been a member of the British Secret Intelligence Service until 1944, when he abruptly resigned. It has been suggested that the reason for his resignation was that he suspected Philby of being a traitor and did not want to actively assist him. Greene, himself a Communist sympathizer and apologist, did not report Philby, who continued his activities for some time after Greene's resignation.

THE STORY: American novelist Holly Martins is invited to take a job with his old friend Harry Lime in postwar Vienna, which is divided into four occupied zones (English, American, French, and Russian). Martins arrives to find that his friend has been killed in an automobile accident. He rushes to the cemetery, where he sees Lime's lovely girlfriend, Anna, and meets Major Calloway, who informs him that Lime was a criminal, dealing in black-market penicillin that he watered down, killing or harming numbers of children.

Martins vows to clear Lime's name and meets with Anna, who believes Lime was murdered. Although Lime's friend Kurtz tells them that Lime lived long enough for his physician to show up, the porter in Lime's building says he died instantly. When Martin and Anna return to question the porter further, they find he has been murdered.

After Martins has seen children hospitalized because of diluted penicillin, he is disgusted by his friend's actions and decides to return to the United States, but not before telling Anna that he has fallen in love with her. As he leaves her rooms, he spots Lime, who is not dead after all. Martins calls Major Calloway, and together they search for Lime, without success. When they arrange to have Lime's coffin exhumed, another man's body is found in his place.

Martins and Lime arrange to meet at a Ferris wheel in an amusement park, where Lime casually talks of his criminal acts, comparing people to little dots on the ground from their great height and warning Martins to stay away from the police. Martins goes to the police anyway, offering to help capture Lime if they will ensure safe passage out of Vienna for Anna, who angrily refuses the offer and now regards Martins as a betrayer of his friend. Martins sets himself up as a decoy, but when Lime arrives, Anna warns him and he flees to his secret escape route in the giant sewers of Vienna. Fleeing, Line shoots a British soldier but is himself shot by Martins.

* * *

There are numerous differences between the film and the book, which was written essentially to be a film treatment without thought to publication as a novel; it was published after the release of the film.

In Greene's book, the main male characters are British, and as the story concludes, Holly Martins and Anna walk away together. In the film version, Cotten waits for her as she slowly walks toward him on a long tree-lined path; she never looks at him as she walks past him.

The first choice to play Holly Martins was Cary Grant, with Noel Coward selected to play Harry Lime. When the film was rewritten to make those characters American, David O. Selznick, the president of London Films, suggested Robert Mitchum for the role of Lime, as his popularity had increased dramatically after the headlines reported his arrest for marijuana possession. His presence, noted Selznick, would be hugely important at the box office, while the other actor considered, Orson Welles, *would not add a dollar to the gross,* he wrote in a memo. When Mitchum was sentenced to jail and therefore unable to work, Welles took the role because he was, not unusually, in dire need of money to finance his film, *Othello.*

The most famous line in the film (see below) was written by Orson Welles, not Graham Greene. In fact, it has been reported that Welles wrote virtually all the dialogue for every scene in which he appears.

There are two versions of *The Third Man.* The British version begins with a voice-over by producer/director Carol Reed, in which the division of Vienna into zones is described. This version is approximately eleven minutes longer than the American, which was somewhat re-edited by Selznick. Here, the voice-over is narrated by Joseph Cotten.

Carol Reed received an Academy Award nomination for Best Director. The only Oscar the film won was for Robert Krasker's black-and-white cinematography. It was named Best Film at the 1949 Cannes Film Festival.

In 1952, the BBC produced a radio series variously titled *The Third Man, The Lives of Harry Lime,* and *Harry Lime Adventures,* with Orson Welles as the voice of the protagonist. Seven years later, BBC Television and Twentieth Century-Fox coproduced a syndicated television series, *The Third Man,* which starred Michael Rennie as Lime, who was now an international adventurer.

The very famous theme music by Anton Karas, known as "The Third Man Theme," was played throughout the film on a zither and became a best-selling record in the United Kingdom; it was also used as the theme for the radio series.

BEST LINE: Harry Lime: "In Italy for thirty years under the Borgias, they had warfare, terror, murder, bloodshed—but they produced Michelangelo, Leonardo da Vinci, and the Renaissance. In Switzerland, they had brotherly love, five hundred years of democracy and peace, and what did they produce? The cuckoo clock."

An Open Letter to Our Valued Readers

What do Raymond Chandler, Arthur C. Clarke, Isaac Asimov, Irving Wallace, Ben Bova, Stuart Kaminsky and over a dozen other authors have in common? They are all part of an exciting new line of **ibooks** distributed by Simon and Schuster.

 ibooks represent the best of the future and the best of the past...a voyage into the future of books that unites traditional printed books with the excitement of the web.

Please join us in developing the first new publishing imprint of the 21st century.

We're planning terrific offers for ibooks readers...virtual reading groups where you can chat online about ibooks authors...message boards where you can communicate with fellow readers...downloadable free chapters of ibooks for your reading pleasure...free readers services such as a directory of where to find electronic books on the web...special discounts on books and other items of interest to readers...

The evolution of the book is www.ibooksinc.com.